"It has been my privilege to play with and to be that kind of man myself. Now, Ra ing to new heights in his book *Man of Honor: Living the Life of Godly Character*. I recommend it to everyone striving to be a man of God."

—TOM LANDRY
NFL Hall of Fame coach

"There are many men of reputation. There are few of character. Ray Pritchard knows that what makes a man exceptional is the strength of his character. A man of great wisdom once penned, 'As iron sharpens iron, so one man sharpens another.' I think that will be your experience, just as it was mine, as you turn every page of *Man of Honor*."

—STEVE FARRAR
Director of Men's Leadership Ministries
Author of Point Man

"As a Major League baseball player, honor was important to me. It is even more important as a husband and father. I also desire to honor my Heavenly Father as I serve Him through Outreach of Hope. If honor is important to you, Ray Pritchard's *Man of Honor* is a must. Get it. Read it. Act on what it says."

—DAVE DRAVECKY
Former Major League pitcher

"For all of us who have searched for how we can become godly men, Ray Pritchard gives us a solid starting point in *Man of Honor: Living the Life of Godly Character*. Focusing on what Paul says in 1 Timothy 3:1-7 and in Titus 1:5-9, Ray combines the biblical qualities with everyday examples from the lives of ordinary men who in their daily lives are striving to be godly leaders in their home, work, relationships, and churches. This book will get you started on the right path and keep you headed toward the goal of becoming a godly man."

—JOSEPH M. STOWELL
President, Moody Bible Institute

"There is a growing fascination today with how to become men of character, integrity, faith, and fidelity. Ray Pritchard has captured that message in this book and shows how any man who really wants to can become a man of honor."

—TIM LAHAYE
President, Family Life Seminars

"Dr. Ray Pritchard is rapidly becoming one of the most effective voices in the American church. With *Man of Honor* he fully arrives. Ladies, get this book for the men in your lives. Men, get it for yourself and for other men important to you. It will make an immediate and positive difference."

—BOB BRINER
Author of Roaring Lambs

"Ray Pritchard has scored a direct hit—practical, interesting, relevant, and useful insights into how we can actually live the walk we usually just talk about as leaders."

—DR. HANS FINZEL
Executive Director, CBInternational

"There is a growing awareness among men of their need to be spiritual leaders. There is no doubt that male leadership is one of the greatest needs in the contemporary church. Dr. Ray Pritchard's book *Man of Honor* is one of the best tools for spiritual growth available. If you want to be a better father, pastor, businessman, or a strong single Christian, this book is a must read. So read it and grow."

—JERRY ROSE
President, TV38 Chicago

MAN OF HONOR

Living the Life
of Godly Character

CROSSWAY BOOKS • WHEATON, ILLINOIS
A DIVISION OF GOOD NEWS PUBLISHERS

Library of Congress Cataloging-in-Publication Data
Pritchard, Ray, 1952-
    Man of honor: living the life of godly character / Ray Pritchard
    p.   cm.
    ISBN 0-89107-899-1
    1. Men—Religious life. 2. Christian leadership. 3. Leadership—
    Biblical teaching. I. Title.
BV4843.P75 1996
248.8'42—dc20   96-10520

04		03		02		01		00		99		98		97		96
15	14	13	12	11	10	9	8	7	6	5	4	3	2	1

This book is dedicated to the nine men who make up my Promise Keepers group. They are Men of Honor and true brothers in Christ.

GEORGE COMINOS

JEFF EATON

DUANE FOLLMAN

ROB GASKILL

ALLAN MACLEOD-SMITH

GARY OLSON

ALEX PIRUS

TOM RENARD

GLENN SWANSON

CONTENTS

FOREWORD

The issue of Christian character among men is a dominant one today. Many books are being written to challenge men to pursue godliness in their personal, family, church, and community lives. And the advent of Promise Keepers has placed the call of God on the lives of men on a "lower shelf" where all who desire to can reach it.

With the publication of *Man of Honor*, Ray Pritchard has joined this distinctive array of Christian communicators as a fresh and provocative voice. He has a unique ability to merge solid biblical training with practical insights and pragmatic, achievable action steps.

Drawing from Paul's description of a godly leader in 1 Timothy 3 and Titus 1, Pritchard offers a contemporary and pragmatic description of a godly man, accompanied by a process for implementation.

He rightly recognizes that for many Christian men the issue is not what they should be, but how they can become what God expects them to be. The crying need of many men is for more clarity about the practical steps they need to take to begin putting into practice what they already know they should be doing.

It is here that Ray Pritchard makes a unique contribution. Rather than simply giving us a biblical analysis, he gives us an outstanding process of spiritual exercise and discipline that, if implemented, will enable a man to begin experiencing real spiritual changes in his life.

Man of Honor is a powerful tool for any man who is serious about his spiritual development. If men will take to heart the instruction of this book, they will be able to tangibly measure their progress in godliness. I recommend it to any man who is tired of making excuses.

Tony Evans
Dallas, Texas

WITH
GRATITUDE

From the very beginning I have had a great deal of help in putting this book together. Many people in my congregation prayed for me daily, and some wrote notes of encouragement. Others sent stories of the Men of Honor they have known. All were inspiring. I have included as many as possible.

I owe special thanks to:

My many friends at Crossway Books who make writing a pleasure and publishing a ministry. With special thanks to Lane Dennis, Len Goss, Ted Griffin, Geoff Dennis, Randy Jahns, Kathy Jacobs, and Brian Ondracek.

Bob Briner, who has been a stalwart friend, wise counselor, and constant source of encouragement.

The elders of Calvary Memorial Church, Oak Park, Illinois, for graciously allowing me the time to finish this project.

Mia Gale and Kathy Duggins, for managing my schedule with so much efficiency.

Lisa King, Brian Bill, and Jeff Eaton—last-minute miracle-workers.

Alex Cominos, who cheerfully allowed me to use his computer.

My wife, Marlene, who smiled through it all.

Josh, Mark, and Nick, who by the grace of God will one day become Men of Honor.

SETTING
THE STAGE

Three years ago I appeared on a national radio broadcast in which the host and I discussed the marks of godly leadership found in 1 Timothy 3 and Titus 1. At the time I was in the process of writing a brief paper summarizing those qualities. As he sometimes does, my friend Jim Warren, the host of *Primetime America*, asked me on the air if I would be willing to make copies of my paper available to anyone who wrote or called asking for it. It seemed like a safe promise to make, because most offers like that net a total of three or four requests.

To my surprise, people began calling my office before the program was over. Later we received a stack of letters from across America. We ended up sending out over 300 copies of that brief paper.

As I read the letters, two facts jumped out at me. First, most of the letters were from women who saw the need for men to assume godly leadership. Second, many of the writers mentioned a need to translate the character qualities of the New Testament into understandable twentieth-century language. After all, you can't obey what you don't understand. If the word temperate doesn't register in your mind, how will you ever become a temperate man?

FILLING IN THE GAP

As I read and re-read those responses, I began to see that lack of desire is not the greatest problem facing Christian men today. Most men want to grow in Christ—to be better husbands, better fathers, better role models, better neighbors and friends; but they don't know how. They don't even know where to begin.

I wrote this book to help fill in the gap between knowing and doing. If by the end of this book you know more than you did, I will have partially succeeded. If you know where you need to grow as a godly leader, I will have mostly succeeded. If you know what to do about those areas of your life that need work, then you and I will both be satisfied. And if you are motivated to put into practice what you have learned, God will be pleased.

Before we begin, let me issue a qualifying statement. The twenty-five character qualities we are going to study were not picked at random. The list is 2,000 years old and comes from the pen of the Apostle Paul. What does a godly leader look like? Answer: He looks like the man described in 1 Timothy 3 and Titus 1. Before we go any farther, I encourage you to set this book aside, take your Bible, and read 1 Timothy 3:1-7 and Titus 1:5-9. Everything in this book is based on what Paul says in those two central passages.

I view these character qualities in three ways. First, they apply specifically to the elders of the local church. Second, they apply in a general way to all Christian men who are called to leadership in any arena. Third, they apply to each one of us because these qualities describe what a godly or mature Christian should look like. No qualification on this list is unique to those called to leadership. That is, when these qualifications are considered in a broad sense, they fit each one of us, or ought to. Indeed, elders must be above reproach, free from the love of money, not quarrelsome, gentle, lovers of the good, and so on. But these are also qualities that all Christians should display. They describe the kind of people all of us should want to become.

So, while the list is written specifically for elders, and then for church leaders generally, we can all benefit from studying this list carefully as we ask ourselves the probing question, "How well do I measure up to these character qualities?"

AIMING FOR THE RIGHT GOAL

On a personal level, I find these standards extremely challenging and convicting. Believe me, it's easier to write about these character qualities than to put them into practice.

Remember, this is an aspirational list. No one lives like this 100 percent of the time. The Bible sets before us a worthy goal, which most of us will work on for a lifetime and still not completely reach. We ought to take this list seriously but also graciously and realistically. While this list is meant to impress us, it is not meant to depress us. No man should read this list and say, "That's impossible." Rather, we should each say, "By the grace of God, that's the kind of man I want to be." Seen in that light, these qualifications describe not perfection, but a mature Christian life—victorious Christian character accomplished only through the grace and power of God.

The book itself is organized very simply. Each chapter considers a single character trait of godly leaders. We will consider what each trait means and what it looks like in real life. We will look at some contemporary illustrations and practical suggestions on how we can develop each trait in our own lives.

Please don't read this book through in one sitting. It's not meant to be devoured like a mystery novel. It is meant to be read and studied a little bit at a time. You may want to use it as part of your daily quiet time with the Lord, or you might enjoy studying it in a small group with several other men. In fact, I think you'll probably grow faster if you study it with other men who are also committed to spiritual growth. Although the book is written for men, Christian women will no doubt find much helpful material in these pages, including how to pray for the men in their lives more effectively. They might even understand more about the way their man is wired.

ORDINARY GUYS

You'll find lots of stories in these chapters, but most of them won't be about famous people. As I wrote this book, I deliberately tried to illustrate the principles from the lives of ordinary men who aren't rich or famous or powerful. I believe that the real heroes today are men who in the course of their daily lives are taking up the challenge of being godly leaders at home, on the job, in their neighborhoods, and in their churches. For the most part these men won't be written up in the local paper—but you won't see their pictures in the post office either.

The men you are about to meet are real men who are pretty much like Christian men everywhere. They love their wives and children; they struggle to balance the demands of home and work and church; in their better moments they want to be Men of Honor (though they probably wouldn't put it in those words). Sometimes they succeed; other times they fail.

If you are single, you may wonder if this book has anything to say to you. The answer is yes. Most of this book will apply directly to you. One chapter applies specifically to married men, and two others apply to men with children. However, even in those three chapters you will find helpful and challenging information.

I don't personally know all the men in this book. Friends from around the country shared these stories with me. Some of the men lived and died years ago. You can find the rest all along the spectrum—from early adulthood to the twilight years. But all of them are Men of Honor. And all of them need the strength Christ gives to live up to the high standards of the Bible.

That's enough introduction for the moment. If you would like to become a Man of Honor for God, turn the page and let's get started!

THE INDY 62,000

The times are changing. Men are beginning to wake up to the challenge of being spiritual leaders at home, on the job, and in the church.

Perhaps no movement has done more for the men of America than Promise Keepers. On an extraordinary June day, I joined 62,000 men in Indianapolis for a life-changing weekend. A few hours after returning home, I jotted down my memories of that unforgettable experience. I include it here because there is a direct connection between what happened that weekend and the writing of this book. Those who have been to a Promise Keepers conference will identify with much of what I express here. Those who haven't attended yet will, hopefully, get a taste of what PK is like.

"THERE MUST BE A MILLION PEOPLE HERE"

"Where's the motel?" . . . "Where's Bob? We can't check in until he gets here." . . . "I'm asking God to do something special for me this weekend." . . . "If the Pacers win tonight, it'll take forever to get out of downtown Indianapolis."

Fathers and sons anticipating a dynamic weekend . . . "Does anybody know how to get to the Hoosier Dome?" . . . Men jumping out of the back of a bus like paratroopers in downtown Indianapolis . . . "There must be a million people here." . . . "Don't forget your red wristband. You can't get in without it."

"GOD IS IN THIS PLACE"

The Hoosier Dome fills to overflowing . . . Hallways jammed with men. Nearly every seat taken, and more men still coming in . . . "Welcome to Promise Keepers." . . . 62,000 men praising Jesus together, singing "Oh, Worship the King," "Crown Him with Many Crowns"—one song after another . . . "God is in this place tonight."

The speaker looks like an ant, so we watch him on the big screen hanging from the ceiling . . . "Where's Tom?" "He's wandering around making new friends."

A sea of hands uplifted in worship . . . "Some of you men didn't want to come. I saw heel marks out in the parking lot." . . . 3,000 men going forward to give themselves to Jesus Christ. . . . Clapping, cheering, raising our hands in worship.

"DO YOUR KIDS KNOW HOW MUCH YOU LOVE THEM?"

"Blessed be the Lord God Almighty." . . . Doing the wave . . . Bill Bright calling us to be filled with the Spirit . . . Gary Smalley telling us to take off one shoe and drop it . . . "Does your wife know how much you love her? Do your kids know much you love them?" . . . "The only thing that matters in life is the love and respect of those who love you the most." . . . Praying in threes that God would help us be better husbands and fathers.

"We're going to dismiss you in sections for lunch. Don't worry. This will work—we think. Remember, Jesus only had to feed 5,000 men." . . . A moving ocean of men rolling down the street toward the big tents where we pick up lunch in little white cardboard boxes . . . It worked. They fed 62,000 men in ninety minutes!

RULE # 4: LISTEN TO YOUR WIFE

"Lord, I love to sing Your praises." . . . John Maxwell talking about sexual purity . . . Rule # 1: Run! . . . Rule # 4: Listen to your wife! "If you followed this rule, the rest wouldn't matter." . . . "Men, you can make a new beginning right here, right now."

"Pastors, stand up please. Now gather around your pastor and pray for him. He bears many burdens. Ask God to keep him faithful." . . . The heavy, warm weight of a dozen hands on my shoulders . . . Tears.

"Pray for me. I need to write my father a letter." . . . Praying together right then . . . "Every man needs an accountability group." . . . "A Promise Keeper is a man of integrity." . . . "Go back and make a difference for God." . . . E. V. Hill on video talking about the Black Panthers . . . Eating dinner in the parking lot—the biggest barbecue in history.

SHOULDER TO SHOULDER
AND BACK TO BACK

"Where did that little airplane come from?" . . . Tossing an apple back and forth . . . "I'm glad our wives aren't here. They'd say, 'Oh, stop that.'"

The final session . . . Joe Stowell's awesome message on being the light of the world . . . "We Christians don't have enough acceptable hand signals when we get mad." . . . Steve Green and Steven Curtis Chapman—accountability partners . . . Singing "Holy, Holy, Holy" with 62,000 men . . . "This is what heaven will be like." . . . "God must love this!" . . . Joining hands and singing "Brother, let me be your servant." . . . Swaying to the music.

"Shoulder to shoulder and back to back." . . . Clapping, cheering, raising our hands in praise to Jesus . . . "America is going to be different because thousands of men have decided to become Promise Keepers." . . . "Share your personal commitment with a friend . . . Don't take off your wristband until you keep that commitment."

"I'VE NEVER SEEN ANYTHING LIKE THIS"

One final song—"Rise up, oh, men of God, have done with lesser things. Give heart and soul and mind and strength to serve the King of Kings. Rise up, the Lord is calling. Rise up, this is the day. Rise up and seize the moment. Rise up, O men of faith!" . . . Final good-byes . . . Christian men hugging each other—strong men, brave men, unafraid to say, "I love you, brother." . . . Thousands of men going home changed forever . . . Driving back in the darkness. Arriving home at 3 A.M. So excited I can't go to sleep . . . "I've never seen anything like it."

Something is happening in our land that we didn't expect. *God is stirring up Christian men, and I believe as never before that Christian men are the hope of America.* This is an idea whose time has come because the foundations beneath us are crumbling. The darkness is moving in all around us. Our homes are breaking up, our marriages are in chaos, and our schools are in trouble. Pastors are stumbling; spiritual leaders are falling left and right. Evil is on the march.

But the darker the night, the brighter the light! At this crucial moment of history God is stirring up Christian men to serve Jesus Christ with total commitment.

We need committed men who will arise, unite, and become Men of Honor for God—men who love Jesus with all their hearts, who love their wives and children, and who love each other and aren't ashamed to say so.

Will you be a Man of Honor? With God's help, you can do it!

WHAT IS A MAN OF HONOR?

Character Quality	Explanation

HIS TEMPERAMENT

Desire (1 Timothy 3:1)	Truly wants to be a man of God
Temperate (1 Timothy 3:2)	Calm under pressure
Self-controlled (1 Timothy 3:2; Titus 1:8)	Stable and well-balanced
Disciplined (Titus 1:8)	Strength under control

HIS EMOTIONAL LIFE

Not violent (1 Timothy 3:3; Titus 1:7)	No abusive words, attitudes, or actions
Not quarrelsome (1 Timothy 3:3)	Doesn't pick fights
Not quick-tempered (Titus 1:7)	Doesn't lose his cool under pressure
Not overbearing (Titus 1:7)	Not a prima donna, but a team player
Gentle (1 Timothy 3:3)	Sensitive to the needs of others

HIS REPUTATION

Above reproach (1 Timothy 3:2; Titus 1:6-7)	No accusation against him can stand
Respectable (1 Timothy 3:2)	An orderly, well-balanced life
Hospitable (1 Timothy 3:2; Titus 1:8)	Opens his heart and home to others
Upright (Titus 1:8)	Committed to honesty and justice
Good reputation (1 Timothy 3:7)	Known, liked, and respected by unbelievers

HIS SPIRITUAL LIFE

Not a new convert   *A growing Christian life—*
(1 Timothy 3:6)   *has a spiritual track record*

Holy   *Makes you aware of God, not himself*
(Titus 1:8)

Sound doctrine   *Committed to the truth of Scripture*
(Titus 1:9)

Able to teach   *Desires to share what he knows with others*
(1 Timothy 3:2)

HIS FAMILY LIFE

Husband of one wife   *Fully committed and faithful to his wife*
(1 Timothy 3:2; Titus 1:6)

Manages his household well *Skillful in leading his family*
(1 Timothy 3:4-5)

Has children who obey him   *A model father*
(1 Timothy 3:4; Titus 1:6)

HIS PERSONAL HABITS

Not given to drunkenness   *Not a habitual drinker*
(1 Timothy 3:3; Titus 1:7)

Not a lover of money   *Does not live for money*
(1 Timothy 3:3)

Not pursuing dishonest gain *Not a cheat or a crook*
(Titus 1:7)

Loving what is good   *Passionate about the best things in life*
(Titus 1:8)

PART I

HIS TEMPERAMENT

SEIZE THE DAY!

A Man of Honor has the right desire.
—*1 Timothy 3:1*

A t a prep school somewhere in New England, on a beautiful fall morning, bright young men have gathered in English Literature class, fearing the worst—long, boring hours arguing about *Beowulf* and the intricacies of iambic pentameter. But lo, it is not to be. Their teacher is brand-new, a graduate who has returned to teach at his alma mater. To him, English Literature is not about names and rhymes; it's about life—living, dying, loving, caring, feeling. He aims to somehow impart this vision to his young charges.

Suddenly he cries, "Follow me" and leads the class out into the hallway and down to the glass cases that contain the pictures of former students from long ago. "Look," he says. "Look closely. Do you see them?" The pictures are old, cracked, faded, but you can still see their youthful faces. "Look at them carefully. They were once young like you are. They had hopes and dreams just like you do. They had grand ideas too." The teacher lowers his voice and says, "Listen, can you hear what they are saying?"

The young men press closer to the glass as if actually expecting to hear the voices of the past come floating up from the cracked and faded pictures.

"They're calling out to you. If you listen, you can hear them. They're calling out, '*Carpe diem.*'"

The young men don't know Latin, so the phrase is a mystery to them. "*Carpe diem*," they mumble to each other.

"Yes!" he cries out. "That's it. *Carpe diem*. They're saying, '*Carpe diem*.' Can you hear them?" Then he turns to the class egghead—the student with the glasses, of course. "Mr. Stevenson, do you know what *carpe diem* means?"

The young man looks puzzled for a moment, until the meaning comes to him. "Seize the day! *Carpe diem* means 'Seize the day!'"

"That's right!" cries the teacher triumphantly. "Seize the day! They are calling out to you from the past—'Seize the day!'"

If you have seen the movie *Dead Poets Society*, that scene is forever etched in your mind. The past calls to the present, "*Carpe diem*"— "Seize the day!" The future also looks to the present and says, "*Carpe diem*"—"Seize the day!"

No message is more timely for Christian men today. Either we rise up and seize the day for the glory of God, or we will let the moment pass and will live to look back with bitter regret at what might have been.

Carpe diem.

THE OVERLOOKED INGREDIENT

"Here is a trustworthy saying: If anyone sets his heart on being an overseer, he desires a noble task" (1 Timothy 3:1). We could easily overlook this verse in our haste to get to the list of qualifications for spiritual leaders. That would be a great mistake because it reveals an overlooked ingredient of leadership: *godly leaders must want the job*.

Spiritual leaders are made, not born. *No one comes into the world as a Man of Honor for God*. To become such a man takes time, effort, diligence, and most of all, desire.

Paul uses two verbs to bring this out. First, he says that a person must "set his heart" on leadership. This verb means to "stretch out in order to grasp," like a football player straining to reach the goal line.[1] Second, he says that a leader must "desire" leadership. This verb means to "eagerly desire" or to "be ambitious for" or even to "covet" (in a good sense).[2]

Notice also that he calls leadership "a noble task." Leadership is a noble calling in and of itself. Consider the following implications of this fact:

- Leadership is a noble thing in the eyes of God, provided it is done with a servant's heart.
- The desire to be a leader is noble if it is accompanied by a desire to grow in grace.
- Being a leader is a noble work—but it is *work*!

A person may desire leadership, but what is he really seeking? A title? A name? A big office? A platform for greatness? A big salary? If he is seeking leadership for the right reason, he desires "a noble task."

Here, then, is the first requirement for leadership. A person must want the job! There should be a God-given desire that moves the heart to action.

HOW MUCH WILL YOU RISK?

The very fact that you are reading this book is a good sign. At the very least it means that you have some desire to be a spiritual leader in your family, on the job, in your neighborhood, or in your church. Simply by reading this book, you've already passed the first test of spiritual leadership.

That leads to the second test: *How much are you willing to risk to become all that God wants you to be?* In the spiritual arena, what you risk is what you get. Those who risk little achieve little. Those who risk the most gain the most.

How far will you go to become a Man of Honor for God?

The greatest men of the Bible were also the greatest risk-takers for God. That should not surprise us because in one sense the life of faith is inherently a life of risk. Go back to the Bible and take a look at the men and women who did great things for God. They were all without exception risk-takers: people who weren't afraid to lay it all on the line for God.

Consider Noah, who built an ark when it had never rained in the history of the world. People thought he was crazy, but here's old Noah with his three boys cutting down that gopher wood and nailing the planks into place. Not only that, but he had to wait 120 years for the rains to finally come.

Consider Abraham, who at the height of his prosperity was called to leave Ur of the Chaldees. Taking his wife with him, he set out for regions unknown because God had promised to show him a better land.

Consider Moses, who led the nation of Israel to the shores of the Red Sea, across the Red Sea, and into the Sinai Desert. And he was eighty years old at the time! At an age when most men are cranking back the La-Z-Boy and reading the sports page, Moses was up on the mountain having a conversation with God.

Consider Joshua, who after 3,000 years is remembered primarily for his victory at Jericho. For six days he led the people in a march around the walls of that impregnable city. For six days it appeared that he had lost his mind. But then Joshua told the priests on the seventh day, "This time march around seven times." After the seventh time around on the seventh day, the priests blew their trumpets, and Joshua called out, "Shout! For the Lord has given you the city." With a mighty roar, the people shouted—"And the walls came a tumblin' down."

Consider David, who walked into the Valley of Elah to face the mighty giant Goliath. Stopping at the stream, he picked up five smooth stones. Though no one else in the whole nation would go down into that valley, David walked in alone. How could a teenager do what brave men were afraid to do? But he did, and the rest is history.

Consider Nehemiah, who left a prosperous career in Susa to return to the rundown city of Jerusalem in order to rally the dispirited people of God to rebuild the walls of Jerusalem. Rousing the nation from its stupor and overcoming hostility at every turn, the walls were rebuilt in only fifty-two days.

Consider Daniel, who when he was thrown into the lions' den, didn't fear for his own life but turned the lions into pillows and slept like a baby all night long.

FAITH WITHOUT RISK IS NO FAITH AT ALL

In the Bible, the men who accomplished great things for God weren't content to accept the status quo. They thought that more could be done if only someone would lead the way. And if no one else stepped forward, they volunteered themselves.

Often no one followed, but they forged ahead, sometimes suffering greatly for their actions. Their path was rarely easy and often cost them their safety and their reputation. But they persisted in their obedience to God and weren't afraid to look foolish in the eyes of their countrymen.

When our children come to Sunday school, what stories do we tell them? The very stories I have just mentioned to you. We tell them about the great heroes of the faith—Noah and Abraham and Moses and David and Daniel and all the rest. We don't talk about the ordinary men and women; we talk about those brave souls who laid it all on the line for God. These are the models we want them to follow.

That is only right and proper because the life of faith is inherently a life of risk. If you are unwilling to take a chance, you cannot discover what living by faith is all about. If you have to have all the answers before you make a decision, if you're afraid to take a step unless you know things will work out to your advantage, faith will always be a mystery to you.[3]

"LORD, PUT ME IN OVER MY HEAD"

Perhaps you have heard the story of Charlie Riggs and his favorite prayer. After his conversion he was being discipled by a young man named Lorne Sanny, who in turn was being discipled by Dawson Trotman, founder of The Navigators. Charlie wanted to grow in Christ, but he was a bit rough around the edges. Sanny wrote to Trotman, telling him that Charlie Riggs was the only man he was working with and that he felt discouraged by Riggs's lack of progress. "Stay with your man," Trotman wrote back. "You never know what God will do with him."

So Lorne Sanny continued to work with Charlie Riggs, teaching him about Scripture memory and the secrets of effective follow-up. A few years passed, and Billy Graham began his evangelistic ministry. In the 1950s The Navigators joined with the Graham team to handle the follow-up of new converts in their early crusades. On the eve of the New York Crusade in 1957, the general director suddenly had to be replaced. Who could they get at the last minute? The lay chairman suggested Charlie Riggs, but Billy wondered if he could handle the job. "I didn't think he could do it. But I had this peace that Charlie so depended on the Holy Spirit that I knew the Lord could do it through him." Charlie Riggs got the job, and the New York crusade became a model for the many campaigns that would follow in later years.

Charlie Riggs retired only after many years of effective service for the Lord. What was his secret? How could a man with little formal training rise to such a high position and hold it for so long?

Here is his answer: "I always asked the Lord to put me in over my head. That way, when I had a job to do, either the Lord had to help me or I was sunk." God delighted to answer that prayer time after time. He kept putting Charlie Riggs in over his head . . . and then bailed him out.

Here's a challenge for every man who wants to become a Man of Honor for God. Let's take Charlie Riggs's prayer as our own: "Lord, put me in over my head." It's always safer to stay in shallow water where you can feel the bottom under your feet, but the real challenge is to jump in where the water comes up over your head.[4]

Are you ready for some excitement? As you read this book, ask God to put you in over your head. God often works His greatest miracles just when we think we're about to sink.

WHERE IS JESUS TODAY?

Let's wrap up this chapter by asking a crucial question: Where is Jesus today? If you're looking for Jesus, where should you go in order to find Him?

He's not in Ur of the Chaldees. He's on the road to the Promised Land.

He's not in Egypt. He's out there in the middle of the Red Sea.

He's not in Jericho. He's outside the walls with Joshua.

He's not in Jerusalem. He's outside the camp at a place called Golgotha.

What am I trying to say? If your goal is to live a life of security and safety, you'll end up with everything but Jesus. Our Lord never took the comfortable road. He never took the easy way. He never took a shortcut in order to play it safe. So if that's what you're looking for, you might as well forget about Jesus, because He doesn't have any part in that.

DYING YOUNG AT A VERY OLD AGE

May I share with you the goal of my life? I want to die young at a very old age. That's not just playing with words; that's a philosophy of life. Growing old is not merely a matter of chronology. It's also a state of mind. You can be old at twenty and young at eighty-five. My goal is to die young at a very old age, doing everything I can to impact the world for Jesus Christ.

You aren't going to live forever. Who knows? You may die tomorrow or you may live another fifty years. The question is, what are you going to do with the life God has given you?

Carpe diem, men of God. Rise up and seize the day.

GOING DEEPER

1. Why is desire an essential component of developing spiritual leadership? What happens when men serve in positions of leadership without passion or desire?

2. Leadership is a noble thing in the eyes of God, and it is also a form of servanthood.
   Do you agree or disagree with that statement?
   What are the marks of a leader who has a true servant's heart?
   How do you spot a leader who is in it for power and prestige?

3. Read Hebrews 11. How did the men in that chapter exemplify the truth that the life of faith is inherently a life of risk? If you could meet one of those men personally, whom would you choose? Why?

4. Consider Charlie Riggs's prayer: "Lord, put me in over my head."
   Have you ever prayed a prayer like that? If so, what happened?
   In what areas is the Lord putting you in over your head right now?

5. Here's a quick-reaction question: What's the first thing in your life that would change if you began to experience increased spiritual growth?

6. Listed below are the twenty-five qualities of a Man of Honor. As you look at this list, which ones are personal strong points for you? Which ones stand out as areas needing special work? Place a check by the five qualities in which you'd most like to see growth over the next six months. Make a point of praying about those five areas each time you pick up this book.

___ *Desire*	___ *Not quarrelsome*
___ *Respectable*	___ *Temperate*
___ *Not quick-tempered*	___ *Hospitable*
___ *Self-controlled*	___ *Not overbearing*

___ *Upright*	___ *Disciplined*
___ *Gentle*	___ *Good reputation*
___ *Not violent*	___ *Above reproach*
___ *Not a new convert*	___ *Holy*
___ *Manages his household well*	___ *Sound doctrine*
___ *Has children who obey him*	___ *Able to teach*
___ *Not a lover of money*	___ *Husband of one wife*
___ *Not pursuing dishonest gain*	___ *Not given to drunkenness*
___ *Loving what is good*	

TAKING ACTION

Why are you reading this book? Since desire is an all-important requirement for spiritual leadership, what do you hope will happen in your life as a result of working through these chapters on spiritual leadership? Jot down at least three positive results you would like to see over the next few weeks as you read *Man of Honor*.

CHAPTER

TWO

COURAGE IN OVERALLS

A Man of Honor is "temperate."
—*1 Timothy 3:2*

The Greek word for *temperate* originally meant "wineless."[1] When Paul uses the word, he means something like "even-tempered," "clear-headed," or "balanced." It refers to a man in whom nothing muddies or muddles his senses. In that sense it certainly touches the use of alcohol but goes far beyond it.

A temperate person is cool, calm, and collected, especially in a moment of crisis.[2] He's not credulous, not easily deceived, not carried away by every wind of doctrine (Ephesians 4:14). He's old enough and experienced enough not to be rattled under pressure. You discover this quality in a person's life as you watch him in a crisis situation. A temperate man doesn't fall apart when his world falls apart. He doesn't lose his emotional equilibrium when the rug is suddenly pulled out from under him. He demonstrates courage in the face of difficult circumstances.[3]

ALWAYS TOO SOON TO QUIT

Two years ago one of my best friends from high school days noticed a lump in his abdomen. When the reports came back, the diagnosis wasn't good. Cancer. Something called Non-Hodgkin's Lymphoma. An avid runner, he had just completed the Boston Marathon when he got the bad news. He went on to endure thirteen rounds of chemotherapy with all the usual side effects—loss of hair, nausea, extreme weakness.

My friend is a strong Christian whose faith has been made even stronger by his ordeal. But he knows that hard days lie ahead of him, and the final result is far from certain. So a few of us who know Rick well decided to get together for a special party in order to cheer him up and to pray for him. I saw old friends I hadn't seen for two decades. We laughed, we hugged each other, we traded stories, we tried to catch up on twenty years of life in two hours. Then we gathered round Rick, laid our hands on him, and prayed for God to heal him. Afterward we sang together "We Will Glorify," "Victory in Jesus," "Jesus Loves Me," and, at Rick's request, "It Is Well with My Soul."

When I arrived back home, Rick sent me a message by E-mail:

> When you are going through difficulties, and you will, the support of close friends becomes a source of strength that enables you to make it through each day. Seeing all of you has renewed my commitment to fight on and has given me what I need to battle this cancer to the very end. I was at a stage where I was weary from the battle and a place where I just wanted to quit. I have been there before when I was running those marathons and you are at the 24-mile mark and others around you are stopping and some are getting into the vans for the ride back. Your body tells you to stop and rest, but you have trained too hard to quit now and so you press on. That's where I was before this weekend. My body wanted out, but my heart says to keep pushing on. I really did need the encouragement you gave me! What's more, now I have the prayers of all you righteous men and I am confident it will accomplish much. Who could lose now? I just hope that I can be of some help to you guys in the same way you have come to my rescue. Keep praying for each other and keep in touch!

FEAR THAT SAYS ITS PRAYERS

How much courage do you have? Would your friends, coworkers, and family members call you a courageous person?

The dictionary says courage is the ability to face and deal with a dangerous or difficult situation. Modern writers offer their own definitions. Someone has said that courage is fear that has said its prayers. General

George Patton expressed it this way: "Courage is fear that holds on for one more minute." Franklin P. Jones called courage "the ability not to let people know how scared you are on the inside," or at least not to let your fear keep you from doing what you know you should. Eddie Rickenbacker said, "Courage is doing what you are afraid to do. Where there is no fear, there is no courage."

It is interesting to think about the various images of courage we have seen or read about. Most of them have to do with men fighting on a battlefield. The soldiers coming ashore at Omaha Beach. The defenders of Bastonge holding out against the Nazis. The Marines landing on Iwo Jima. Pickett's charge at Gettysburg. President Kennedy standing strong during the Cuban missile crisis.

THE MANY FACES OF COURAGE

But there are many faces of courage that have nothing to do with soldiers on the battlefield. Consider the courage of a family dealing with terminal cancer. A single mother fighting to raise her family. A widow who faces the last years of her life without her beloved husband by her side. A child of divorce struggling with doubt and anger and feelings of rejection. A single person who chooses purity over promiscuity. An engaged couple who will wait even though the world says go ahead. President Reagan telling the nation he has been diagnosed as having Alzheimer's disease. A newly-graduated MBA who moves into an inner-city community, hoping to help those less fortunate than himself. An employee who sees corruption and has the courage to blow the whistle. A dad facing a difficult surgery.

What do these situations have in common? Four qualities are evident in people with courage:

- Bravery in the face of danger—"I won't be held back by fear."
- Steadfastness in the face of opposition—"I won't give up."
- Action in the face of resistance—"I won't be intimidated."
- Optimism in the face of despair—"I won't lose heart."

Although it may not seem so at first glance, temperance and courage are tandem qualities. The biblical quality of temperance is courage in overalls. It's standing strong when you would rather turn and run. Listen to God's Word on this subject:

> "Be strong and courageous, because you will lead these people to inherit the land I swore to their forefathers to give them. Be strong and very courageous. Be careful to obey all the law my servant Moses gave you; do not turn from it to the right or to the left, that you may be successful wherever you go."
>
> —*Joshua 1:6-7*

> "Have I not commanded you? Be strong and courageous. Do not be terrified; do not be discouraged, for the LORD your God will be with you wherever you go."
>
> —*Joshua 1:9*

> The LORD is my light and my salvation—whom shall I fear? The LORD is the stronghold of my life—of whom shall I be afraid? When evil men advance against me to devour my flesh, when my enemies and my foes attack me, they will stumble and fall. Though an army besiege me, my heart will not fear; though war break out against me, even then will I be confident.
>
> —*Psalm 27:1-3*

> For God did not give us a spirit of timidity, but a spirit of power, of love and of self-discipline.
>
> —*2 Timothy 1:7*

> Perfect love drives out fear.
>
> —*1 John 4:18*

How can we develop this quality of daily courage that will keep us cool, calm, and collected—temperate? Three principles will help us.

PRINCIPLE #1:
REMEMBER WHO YOU ARE

Proverbs 28:1 says, "The wicked man flees though no one pursues, but the righteous are as bold as a lion." The *righteous* are bold, not the wicked. The wicked are scared to death. If you are a Christian, the first step to courage is to remember who you are in Jesus Christ. In Him, you are strong, victorious, accepted, justified, redeemed, saved, completely forgiven. Your sins have been washed away. You are seated with Jesus Christ in the heavenlies.[4] You were born for courage, not for fear. Second Timothy 1:7 tells us that God has not given us a spirit of fear, but love, power, and a sound mind. If you have a controlling spirit of fear, timidity, or anxiety, it didn't come from God.[5]

You were born again for courage, for bravery, for strength. God means for you to be an overcomer. If you are a believer, God has given you His Holy Spirit. You are not a loser. You were born again through Jesus Christ, and through the power of the Holy Spirit you can be victorious over the problems, struggles, and trials of life.

PRINCIPLE #2:
FACE YOUR FEARS

Fear will win every day until you stand up, look that fear straight in the face, and say, "You are not going to win over me anymore. By the help of God and with the power of the Holy Spirit, I am going to defeat you." You will never triumph until you confront the thing that is dragging you down.

Courage is nothing more than seeing the fear and taking action against it. In this sense our battle against fear is like our fight against worry. Ninety-five percent of the things we worry about won't ever happen. I tend to be a worrier. Fortunately, at least once a week my wife will tell me, "Stop that. You're worrying about something that will never happen—and even if it does, we'll deal with it when it comes."

God has given us a sound mind so we can look at our problems honestly and draw a proper strategy against them. He's given us power so we can overcome. And He's given us love so we can act in His strength—His life and love working through us.

There is no reason for a child of God to be gripped or destroyed by fear.

PRINCIPLE #3:
FOCUS ON GOD, NOT YOUR FEAR

First John 4:18 says, "Perfect love drives out fear." You can either allow the love of God or fear generated by Satan to reign in you—the choice is up to you. But both cannot dominate your life at the same time. Either fear will push the love out, or the love of God will push the fear out. How does the latter come to pass in our lives? Three practical steps will help us maintain that focus.

THANK GOD FOR THE THING THAT IS CAUSING YOU TO FEAR. Are you afraid of losing your job? Then pray, "Lord, I'm scared that I might lose my job soon; and if I do, I don't know how I will take care of my family. Father, I'm worried about my future. I don't know what to say to my wife and children when they ask me if I'm going to lose my job. Sometimes I wonder if You have forgotten me. I didn't need this, and I'm not sure I deserve this. But I thank You for allowing this to happen, even though I don't know why. You are a mighty rock, a strong tower, and a shelter in the time of storm. You have never failed me or my family. Your faithfulness stretches far beyond my need. By faith I affirm Your complete control of my life, and I trust You to help me keep this job or find another one. I choose to glorify You even while I am unemployed, if that is Your will for my life. Amen."

Prayer like that allows you to pour out your soul to God. It also allows you to focus your mind on God's character. By thanking Him for the thing that causes you to fear, you are affirming that God is greater than your problems. This is always the first step in overcoming your fear.

LIST THE BLESSINGS THAT HAVE COME INTO YOUR LIFE BECAUSE OF THE THING THAT YOU FEAR. What positive changes has God made in your life—in what ways have you grown spiritually—as a result of the situation you have dreaded? Your list might include items such as:

- Praying all the time.
- No longer sweating the small stuff.
- Reading the Bible daily.
- Asking friends for their prayers.
- Getting rid of the clutter.
- Having long talks with my wife.
- Having a clearer sense of important priorities.

- Saying no when I used to say yes too quickly.
- Discovering the importance of worship.
- Focusing on God as the only hope.
- Truly desiring Christian fellowship.
- Living out the truth of *carpe diem*.

Most importantly, God now has your undivided attention, which is what He wanted all along.

EACH DAY SHARE ONE OF THOSE BLESSINGS WITH ONE OTHER PERSON. A man in my congregation, Fred Hartman, died of cancer a little over a year ago. As a deacon and a leader of our Awana program, he was one of the most admired men in our church. I visited him not long before the end. The cancer had sapped his strength, and he was barely able to stand. But when I went into that house, I felt peace—the presence of the Holy Spirit even while a godly man was losing his battle with cancer.

I thought back to something Fred had told me two years earlier, when the cancer was first discovered: "When people get cancer they want to ask, 'Why me?' Instead, I have asked the Lord, 'Why not me?' All my life I have known God's blessings. He's been so good to me. He has watched over me, brought me back when I strayed from Him, gave me a wonderful wife, a son, a good business, a wonderful home, a church, and more friends than anybody should ever be allowed to have. I have received so many of God's blessings. If this happens to other people, why shouldn't it also happen to me?"

That is what courage looks like—the courage and confidence of a man who knows God and who has allowed the Lord to develop the character of Christ within him.

That's the kind of leaders—the kind of Christian men—God wants to grow in America's homes, communities, businesses, and churches today!

DON'T ADD COURAGE

Am I telling you to add courage to your Christian life? No. You already have it. God put it in you the moment you trusted Jesus Christ as Savior. Now you must use the courage God has given you. You already have victory in Jesus Christ. Now live out that victory. You already have power. Use the power God has given you.

What is courage? It is facing and dealing with the dangerous and difficult situations of life with the very strength and love of God—not giving in to fear, but stepping out for and with Christ.

A Man of Honor doesn't cut and run when the going gets tough. He stands tough, he takes the heat, and he doesn't lose his cool.

GOING DEEPER

1. A temperate man doesn't fall apart when his world falls apart. Describe three crisis situations you have experienced in the last five years. How well did you handle those situations? What have you learned about yourself as a result?

2. In your own words, define temperance. Describe the telltale marks of a man who has this quality and the marks of a man who doesn't.

3. Take a piece of paper and write down the names of the five most courageous people you know or have known. What specific qualities do these people have in common?

4. Read Joshua 1:1-9 carefully.
   What promise did God make in verses 3-5?
   What responsibility did Joshua have according to verse 7?
   Can the promise of verse 8 be claimed today? Explain.

5. You were born for courage. You were not born to be a loser.
   Do you agree with those statements?
   How do they square with your own experience?
   How do they square with the story about Fred Hartman?

6. If it's true that 95 percent of the things we worry about never happen, why do we still worry? Is worry always a sin? How do you know when you've crossed the line from legitimate concern into sinful worry?

7. How would your life be different if you began to face your fears?

TAKING ACTION

Pinpoint one area of fear in your own life. Write down three concrete steps you could take this week to deal constructively with your fear. Write down three positive things that have come into your life because of the thing you fear the most. Spend time each day reviewing both lists until you can say, "Lord, I thank You for the thing I fear because it has taught me to trust You more than ever before."

THE FINE ART OF SELF-CONTROL

A Man of Honor is "self-controlled."
—*1 Timothy 3:2; Titus 1:8*

T he original Greek expression in these verses describes a person who has a "safe mind." The *New International Version* translates this Greek word with several different English words in various passages—"self-controlled," "reasonable," "clear minded." Other translations use words such as "prudent," "sober," "discreet," and "master of himself."[1]

That last phrase is fascinating. What does it mean to be "master of yourself"? *It implies that you are in full control of yourself at all times.* Sometimes we men are accused of thinking with our stomachs or of being walking hormones. And sometimes those accusations are all too true. As I write these words, I am thinking of a respected man who left his wife of many years for a young woman barely out of her teens. I know another man who left his wife a year ago and is now with his second young woman. Both men have achieved some degree of success in their chosen professions, both have risen to a degree of prominence, and both had wives who love the Lord and would have been happy to stay with them forever.

What happened? How can smart men be so stupid? They have lost so much—their wives, their families, their reputations, the admiration of their friends. They traded it all for the thrill of a fling with a younger woman. Neither man will get away with it. Even pagans appreciate the value of faithfulness and understand the importance of keeping your commitments. If nothing else, these men will find themselves silently passed over when promotion time comes because the top positions in most companies are reserved for men who can be trusted to keep their promises. If a man won't keep the most sacred promise he ever makes, how can you trust him with something as trivial as a billion-dollar portfolio? A man who would "cash in" his wife might do the same with the company gold.

NOT A FLAKE OR A GOOF

A Man of Honor is master of himself. He is balanced, reasonable, and discerning—not given to extremes. He is experienced and mature enough to keep his balance when life throws him a curveball. "Self-controlled" also implies a sober and serious attitude. He's not a goof or a flake. He is a man who is serious about spiritual things.[2] *He's a great man to have around when a tough decision needs to be made because he doesn't jump to conclusions or act solely on the basis of his emotions.* This quality comes from long experience with life and long-term growth into spiritual maturity. Not many young men have this quality in abundance; it is more often seen in older men who have walked with God for many years.

AN OLD TESTAMENT MAN FOR THE 90S

The Bible offers many examples of men who failed because they lacked this essential element of self-control. But perhaps paramount among them all is Samson, the undisputed heavyweight champion of ancient Israel. His story is found in Judges 13–16. His life offers us many valuable spiritual lessons and practical applications.[3]

In one sense Samson is one of the best-known heroes in all the Bible. Generations of children have marveled at the story of Samson defeating the Philistines with the jawbone of a donkey. Many teenagers know about Samson's long hair and how Delilah tricked the secret out of him. Most of us know that he had his eyes poked out and how, as he was dying, he pushed the pillars apart and killed 3,000 Philistines. If you go to church at all, you know about Samson. His story is both heroic and tragic.

Sometimes we read the stories of men like David or Moses or Abraham and think, "I could never be like them." They seem to be in a different category, as if they were "special cases" and the rest of us are just "regular people." After all, Abraham was the friend of God, and Moses saw God face to face, and David was a man after God's own heart. Those are great stories, and we profit greatly from reading them; but those men don't seem very much like us.

Not so with Samson. He's a lot like us; the resemblance makes us uncomfortable. Many of us know what it's like to come from a godly home. And many of us entered life with great expectations laid on us by other people. Most men know what it means to be tempted by women. All of us struggle at times with the desire for revenge. We've been there, we understand; and when we see Samson struggling and falling, we know exactly what he is going through.

Here is a man who would feel right at home at the end of the twentieth century. He'd have a ball "looking out for Number One." Recently I received a brochure advertising a seminar on how to reach baby boomers. It said that boomers desire self-fulfillment above everything else. They are materialistic, nontraditional, and heavily into lifestyle issues. They lack institutional loyalty and crave a cause in which to believe. They will give of themselves but always expect something in return.

That sounds just like Samson. Give him some Dockers, a BMW, and a condo, and he would fit right in. Cindy Crawford would find him fascinating. Donald Trump would party with him. Geraldo would interview him. Jay Leno would make jokes about him. Kids would hang his posters on their bedroom walls. Somebody would make a rap song about his affair with Delilah. He'd feel right at home in America in the 90s. Perhaps more than any other Bible character, to our discredit, Samson is one of us.

SAMSON'S TWO SPIRITUAL FLAWS

In the end he stands out as a man who wasted his life on things that didn't matter. Although he started out with every spiritual advantage, he threw it all away. How could a man who started so well end so poorly? There are at least two answers to that question:

He Never Appreciated His Spiritual Heritage

In the beginning he had godly parents and a godly family and a godly calling. He knew the will of God, and he knew the Word of God. An angel personally announced what God wanted him to do. Plus, he had good looks, a winning personality, and enormous leadership ability. Samson inspired people. He was born for greatness. Samson had it all!

But he failed to appreciate all that God had given him. He dillied and he dallied. He went this way and that way. He messed around with lesser things, and in the process he basically frittered his life away.

What happened to him can happen to any of us, especially those of us raised in the Christian faith. In fact, the "better" your background, the more likely you are to do the same thing Samson did. The more you've been given, the greater the punishment for neglecting it.

He Couldn't Control His Emotions

This is a key point. When we read Samson's story, we tend to think that his problem was all in the sexual area. Actually, his problem was not in the sexual area at all. His most basic problem was that he never learned how to control his emotions.

First he was filled with lust, and then he was filled with anger. Then he was full of lust again, then anger again, and then lust again, and then anger again . . . He was riding an emotional roller-coaster—from the peak to the valley, then around a sharp corner, and then he did it all over again. One moment he was worshiping God, the next he was flirting with Philistine women. On one occasion he led the army of Israel to a stunning military victory by the power of the Holy Spirit. Later he slept with a Philistine prostitute. Not long after that he met Delilah, who tricked him into revealing the secret of his power, which led to his imprisonment and death. What a breathtaking but deadly spiritual odyssey!

Samson never learned to control his emotions, and consequently they controlled him completely. Proverbs 16:32 could have been written about Samson: "Better a patient man than a warrior, a man who controls his temper than one who takes a city." In his day Samson had taken more than one city. But he never learned to control his temper. He never learned how to rule his spirit. He never knew the first thing about self-control. As a result, in the end his runaway emotions ran away with him.

THREE TIMELY LESSONS

It has been well said that we learn much more from defeat than we do from victory. Failure is a wonderful teacher if we are willing to learn. Samson's story brings three timely lessons to mind. These apply to every man who desires to develop the spiritual quality of self-control.

LESSON #1:
UNLESS WE DEAL WITH OUR PROBLEMS THEY WILL
COME BACK TO HAUNT US AGAIN AND AGAIN AND AGAIN

Many men never deal with the real problems they face—anger, bitterness, an unforgiving spirit, an undisciplined life, greed, uncontrolled lust.

Perhaps *you* have neglected to meet the problem head-on. You have lifted up the carpet and swept that sin or that anxiety or that trial under the rug and have said, "That hasn't bothered me for four or five or six years, so I'm basically okay now." I beg you not to say that. Some of us need to take a good look in the mirror and see the way we really are. The hardest thing you'll ever say is, "I need help. I have a problem I can't handle." But isn't that the first step in any recovery program? You'll never get better until you are willing to say, "I really need help in this area of my life." If we do not learn to deal with our problems now, we will certainly have to deal with them later. Samson is Exhibit A of that principle.

LESSON #2:
UNLESS WE LEARN THE DIFFERENCE BETWEEN BEING
EMPOWERED BY THE SPIRIT AND CONTROLLED BY THE SPIRIT,
WE WILL FALL JUST LIKE SAMSON DID

Does that sound odd? It shouldn't. It is possible for a Christian to be empowered by the Spirit of God to do certain things and yet not to have his life yielded to the full control of the Holy Spirit. How else do you explain noted Christian leaders falling into open sin? I do not doubt that they were empowered by the Spirit of God, but at the point of their fall they were not *controlled* by the Holy Spirit. Samson at certain points was empowered by the Spirit of God. But there was never a point in his whole life when for a long period of time he remained under the control of God's Spirit.[4]

It's not enough just to be able to accomplish good things or win stunning battlefield victories. Unless your life is under the control of the Spirit, you're going to fall just like Samson did.[5]

LESSON #3:
UNLESS WE YIELD OUR SEXUAL DESIRES COMPLETELY TO GOD, WE RISK FALLING PREY TO THE DELILAHS OF THIS WORLD

To say it that way makes Delilah look bad, but I don't mean to smear her name. I suspect that she was just a woman who was hungry for a relationship. She was looking for love. She wanted somebody to spend some time with her. And who better than the handsome, powerful, famous Samson? I am not saying that the situation was all Delilah's fault or that Samson was just a victim. She was ready, he was willing, and they were both able.

But remember, Samson was the one who went down and found Delilah. Men, unless we lay the sexual area of our lives before God, we risk falling prey to the Delilahs of this world. It can happen to you; it can happen to me. "If you think you are standing firm, be careful that you don't fall!" (1 Corinthians 10:12).

LAUGH MORE AND WORRY LESS

Before we wrap up this chapter, let's end on a positive note by asking what self-control looks like on a daily basis. Samson shows us what happens when a man lacks this quality. But what will you look like when your life is controlled by the Holy Spirit?

You will . . .

- Live for God on Monday just as much as you do on Sunday.
- Bend your powers toward righteousness.
- Take your intellect and put it into the service of the King of kings.

- Transform the fire of worldly desire into passion for Jesus Christ.

- Establish some "hedges" in your relationships.

- Invest your time and talent and energies to win others to Jesus Christ.

- Make your wife and children your first priority.

- Say no to temptation and yes to purity.

- Decide to be as strong morally as you are physically.

- Choose to be a giver rather than a taker.

- Do what's right the first time.

- Admit mistakes without making excuses.

- Keep your New Year's resolutions.

- Allow others to rebuke you without getting angry.

- Laugh more and worry less.

Someone has said that freedom is not the right to do what you want, but the power to do what you ought. God reserves His choicest blessings for the man who has discovered the power to do what he ought to do. Blessed is that man, for he will become all that God wants him to be.

GOING DEEPER

1. Why is self-control so important for spiritual leaders? What happens when this quality is absent?

2. Even pagans appreciate the value of keeping your commitments. Do you agree with that statement?
   If it is true, why are immoral men often promoted to positions of power?

3. Not many young men have this quality in abundance; it is more often seen in older men.
   Do your own observations back up this statement? Explain.
   How can a younger man learn to develop this quality?

4. Read Judges 13.
   List at least three signs of Samson's godly heritage.
   How does your own spiritual heritage compare to Samson's?

5. Read Judges 14.
   Why do you think Samson was so attracted to Philistine women?
   What practical steps can men take to protect themselves from sexual
   temptation?

6. What is the essential difference between being empowered by the
   Spirit and controlled by the Spirit?

7. "Freedom is not the right to do what you want, but the power to do
   what you ought."
   Name three things you know you ought to be doing that you aren't
   doing right now. What's keeping you from doing those things?
   List one small step you could take in each area that would get you
   moving in the right direction.

TAKING ACTION

Evaluate your own sexual life. What words would you use to describe it?
Are you involved in any areas of sinful activity? Ask yourself this question:
"Do I truly want to yield my sexual desires to God?" Ask a good friend to
hold you accountable to moral faithfulness and sexual purity. Set a definite time (next Thursday? once a month? once a week?) when your
friend will check with you to see how you are doing.

THE ULTIMATE
HE-MAN

A Man of Honor is "disciplined."
—*Titus 1:8*

The Greek word translated "disciplined" describes a person who has his "strength under control." He eats, but he is not a glutton. He sleeps, but he does not sleep forever. He loves, but he does not love indiscriminately. He bargains when he shops, but he knows how to say no. He has a credit card, but he knows when not to use it. He gets angry, but he never loses his cool. He is strong physically, but he doesn't want to intimidate others.[1]

Proverbs 25:28 warns of what happens when this quality is not present: "Like a city whose walls are broken down is a man who lacks self-control." Such a man is easy prey to sexual temptation, financial temptation, uncontrolled anger, arrogance, envy, sloth, and a critical spirit.

Seneca said, "Most powerful is he who has himself in his own control." Many gifted men fail at precisely this point. Great promise is squandered by a failure of self-discipline. This is the difference between an NBA player who washes out because of drug abuse and a superstar like Michael Jordan.

The comparison is apt because the New Testament often compares the growing Christian to an athlete in training. For instance, 1 Corinthians 9:24 tells us to "run in such a way as to get the prize." But the following verses remind us that winning the prize requires "strict training" (verse 25), that we must not "run aimlessly" or be like a boxer "beating the air" (verse 26), that we must each "beat my body and make it my slave" lest through careless sin we should be "disqualified" from winning "the prize" (verse 27).

IT'S NOT BRAIN SURGERY

Every football coach knows that championships are won in the weight room and on the practice field, not just in the actual games. The same is true in every area of life. Those who discipline themselves sooner or later rise to the top of their chosen profession. When faced with a simple job, we often jokingly say, "It's not brain surgery." Of course not, because if it were, most of us couldn't do it. There aren't many brain surgeons because there aren't many people willing to pay the price of fifteen years of specialized training, hundreds of sleepless nights, and thousands of hours spent learning proper surgical techniques.

Discipline may be out of style, but when you watch your son or daughter being wheeled into the operating room, more than anything else you want a doctor who paid the price over the years so he won't make a mistake when he picks up the scalpel.

A disciplined, godly life doesn't happen by accident. No one just happens to grow into spiritual maturity. To put this into a simple formula: Time + Discipline = Growth.[2]

Paul challenged Timothy to "train yourself to be godly" (1 Timothy 4:7). Men, what are you doing right now to develop your spiritual life? The word "train" comes from the Greek word *gumnos,* which originally meant "naked" and from which we get the English word *gymnasium.* The word suggests sweaty shoes, worn-out jerseys, scarred helmets, callused hands, and aching muscles.[3]

No one becomes godly by accident.

You can't sleep late and lounge around like a couch potato if you want to win the prize of a godly life. And you can't indulge yourself physically, mentally, or spiritually. You're going to have to get in shape in every sense of the word. Too many men have developed a spiritual beer gut from lazy habits of life.

Through Christ you can be a winner, but it won't be easy and it won't come quickly. There is a price to pay.

IT STARTS IN THE MORNING

Where does such discipline come from? Let me share a story sent to me by a missionary serving in Central America.

> No doubt the man who most influenced me after my own father was Dr. Pierre Wildes DuBose. He founded a Christian boarding school named after his father—the Hampden DuBose Academy in Florida. I spent my junior and senior high years there because my parents were missionaries in Honduras.
>
> Dr. DuBose—Doc to all the students and staff—handled all the discipline for the students. Whenever a boy was called in or sent in, Dr. DuBose would be sitting at his desk, looking over his glasses, and his first question always was, "How are you doing with your private devotion? Your quiet time?"
>
> Failing to spend personal time with the Lord affected school work, domestic work, sports, relationships with other boys or with the girls. One could almost become superstitious and spend time in the Word and prayer just to keep the evil away . . . but it is a fact that starting the day with the Lord does improve the whole day.[4]

Such discipline is not optional if we are going to be Men of Honor for God. You won't have a quiet time by accident. It just doesn't happen that way. You have to schedule the time or you'll end up watching TV or reading the newspaper.[5] Dr. Ron Blue, president of CAM International, actually writes his quiet times in his daily appointment book. That way they actually become part of his schedule, so he knows (and his secretary knows) that when the appointed hour comes, he will be meeting with the King of kings and is not to be disturbed for any reason.

IT WON'T HAPPEN ALONE

You *can* be godly, but it probably won't happen without some help from your friends.

Even though I have been a Christian for over twenty-five years, I find the temptation to laziness as great today as I ever did. My greatest encouragement to godliness comes from a Promise Keepers group that meets every other week. There are nine of us right now—an attorney, a cardiologist, a publisher, a printer, a pastor, an architect, a coach, a pediatric surgeon, an options trader, and a sales manager. Whenever I'm tempted to give up or give in or get grumpy or lazy or start slacking off on my commitments, one of the guys will give me a pat on the back or, if necessary, a kick in the seat of the pants. I find it encouraging to meet together because if one or two of us have had a rough week, there are always a couple of others who have seen some amazing answers to prayer.

As part of our group covenant, we agree not to share with anyone else the things that happen in the group. That creates a safe environment for men to open up and share their struggles—sometimes with painful honesty. But after a year and a half of meeting together, I can safely share one secret: mostly, we laugh together. Someone (usually Allan) will say something off the wall; then Glenn will chime in; then Gary will start chuckling; then Duane will tell a crazy story from the hospital; George will roll his eyes and say, "You guys are nuts." That makes Rob smile and Tom and Alex laugh. The other night Jeff said he felt like he had been "rode hard and put up wet," so it took about an hour to get him to laugh. But we did it.

Always—and I emphasize that word—I leave the meeting feeling more committed to be a godly man in all my relationships.

God never meant for you to make it on your own. Men, whom are you meeting with on a regular basis? Who holds you accountable to be a man of God? Who encourages you when you are down? Who cuts through the baloney and tells you the truth? Who knows you well enough to smell an excuse? Who knows when you need some extra prayer?

THE HARD WAY VS. THE EASY WAY

You *can* become a man of God, but it won't come quickly. There are no shortcuts on the road to godliness. You can't take the easy way if you want to win the prize.

Every day you face a choice of going one of two ways. You can go the easy way or the hard way.

The easy way is the way of procrastination. It is the way of staying in bed when the alarm clock goes off. The way of saying the boss isn't around, nobody is seeing me, it's good enough for government work. The way of no plans, no forethought, no enthusiasm, no diligence.

The hard way means getting up early to have your daily devotions whether you feel like it or not. It means paying the price to cross racial lines for the sake of Jesus Christ. The man who takes the hard way doesn't send his children to church—he takes them with him. He sacrifices time out with his buddies so he can spend time with his wife. The hard way means putting God's kingdom ahead of your own interests, even at the expense of career advancement. If you decide to go the hard way, you're going to have to get in shape mentally, physically, socially, emotionally, and spiritually.

GOD IS ON THE HARD ROAD

Here's an important insight that many men never discover: *God is on the hard road. He's not sitting with the couch potatoes.* The hard road looks difficult and daunting. All of us would rather be on the easy road. But God is calling you and me to stop making excuses and get into the ball game.

Do you want to know the ironic difference between the easy road and the hard road? The easy road looks easy, but once you get on it, it turns into the hard road. And the hard road looks hard, but once you do the hard thing in life, it turns out to be easy. The easy road is deceptive. It is the way of destruction, poverty, starvation, and desperation. It is the way to wasted days, wasted weeks, wasted months, and wasted years. The hard road, which appears to be so difficult, is ultimately the road of blessing, fulfillment, and lasting spiritual growth. It is the road that leads you to the top. The easy road takes you down to the bottom. The only road that goes to the top is the hard road. It is tough, but it is the only one that goes where you want to go with your life—and where God wants you to go.[6]

SHIFTING SANDS OR A FIRM FOUNDATION

One summer our family vacation took us to the Deep South. As we were meandering our way back up toward Chicago, our path led through Knoxville and onto I-75 heading north toward Lexington and Cincinnati.

We weren't in any hurry, and soon it was past lunchtime. Sounds floating from the backseat indicated that an imminent stop would be well advised. We exited and made our way to the little town of Corbin, Kentucky, looking for a fast-food restaurant.

As we drove along, I spotted a sign that said, "Visit the original Kentucky Fried Chicken." We discovered that it was a combination restaurant and museum. It seems that in the 1930s Harland Sanders bought a restaurant and built a motel next to it. The number one recipe in the restaurant at the motel was the best fried chicken in the state of Kentucky.

By 1956 he was successful but not known. He was sixty-six years old, the time when most men retire. Then calamity struck: I-75 was being built, and the new interstate would bypass the town of Corbin, Kentucky, meaning nobody would stop at the motel or eat at his restaurant. If he was going to survive, he had to do something else. So he sold his restaurant and the motel and went into the chicken spice business, supplying restaurants in several states. Out of that little business came the idea to start a restaurant where people would come and buy nothing but fried chicken cooked with the colonel's special herbs and spices. He decided to call his first restaurant Kentucky Fried Chicken. The rest is history.

A sign on the wall of the museum contains the credo of Harland Sanders. It is called "The Hard Way."

> It is comparatively easy to prosper by trickery, the violation of confidence, oppression of the weak, sharp practices, cutting corners, all those methods we are so prone to palliate and condone as business shrewdness. It is difficult to prosper by the keeping of promises, the deliverance of value and goods and services and denouncing the so-called shrewdness with sound merit and good ethics. The easy way is efficacious and speedy, the hard way arduous and long. But as the clock ticks away, the easy way becomes harder, and the hard way becomes easier. As the calendar records the years, it becomes increasingly evident that the easy way rests upon a hazardous foundation of shifting sands, whereas the hard way builds solidly a foundation of confidence that cannot be swept away. Thus we builded.

The next time you go to Kentucky Fried Chicken, remember that those thousands of restaurants were started by a man who decided he was not going to go the easy way. People around the world know the Colonel's profile even if they don't know the story behind it.[7]

In the Sermon on the Mount, Jesus told about two houses—one built on the sand and the other on solid rock (Matthew 7:24-27). When a storm came, it destroyed the first house; but the second one lasted because it was built on a firm foundation. Jesus said that the "rock" was hearing His words and putting them into practice.

Men, what's the foundation of the "house" you are building with your life? Without discipline you will never become a godly man. Your "house" may look strong, but it won't stand up to the storms of life. If you take the easy way, in the end you will be disappointed, and all you have worked for will come to nothing.

Rare is the man who takes the hard road of discipline. It will cost him all he has; but in the end the prize of godliness will be worth the pain.

God is looking for a few good men who will pay the price. Are you one of them?

GOING DEEPER

1. Time + Discipline = Spiritual Growth.
   How much time do you spend each week focusing on your spiritual growth? Are you satisfied with your answer? If not, what are you planning to do about it?

2. Read Proverbs 25:28.
   How does discipline build a "wall" of protection around your life? How can your discipline also protect your entire family? Do you know anyone whose lack of discipline has hurt his own family? Explain.

3. Read 1 Corinthians 9:24-27.
   What is the "prize" Paul mentions in verse 24? When will he receive it? Why is strict training necessary in order to win the prize? In running terms, spiritually are you a sprinter, a walker, a jogger, or a marathon man? Describe your current "training" program to get into top spiritual shape.

4. No one becomes godly by accident.
   Do you agree with that statement? Why or why not?
   Why is discipline an indispensable part of spiritual growth?

5. Would the people who know you best call you a disciplined person?
   Why or why not?

6. Consider the hard way vs. the easy way. Describe the characteristics
   of the two paths. How can you spot a person on the hard way? The
   easy way? Do you know anyone who has chosen the easy way in life?
   What has happened to him or her or them?

TAKING ACTION

For most men, spiritual growth begins with a commitment to spend time
with the Lord each morning. Make a commitment to spend at least ten
minutes each morning for the next week reading your Bible and praying. If you make a weekly plan, add "Daily Devotions" to your schedule.
Ask a friend to hold you accountable to keep this commitment.

PART II

HIS EMOTIONAL LIFE

THE MAN
I NEVER MET

A Man of Honor is "not violent."
—*1 Timothy 3:3; Titus 1:7*

I like the King James rendering—"no striker." That says it all. A "striker" is a violent person who is easily angered. Such a man tends to be assertive, manipulative, demanding, coercive, and highly critical of others. He is quick to pick fights and slow to make up afterwards.[1]

This term warns against persons who use physical, verbal, mental, or emotional abuse in order to get their way. They are masters of intimidation, quick to raise their voice, quicker still to raise their fists, always ready to do whatever it takes to have their own way. Such men have a Rambo mentality, loving violence for its own sake.[2]

FRIDAY AFTERNOON MASSACRE

Carlos died on Friday afternoon. I never met him because he never made it to our church as planned for the following Sunday night. He was going to share how Jesus Christ had radically changed his life, but bullets from members of his gang silenced him forever. Ironically it happened because he was witnessing to two young men from another gang. He himself had been led to Christ by Glen Fitzjerrell, who works with the gangs on the north side of Chicago. As part of his discipleship program, Glen asked Carlos to speak at our church. He readily agreed and said he'd be glad to come and tell what the Lord had done for him.

One week later he was standing at the same spot in the alley when he struck up a conversation with two members of a rival gang. At precisely that moment, a carload of his buddies drove by and saw him talking to their bitter enemies. Assuming he was selling out gang secrets, his friends began shooting at him and the two young men. Before coming to Christ Carlos would gladly have fired the first shot. But in a split second he decided to jump in front of the two young men and take the bullets that were intended for them. He died two days before he was to have shared the love of God with my congregation.

Lots of people die in Chicago every year, so the news of his death never made the front page. In a city grown weary of gang-related violence, Carlos hardly rated more than a few lines in a forgotten obituary. "Another gang member gunned down," said the reporter. No one knew why he died.

But Glen started his sermon that Sunday morning with the story of Carlos's giving his life for two men from a rival gang. It's easy to ask yourself what you would have done in a similar situation. I'm sure we all like to think that we'd take the bullets just like Carlos did. But in truth, if pressed to the wall, I can count on the fingers of one hand the number of people I *know* I would give my life for, no questions asked. I don't feel either noble or guilty coming to that conclusion; it's just a statement of bare facts. Maybe in a moment of crisis I would do better than that, but I'll probably never be put to the test.

At least not like Carlos was.

HOTHEADS IN THE RING

One of my best friends has been studying martial arts for almost eight years. Three times a week he goes to the top gym in Chicago to work out. In a year or two he hopes to have his black belt, but not until he has mastered all the major forms of fighting. My friend loves the challenge and discipline and the sheer hard work required to become one of the best fighters in the Midwest. "Have you ever used your martial arts in an actual fight outside the ring?" I asked one day, thinking that surely the answer would be yes. "No, and our instructor constantly tells us that the purpose of martial arts is not to win a fight, but to gain self-control." My friend went on to say that hotheads rarely do well in the martial arts because they lack the discipline necessary to succeed.

Men of honor don't have to fight to prove their manhood. They don't need to prove they are men by shoving other people around. They are strong enough to walk away without saying a word.

Before Carlos came to Christ, he was as tough as any man in his gang. He knew how to use his fists, and he knew how to use his gun. Growing up in the inner city means living on the raw edge of danger every day. Glen says that's why most kids join gangs—to find the security and acceptance they can't find at home. The gangs provide a measure of safety for ghetto kids in a world where Dad is absent and Mom works all day. In exchange for security, the gang members learn to protect their turf and to use whatever force is necessary to protect themselves.

Not long ago I ate lunch with the editor of a local newspaper. He talked about the rising influence of gangs in the area where I live and minister (Oak Park, Illinois, just west of Chicago). For many years most local leaders denied we had a problem, even though all the teenagers knew the truth. Gangs have now become a national problem, with some of the larger gangs establishing local branches in many major cities. Our town's first drive-by shooting ended with one dead and many others arrested. As the editor spoke about this crisis, he made a profound observation: "For too long we've sought a government solution to problems that begin inside the home. I believe that once a fifteen-year-old joins a gang, he won't be changed short of divine intervention." We need "faith-based solutions," he said.[3]

Carlos proved the truth of those words. *Jesus Christ did what welfare assistance and job training could never do.* Jesus reached down into the heart of a Spanish Cobra and changed it into the heart of a Christian. That's a pure miracle, made possible only by the grace of God.

Why did Carlos do what he did? More than once I have wondered what happened in that microsecond before he jumped in front of the two young men. Did he pause to weigh the alternatives? Did he think about the irony of being shot by his own friends who thought he had become a traitor? Did he wish for a gun so he could fire back?

I'm sure that the answer to the last question is no. Carlos understood that violence begets violence, hatred leads to more hatred, and one bullet leads to a thousand more.

WHO IS MY ENEMY?

In the Sermon on the Mount Jesus declared that His disciples would follow a revolutionary policy of nonretaliation against violence: "You have heard that it was said, 'Love your neighbor and hate your enemy.' But I tell you: Love your enemies and pray for those who persecute you" (Matthew 5:43-44). It might help to define who the "enemy" is in this verse. The "enemy" is almost always a friend, a colleague, or a family member who has hurt me in some way. *My enemy by definition will almost always be someone close to me.* I don't have any enemies in Iraq or Bosnia because I don't know anybody over there. But it's not hard to have enemies in my own town because I know lots of people there.

It is also true that an enemy is a person God uses to reveal my weaknesses. An enemy is like a chisel God uses to chip away at the rough spots in my life. That's why if you are married, your wife will be your enemy from time to time. No one knows your weaknesses like she does. She sees hidden blemishes, secret sins, bad habits that the rest of the world never sees. She knows the real you because she lives with you every day. If she loves you, she'll have to be your enemy from time to time. Painful as it might be for you, God will use her loving honesty to help you grow.

That's why you have to feed your enemy. Romans 12:20 instructs us, "If your enemy is hungry, feed him; if he is thirsty, give him something to drink." You can't let your wife or your children starve to death. It wouldn't look good in the newspaper. That's why you have to give your boss or your teacher or that obnoxious person in the next office something to drink. These are people who are close to you, and because they are close to you, God is using them to expose the weak areas of your life.

LIVING WITH A RAGEAHOLIC

"If it is possible, as far as it depends on you, live at peace with everyone" (Romans 12:18). I like this statement because it strikes me as utterly realistic. In a fallen world, it isn't always possible to live at peace with everyone. Sometimes despite our best efforts, we'll rub people the wrong way.

Sometimes you are thrown into a situation at school or at work with people who are Grade A, board-certified, 100 percent jerks. And you can't do anything about it! Such people don't want peace—they want to make trouble.

Not long ago a friend spoke about a colleague at work who yells at everyone all the time for no particular reason. She just yells and yells and yells. He called her a "rageaholic." That's a picturesque word to describe a very sick person. Unfortunately, she's not the only one out there. You can find at least one person like that in every school, every business, and usually on every block.

Paul's advice in such cases is simple: "Live at peace with everyone." If that doesn't work, make sure that you aren't part of the problem. Note that little phrase, "as far as it depends on you." The only person you can take care of is you. Do you remember the saying, "It takes two to tango"? It also takes two to tangle. *If you refuse to fight, at least you can't be blamed for causing the problem.* You can't control other people or how they respond to you. But you can create an environment that makes it either more or less likely for them to blow up at you. So the principle is, be a peacemaker to the point that if someone makes trouble for you, no one can legitimately blame you.

JESUS OUR MODEL

If you want a biblical example, consider Jesus. He wasn't born in a palace, but in a stable in an obscure village in Judea. From the very beginning He faced murderous opposition from a "rageaholic" named King Herod.

That was a sign of things to come. Whispers and rumors abounded regarding His parents. When He grew up, His own family doubted His true identity. As He began His ministry, the common people heard Him gladly, but the religious leaders saw Him as a threat to their interests. They feared the multitudes of people who flocked to hear Him preach. Trying to trip Him up, they sent their best scholars to ask Him hard questions; but every time He made them look foolish, which infuriated the leaders even more.

Eventually they decided, "This man must die!" Fueled by hatred, jealousy, and blind rage, they schemed and plotted and bided their time. Surely this upstart rabbi would make a mistake sooner or later, and when

He did they would pounce on Him like a fox on a rabbit. But knowing their evil plans, He calculated every word, and He too bided His time.

The day came for the showdown in Jerusalem. Late one night He was arrested and taken away. Witnesses appeared who made absurd charges against Him, claiming He was an extremist, a rebel, a troublemaker, an insurrectionist, a traitor to the nation. But the truth didn't matter that night. His fate was already sealed, the die cast, the verdict rendered.

They beat Him with their fists, then ripped off His beard, then spat on Him. Finally they scourged Him with a whip, shredding His back. In the end He could barely stand up because of the torture He had endured.

On Good Friday they crucified Him along with two thieves. As He hung on the cross, His first words were a prayer for His tormentors: "Father, forgive them, for they do not know what they are doing" (Luke 23:34). Shortly after that, He died.

What a great man He was. Only God's Son could have done what He did. If God were not God, He could not have sent His Son to die for the sins of the world. Only an infinite God could offer an infinite sacrifice with infinite results.

CARLOS AND JESUS

How much of this did Carlos understand on that fateful day when he took the bullets intended for his enemies? I'm not sure of the answer, but I do know this: in that microsecond before he moved, Carlos decided to follow Jesus even though it meant going to his own grave.

I never met Carlos, but he taught me a great deal about God. In choosing the path of nonviolence, he himself died a violent death. I expect to meet him in heaven and to hear the message he never gave that Sunday night. He was a Man of Honor who died in the service of his Master, following in His steps. He knew that Jesus died for him; that's why he could die for his enemies. "And by faith he still speaks, even though he is dead" (Hebrews 11:4).

GOING DEEPER

1. The chapter began with a description of the man with a Rambo mentality who uses force and intimidation to get his way.

Have you ever known anyone like that? Were you ever like that yourself? Would your close friends say you're a lot like Rambo? Why do so many men confuse manliness with meanness? What is the essential difference between the two?

2. Consider the story of Carlos taking the bullets.
Why would a man do such a thing? What would you have done? List the people you know you would die for. Are you surprised by who is on your list . . . and by who isn't?

3. Men of Honor don't have to fight to prove their manhood.
Why is that statement true? What does it really mean? When was the last time you walked away from an argument? When was the last time you wished you had? In what situations do you believe the use of violence might be justified?

4. Most of us would agree that the Gospel of Christ is the only hope for changing America's inner cities. In a practical sense, how does faith in Jesus Christ break the cycle of violence? What other "faith-based solutions" would help put broken families back together again?

5. An enemy is any person God uses to reveal our weaknesses.
Do you agree that your wife could sometimes be your enemy? Describe a time when someone you loved revealed a weakness in your life. How did you respond?

6. Read Romans 12:17-21.
What does it mean to "heap burning coals" on someone's head? Why does God forbid His children to seek revenge? What happens when we seek it anyway?

7. What does the example of Christ say to you about the possibility of living a nonviolent life in a world filled with hatred? Is it unrealistic to expect men to live the way He did? Explain your answer.

TAKING ACTION

Take an enemy inventory of the people closest to you. Be sure to include your wife, your children, and your closest friends. What things have you learned about yourself from them that you wouldn't have discovered any other way? Spend time thanking God for your beloved enemies.

STOP ARGUING!

A Man of Honor is "not quarrelsome."
—*1 Timothy 3:3*

T he *King James Version* uses a picturesque phrase here—"not a brawler." Other translations use phrases such as "not pugnacious," "not combative," or "not thin-skinned."[1] Some people just love to pick fights. They love to argue, to mix it up, to trade insults and put other people down. Such a man is the master of the cutting remark, the king of the snappy comeback. Proverbs 20:3 says, "It is to a man's honor to avoid strife, but every fool is quick to quarrel." Do you know how to spot this person? In any group this man dominates the discussion by arguing every point into the ground. He can always find a thousand reasons why a new idea won't work. When challenged, he sends out the clear message, "My way or the highway."

By contrast, the godly leader is uncontentious, willing to listen, not argumentative, not given to a fighting spirit. He is a peacemaker, but not a peace-breaker.

"HIS OTHER FACE"

Assistant Prosecutor Christopher Darden set the tone in his opening statement in the O. J. Simpson murder trial. "It is not the actor who is on trial here today, ladies and gentlemen. It is not that public face. It is his other face." What a chilling phrase—"his other face." The face we never see running through airports or driving rental cars. The face that never appears in the movies or on the talk shows.

It is, Mr. Darden said, the face Simpson wore behind the walls in his Brentwood home. It is, he said, the face of a batterer, a wife beater, an abuser, a controller.

Was it also the face of a brutal murderer? The jury said no and acquitted him.

For the moment we do not know who killed Nicole Brown Simpson and Ronald Goldman. But we do know this much—there is such a thing as the "other face" of O. J. Simpson.[2] We know it's true because we all have the same "other face." There is within the human heart an enormous capacity for evil. The Bible says in Romans 3:23 that "all have sinned and fall short of the glory of God." Jeremiah 17:9 tells us that "the heart is deceitful above all things and beyond cure. Who can understand it?"

ANGER CAN BE USEFUL

Anger is a powerful emotion that can be used for good or for evil. Anger isn't always wrong. We know, for instance, that anger is one of God's emotions and that God never sins, and yet the Bible speaks repeatedly of His anger—in over a hundred different passages. We also know there are times when anger is justified and even righteous. Ephesians 4:26 says, "In your anger do not sin."

When we see people hurting other people, when we watch the wholesale slaughter of the unborn, when we see children being lured into drugs and prostitution, when we see families torn apart by sin, *that ought to make us angry*. If we sit idly by while the world goes to hell, if we don't get angry, if we don't weep, if we don't care, then something is wrong deep inside us.[3]

BEFORE THE SUN GOES DOWN

However, even righteous anger can quickly lead us in the wrong direction. The same verse that says, "In your anger do not sin" adds, "Do not let the sun go down while you are still angry." That is, don't go to bed angry. Even if your anger is justified, don't go to sleep that way. Deal with it, talk it out, pray it out, walk it out, but don't try to sleep it off. That won't work.

Recently I talked with a friend who mentioned another couple having serious marriage problems. He said, "I think for a long time they just neglected their relationship." You could say that about most couples who have problems. Little things build up . . . build up . . . and build up like the lava in Mt. Saint Helens and then, *Boom!*—the top blows off.

There is a divine time limit on your anger. Solve your problems before you go to bed. Don't go to sleep angry. Why is that so important? Because what you think about as you drift off to sleep becomes part of your subconscious. What starts as anger overnight becomes a grudge by morning. The anger sinks in and slowly turns to resentment. Over time it hardens like concrete. Each little grudge becomes another brick in the wall that separates you from your mate.

As long as you carry a grudge, you can't communicate with your wife or your children. You talk, but your mate hears only the anger inside. You listen, but your resentment blocks the message from coming through clearly. The sludge of negative emotions clogs up the communication line and nothing can get through.

Commenting on this principle, a friend wrote the following note:

> Beth and I were challenged to make a vow before we were married to not ever let the sun go down on our anger. The pastor who married us read from Ephesians 4, and we then vowed before God and the pastor to not ever go to bed angry. That was over 10 years ago. I can say that this has been the best single bit of advice we have ever received. We have never gone to bed angry yet—but we've sure had some late nights talking things out before we fall asleep.[4]

What happens when you don't deal with your anger? It settles deep in your heart; it hardens like concrete; it distorts your personality; it squeezes out your joy; it oozes the smelly black gunk of unhappiness over every part of your life. That's why the very next verse in Ephesians offers this warning: "Do not give the devil a foothold" (Ephesians 4:27).

All rock climbers understand that verse. In order to get up the side of a mountain, you have to get a firm foothold. That's what Satan wants to do in your life. He wants to use your anger (even your legitimate anger) to get a foothold in your heart and so shoot his laser-lies deep into your life.

DADDY KING

When Martin Luther King, Sr., respectfully called "Daddy King," died in 1984, he was eulogized as the father of the civil rights movement in America. One black leader said, "If we started our own country, he would be our George Washington."

In his eighty-four years he endured more than his share of suffering and hatred. During his childhood in Georgia he witnessed lynchings. The first time he tried to register to vote in Atlanta, he found that the registrar's office was on the second floor of City Hall—but the main elevator was marked "Whites Only," the stairwell was closed, and the elevator for blacks was out of order.

He is mostly remembered for the accomplishments of his son, the Rev. Martin Luther King, Jr.—leader of the nonviolent civil rights movement, cut down by an assassin's bullet in 1968. One year later, Daddy King's second son drowned in a backyard swimming pool. The crowning blow came in 1974 during a church service. As his wife played "The Lord's Prayer," a young man stood in the congregation and began shooting. Mrs. King collapsed in a hail of gunfire, while Daddy King watched in horror from the pulpit.

NO TIME TO HATE

Near the end of his life, reflecting on the loss of his wife and oldest son, he spoke of the policy of nonviolence he had come to embrace. "There are two men I am supposed to hate. One is a white man, the other is black, and both are serving time for having committed murder. I don't hate either one. There is no time for that, and no reason either. Nothing that a man does takes him lower than when he allows himself to fall so low as to hate anyone."

How can a man not hate when his wife and oldest son have been murdered? It seems natural and even proper to hate killers, doesn't it?

The answer comes back, "There is no time for that." To hate is to live in the past, to dwell on deeds already done. Hatred is the least satisfying emotion, for it gives the person you hate a double victory—once in the past, once in the present.

No time to hate? Not if you have learned how to forgive. *Forgiving does not mean whitewashing the past, but it does mean refusing to live there.* Forgiveness breaks the awful chain of bitterness and the insidious desire for revenge. As costly as it is to forgive, unforgiveness costs far more.

FOUR STEPS TO FREEDOM

I wonder how many of us have gotten in trouble because we gave in to our anger. Perhaps we have said things in a moment of tension that we later longed to take back but could not. Marriages have been broken, friendships have ended, jobs have been lost because we lost our temper and said and did things we later regretted.

Is there a better way? How can we handle our anger so that it doesn't destroy us and those we love? Let me offer four suggestions to help you deal with your anger.

STEP #1:
HAVE THE COURAGE TO FACE YOUR ANGER

It all begins here. Until you can admit to the "other face" that no one ever sees, you will never get better. So many of us have a public face that looks good and a private face that we keep behind locked gates and stone walls, a face of anger and hatred.

STEP #2:
SHARE YOUR STRUGGLES WITH A FRIEND

As the evidence came out in court, it seemed that many of his friends knew O. J. Simpson had a strong temper and that he was prone to violent behavior. The police knew it. But no one confronted him with the ugly truth. What if he had said, "I need some help. I've got some anger in me that I'm not handling very well"? Would things be different today? (I am not assuming by these comments that O. J. is in fact guilty of murder. But clearly he has been a batterer.)

Men especially seem to struggle in this area. We harbor deep feelings of bitterness and anger and don't know what to do with them. What's worse, we're afraid to tell anyone because we think that sharing our struggles is a sign of weakness. How wrong we are. The weak cover up; only the strong have the courage to admit they need help.

A friend recently stopped by to see me, and we ended up spending several hours together. In discussing one sensitive matter, I asked my friend to pray for me that I would not lose my cool and say something under pressure that I would later regret. Years ago I probably wouldn't have done that, but having learned the truth about myself, I now find it easier to admit my need and ask for prayer than to wish I had.

STEP #3:
DO A RELATIONSHIP INVENTORY BASED ON EPHESIANS 4:30-32

> And do not grieve the Holy Spirit of God, with whom you were sealed for the day of redemption. Get rid of all bitterness, rage and anger, brawling and slander, along with every form of malice. Be kind and compassionate to one another, forgiving each other, just as in Christ God forgave you.

These words are incredibly specific. Check your life for any signs of bitterness, anger, rage, slander, brawling, and malice. If you find even a trace of those things, get rid of them with Christ's help! They are like a deadly virus in your spiritual bloodstream.

Anger kills!
Bitterness kills!
Slander kills!
Rage kills!
Resentment kills!
It doesn't just kill other people. It kills you too!

STEP #4:
YIELD CONTROL OF YOUR LIFE TO THE HOLY SPIRIT

Ephesians 4:30 warns us not to grieve the Holy Spirit by harboring bitterness in our hearts. You can allow the Holy Spirit to be in control, or your anger can take control. There is no third option, no middle ground.

Jesus has shown us the way. You don't have to live in anger and bitterness over the way people are treating you and/or have treated you. Through the power of the Holy Spirit, your life can be different. God's Spirit can set you free from the chains that have bound you to the past.

The price is simple, but it's not cheap. You have to give up your anger, let go of your bitterness, say farewell to your hurtful memories. Then and only then will the Holy Spirit be free to take control of your life.

I'd like to suggest a simple prayer for the Holy Spirit to take over your life. Saying words alone won't change your heart, but if these words reflect your deepest desire, today could be a new beginning for you.

> *Father, for too long I have tried to solve my own problems. I thought I could handle things on my own, but it didn't work. I've made a mess of my own life. I've tried and tried, and now I'm tired of trying.*
>
> *Lord Jesus, thank You for showing us how to live. Thank You for showing us how to die. Thank You for taking all my sin away when You died on the cross. Thank You for showing us how to forgive the people who have hurt us the most.*
>
> *Holy Spirit, here and now I yield control of my life to You. From this day forward I want You to run my life. Please fill me with Your power so that I might become a truly different person. With all my heart and all my soul, with everything that is in me, I now say that I want You to take control.*
>
> *Lord Jesus, You're in charge now. Lead on, and I will follow You from this day forward. Amen.*

May God grant you new life through Christ in the power of the Holy Spirit. And may you experience the freedom of forgiveness and the joy that comes from letting Him take control.

GOING DEEPER

1. Every group needs men who will ask good questions—even if the questions are difficult to answer. Yet we've all met people who like to

argue things into the ground. Where is the line between fair questions and a quarrelsome spirit? How do you know when you've crossed it?

2. We all have that "other face."
   What does that sentence mean? Is it true?
   Have you ever worried about what would happen if people found out what you were really like? Why does that bother you?

3. Read Matthew 23:13-28.
   Who were the Pharisees, and why did Jesus condemn them?
   Why are religious people especially prone to hypocrisy?

4. Anger isn't always wrong.
   Do you agree with that statement? Explain your answer.
   Name at least three examples of justified anger.

5. Why is it especially important for husbands and wives to settle their differences before the sun goes down? What happens when you don't?

6. What does the example of Dr. Martin Luther King, Sr., say to you about the possibility of racial reconciliation in America? Why is hatred such an unsatisfying emotion? Why is forgiveness always the better way?

7. What practical steps can a person take to heal anger and past hurts? What can you do if the person is dead or in some other way completely unavailable to you?

TAKING ACTION

This chapter ended with a prayer for the Holy Spirit to take control of your life. Before going any further in this book, please take time to ponder that prayer carefully. If it truly represents the desire of your heart, pray it slowly and sincerely to the Lord.

ANGRY MAN ALERT

A Man of Honor is "not quick-tempered."
—*Titus 1:7*

The day is over at last. You climb into bed ready to sleep, but sleep won't come. You toss and turn. You try sleeping on your side, your back, your front. You cover your head with the pillow. You turn on the fan. You open the window. You get up and take a shower. You go to the kitchen and make a sandwich. You sit down and watch TV, but you can't concentrate.

Nothing helps. You're dead tired, and you had a rotten day. Your body cries out for rest, and your eyes will hardly stay open. But your mind won't cooperate.

What was it you said at supper? Ah, now it all comes back. The kids heard it too, didn't they? You said it in a blinding flash of anger. Now you wish you could take it back. Too late.

Now it's nearly midnight, and you can't sleep. But you aren't the only one. Someone else is awake, too. Maybe she is crying. Or maybe she is silent, wondering when you will strike again. Take a good look at yourself. How many nights has it been lately? Maybe that's why you are so irritable and grouchy.

There is no easy way out . . . and you don't deserve one. No need to pray or wait for God's leading. You know what you have to do. Someone else is waiting for you to make the first move.

"Sweetheart, I was wrong, and I know it. Please forgive me."

A MESSAGE FOR HOTHEADS

How difficult those words are to say. But every married man must say them sooner or later. And most of us will say them many times.

Sometimes we speak of "losing" our temper as if we don't know where it is. The truth is, you never "lose" your temper; you simply turn it loose on someone else, usually someone close to you, often against those you love the most.

A recent survey showed that 63 percent of American children aged seven to ten fear dying young, 71 percent fear being shot or stabbed at school or home, and 70 percent worry about being hit or slapped by an adult. Where does that fear come from? Perhaps from the fact that many fathers resort to violence in dealing with their children. Most of the children surveyed said they felt comfortable talking with their mothers about their fears, but few felt the same way about their fathers.[1] Dads, that hurts, doesn't it?

ANGER UNDER CONTROL

Do you want to be a spiritual leader in your home? Then heed the words of Titus 1:7. A Man of Honor is "not quick-tempered." The word literally means "not passionate." Moffatt translates it as "not hot-tempered," while *The New Testament in Basic English* says, "not quickly moved to wrath." It describes a person who doesn't blow his top whenever he gets angry, who doesn't suddenly, without warning, become upset and disturbed.[2] Proverbs 29:22 warns us about this tendency: "An angry man stirs up dissension, and a hot-tempered one commits many sins."

Remember, there is such a thing as righteous anger (Ephesians 4:26), and there are times when leaders need to be angry. No one wants a leader who always smiles and never frowns. No one wants a leader who lives in Fantasyland and thinks every day is Christmas. We need leaders who know how to get angry at the right time for the right reasons in the right way.

But in his letter to Titus Paul is warning us against putting a hothead in a position of spiritual leadership. One hothead can destroy the work of a dozen godly men. Leaders deal with people and their problems, and sometimes people can be frustrating and the problems can be annoy-ing. *Godly leaders know how to remain calm under pressure and provocation.*

WHEN THE TRUTH HITS HOME

This is an area where I have learned a lot about myself in the last few years. There was a time when I would have said I don't have a temper, but now I know the truth about myself. As I write these words, my mind goes back to a night many years ago when I sat in my living room with my wife and two close friends. The two friends had quite literally become closer to me than my own brothers. We had spent hundreds of hours laughing together, talking together, praying together, working together. To say that they knew me well would be an understatement. In some ways they knew me better than I knew myself. Certainly they knew my weak-nesses better than I did. That night they had come to talk to me about some areas in my life that needed to change.

Before I tell you what happened, let me say that I've been on the other side more than once, and I know from experience how difficult it is to say hard things to someone you love. And my friends did love me, though I didn't feel it that night. I know that some people say you can do a painless confrontation, but trust me, there's no such thing. I know what it is to deliver the bad news, and I know what it is to receive it. That night I was on the receiving end.

For over two hours we talked and danced around the subject. I knew what was coming because I knew my friends. They didn't want to say what they had to say because they were my friends. But sometime after 10 o'clock that night the words came out, laying bare some painful short-comings in my life. For a few moments I struggled to gain my compo-sure as we talked about what I could do to face my problems. Then one of my friends said something that in that moment, loaded as it was with ragged emotion, coming at the end of a long, long day, after months of struggling against problems not entirely of our own making, seemed to be a personal attack on me.

Looking back, I see clearly now that he didn't mean it the way I took it. But I was angry and hurt and not thinking clearly. Perhaps the truth cut too close to the bone. In any case, I'm not proud of what happened next.

I felt something begin to happen on the inside, a slow explosion of anger rising from the soles of my feet. It was as if someone had pushed a button inside me and released a time bomb. I sensed the anger rising, and I knew that when it hit my lips, something terrible would come out. But I felt helpless to stop it.

All of this seems so clear in retrospect, but in the confusion of the moment I was simply overwhelmed with uncontrolled fury. When I finally began to speak, I said things that make me blush with shame today. Awful words. Hurtful words. Personal insults. On and on I went, glaring at the men who had been my close friends.

All the while my wife sat watching me, frozen in shock and fear. It was rage, pure and simple. Beyond anger, beyond frustration, beyond bitterness, at a depth I had never experienced before and have never experienced since. Hot molten lava poured out of me as Mt. Saint Helens erupted in my living room.

Then suddenly it was over. The volcano within me quieted down, and we looked at each other, no one knowing what to say next. Soon we prayed and parted for the night.

Like feathers in the wind, angry words once spoken can never be recalled. Hot lava eventually cools, but the hardened pumice remains as evidence of the explosion.

In the next few days I learned the price of my passion. The worst part for me was dealing with the guilt and shame of what I had said to men who had been my dear friends. To make matters worse, like a volcano after an eruption, I kept spewing forth hot steam and ashes. For some time I alternated between guilt and anger—guilt for what I had done, anger at those I felt had mistreated me.

THE TURNING POINT

The turning point came about a month later when I attended a conference in a neighboring state. I roomed with a man I had never met before, and when he asked why I had come, I began to pour out my story to this total stranger. During every break between sessions, I told him my story.

It was long and involved and stretched back four or five years, a story of the highest highs and the lowest lows I have ever known. I made sure he knew who the real villains were. That night, after the final session, we went back to our room, and I continued to share the story of what had happened. Finally I got to that fateful night at our house. In excruciating detail I repeated the terrible things I had said and what they had cost me. As I told the story, I found myself getting angry all over again, ready to fight again, daring my friends to move a muscle.

Finally it was over. I looked at the clock, and it read 1:45 A.M. Although he was dead tired and no doubt exhausted from listening to my long story, my roommate looked at me and said words that changed my life. "Ray, God has been very good to you in allowing this to happen." Good to me? Had he missed the point of my story? But he knew me better than I knew myself. "God has shown you His grace by allowing you to lose your temper like that." How could losing my temper show God's grace? "For years you've had the reputation of being a laid-back guy who laughs his way through life." How could he know me that well when he'd never met me before today? "People who don't know you well think that you don't have a worry in the world. And you've cultivated that image because it makes you popular and easy to like. But the truth is far different. There's a seething cauldron inside you that you've managed to keep a lid on for a long time. But that night the lid came off."

Then he went on to explain a fundamental truth about the Christian life. "As we grow in Christ, most of us come to the place where we think there are some sins we just won't commit. Maybe we don't say it out loud, but in our hearts we think, 'I would never do that.' That's what happened to you and your temper. You covered yours for so long that you thought it had gone away. But it was there, like a snake coiled in the grass, waiting for the chance to strike.

"That night God pulled back the cover and let the world see the depravity within your own heart. From now on, whenever you stand up and speak, you can never say, 'I don't have a temper,' because you do. The grace of God is forcing you to admit the truth about yourself."

Having said those words, he rolled over and went to sleep. But I stayed awake a long time. For me, it was one of those moments when the light suddenly went on and I could see clearly what had happened.

NO DIFFERENCE!

I did have a temper, but I didn't want to admit it. For years I had managed to cover it up, and for the most part had done a good job. But that night, under extreme pressure, the truth came out, and the volcano erupted.

Do I have a temper? Yes. And now I know in a deep way why Jesus said that hatred is like murder (Matthew 5:21-22). I also understand what James meant when he said that the tongue is set on fire by hell (3:6).

Apart from the grace of God, I am capable of terrible crimes. Without Jesus Christ, there is no sin beyond me. I don't mean to say that I'm not as good as I think I am. I mean to say that without Jesus Christ and apart from His life flowing through me, I am not good at all. Surely this is what Paul means when he says in Romans 3:22-23, "There is no difference, for all have sinned and fall short of the glory of God."

"No difference." Is the apostle kidding? He's absolutely serious. No difference between me and Charles Manson, or between me and Jeffrey Dahmer. Their crimes are worse in degree, but not in kind. We are all sinners by nature, by choice, by word, and by deed. Most of us simply find more acceptable ways to express our sin. But there is no difference.

WHY JESUS CAME

It is at this point that the Gospel message becomes relevant to men. Left to ourselves, we are like wild stallions, untamed and untameable. We serve our own interests, follow our instincts, and are slaves to our own passions. That's one reason we love to watch bloody, violent movies. It's vicarious entertainment because we know that in a certain situation we would be capable of blowing people away. Apart from the Holy Spirit's restraint, our sins would consume us.

That's why Jesus came—so we wouldn't spend our days blowing people away . . . or wishing we could.

The great news of the Gospel is that Jesus Christ comes into a life filled with selfish passion and totally remakes it from the inside out. The passion is still there, but now through Christ it is aimed toward righteousness.

A Man of Honor is "not quick-tempered." Such a simple phrase, but for me at least, it contains an enormous challenge. It's not the passion that gets us in trouble, and often it's not even the anger, but it's our unwillingness to face the hard truth about ourselves. If you truly don't have a temper, then perhaps what I have said does not apply to you. But for the rest of us, which I think is most of us, these words stand as an enormous challenge.

One final word: you'll never become "not quick-tempered" until you admit you have a temper in the first place.

GOING DEEPER

1. Why is it difficult for men to say, "I was wrong" even when we know we were?

2. Have you ever had an experience of losing your temper similar to the one described in this chapter? Describe the circumstances that led up to it and the aftermath. As you look back, how can you see the grace of God at work in your own experience?

3. Many fathers resort to violence in dealing with their children. What is the difference between legitimate discipline and unhealthy violence?
   List some signs that a parent has crossed the line in the wrong direction.
   What factors underlie abusive actions by parents toward their children?

4. Read 2 Chronicles 26:16-23.
   Why did Uzziah get angry with the priests who confronted him?
   What sin had he committed? How did God judge him?
   How have you suffered in the past from losing your temper?

5. Why do you think many children feel more comfortable talking with their mothers about their fears than with their fathers? As a child growing up, did you find it easier to talk with your mother or with your father? How much time have you spent talking with your

children in the last twenty-four hours? Fathers, what can you do to become more tender so that your children will want to open up to you?

6. Anger is the most powerful human emotion. What happens when anger clouds our thinking? According to Proverbs 19:19, why is it futile to rescue a man given to anger?

7. Why is it dangerous to put a quick-tempered man in a position of leadership? How can you deal with such a man in a Christlike fashion?

TAKING ACTION

What commitment do you need to make in order to be "not quick-tempered"? Write a sentence beginning with this phrase: "With God's help, I _____." Spell out your intention to be free from outbursts of sinful anger, whether large or small. Write below that the words of James 1:19-20. Sign the page, put it in an envelope, seal it, address it to yourself, and stamp it. Then give it to a trusted friend, asking him not to open it but to mail it to you four months from now as a reminder of your commitment to control your temper.

SERVANTS UNLIMITED

A Man of Honor is "not overbearing."
—*Titus 1:7*

The Greek word translated "overbearing" literally means "self-pleasing." It is sometimes translated with words such as "obstinate" or "pushy." Such a man is

> stubborn, arrogant, and inconsiderate of others' opinion. A self-willed man is headstrong, independent, self-assertive, and ungracious toward those of a different opinion.[1]

He is a not a team player because he doesn't care about anyone but himself. He speaks his mind, defends his turf, stakes out his position, all with a reckless disregard for the feelings of others. If someone gets hurt in the process, so be it, because "you can't make an omelette without breaking a few eggs." Don't get in an argument with this man. You won't win, you won't break even; you'll be crushed, and he'll walk away laughing.

What's the opposite of an overbearing man? One word comes to mind: *servant*. A true Man of Honor is a servant, not a master. He enjoys being a team player, even if all he does is clean up the locker room while someone else gets the glory.

SERVANTS I HAVE KNOWN

Not long ago I sat down and started making a list of great servants I have known, going all the way back to my childhood days. Faces from the past floated into my memory, people who over the years have impressed me by their servant heart and servant spirit: Betty Jahns, Rick and JoAnne Hale, Caleb Lucien, Delores Bolton, Buford Thornton, Hal Kirby, Libby Redwine, Alvin Johnson, Kim Lewis, James and Sherry Cagle, Jerry and Beverly Hansen, Dennis Greene, Jesse Sandberg, Bob Cauthon, Vern Henriksen, John Sredl, Shirley Jager, Bernie Fillmore, John Tahl, Irma Csakai, James Warner, Helen Scharama. I am sure you could come up with a similar list of Christ's servants you have found to be special blessings in your life.

As I made my list, I made an interesting discovery. It is difficult to say exactly what a servant does, but you know one when you see one. On the surface, most of the people have nothing in common. I thought about Delores Bolton, a church secretary for forty years, one of the most retiring, shy, unassuming people I have ever known. Buford Thornton was one of my father's best friends. Vern Henriksen has spent hundreds of hours as the receiving treasurer at the church I pastor. Hal Kirby brought words of encouragement the day my father died. None of these people are famous as the world counts fame. There is no reason that you would know any of them. Yet their faces came to mind when I thought of the word *servant*.

SERVANTS COME IN MANY SIZES

I draw four conclusions from the fact that servants are hard to define but easy to spot.

Being a Servant Is an Attitude, Not an Action

So many of us think, "Tell me what I need to do if I'm going to be a servant." Being a servant doesn't start with what you do; being a servant starts with the attitude of the heart. It's not *what* you do, but *why* you do it that matters.

Servants Come in All Sizes, All Shapes, and All Colors

Servants of God may be very ordinary persons with a very ordinary manner of life.

Anyone Can Be a Servant If He Has a Servant's Heart

What is it that makes the difference between being a servant and not being a servant? Is it visiting a nursing home? Is it coaching a youth baseball team? Is it giving money to those who are in need? No, because you can visit a nursing home with a servant's heart or you can do it out of a sheer sense of obligation. You can coach baseball because you want to serve others or because you want to win favor and have others praise you. You can give money because you really want to serve or you can give money in order to curry favor with someone. The same action can be the action of a servant or of a proud person. What makes the difference is the motivation inside the human heart.

JESUS CHRIST IS THE MODEL SERVANT FOR THE PEOPLE OF GOD

There are two verses that you ought to tattoo on your soul. The first is Mark 10:45, "For the Son of Man did not come to be served, but to serve." The second is Philippians 2:5, "Your attitude should be the same as that of Christ Jesus."

Where do you find servanthood in the life of Christ? There are many answers to that question, but I find myself drawn again and again to the Upper Room as the disciples gathered with Jesus for their final meal. They were all there—James and John, Judas, Peter, Matthew, Bartholomew, Simon the Zealot, and the rest. The men knew that something was up. Jesus seemed pensive and quiet. He talked, but He obviously had something on His mind. Jesus knew that before long Judas would leave, only to return with a kiss of betrayal. The Roman soldiers would arrest Him, and soon He would stand before Herod and Annas and Caiaphas and Pilate. In a matter of hours, He would be hanging on a cross.

The chatter in the Upper Room went back and forth, and Jesus listened. Suddenly, without a word, He stood up, took off His tunic, and wrapped the towel of a slave around His waist. Taking a pitcher of water, He went to the end of the table and knelt down. Without a word He took the feet of the first disciple, brushed the dirt off, and began to splash water on his feet. When they were clean, He took the towel and wiped them dry. He went on to the next man and did the same thing. In the room there was total silence. No one dared to speak. They could not believe what Jesus was doing.

THREE FACTS ABOUT FOOT WASHING

In order to understand what this meant, we need to know three facts about foot washing.

Foot Washing Was Considered an Ordinary Sign
of Common Courtesy

To us what Jesus did was bizarre and unusual, but in those days foot washing was a common practice when a visitor came to your house. The roads in Palestine were dry and dusty, except when it rained and they turned into a quagmire of mud. So even if your feet were clean when you left your house, by the time you got wherever you were going, your feet would be covered with dust and dirt and grime and grit. So it was common in those days that if you came to my home for the evening, when you arrived I would greet you with a kiss on the cheek, I would offer you oil to rub on your face, and then I would call my servant, who would kneel down and take off your sandals and wash your feet.

But it was not common for the *host* to wash the feet of his guests. Foot washing was the work of slaves. A rich man never washed anyone's feet because he had enough servants to do it for him. But Jesus broke the rules, and that's why they were so shocked—not that somebody would wash their feet, but that *Jesus* was the one doing it.[2]

Foot Washing by Definition Is Dirty, Smelly, and Humiliating

Have you ever tried to wash somebody's feet at the end of a long, hard day? Have you ever tried to wash somebody's feet covered with smelly grime and perspiration? Have you ever put your face right next to an ingrown toenail? The very idea seems repulsive.

Foot Washing Will Never Go out of Style Because
You'll Never Run out of Dirty Feet

Everyone has dirty feet. That's one good thing about foot washing. Everyone around you has dirty feet. Think about your feet right now.

Unless you happen to be reading this early in the morning, your feet are probably less than perfectly clean.

Jesus came to a world of dirty feet. He came to clean those dirty feet, which means He came for *you* because your feet are dirty too.

When Jesus finished, He asked His disciples, "Do you understand what I have done for you?" In one sense the answer was yes; they understood that Jesus had just washed their feet. But His question went deeper. "Men, do you grasp the meaning of what I have just done?" In washing their feet He was giving them a parable, an acted-out object lesson. He wasn't just washing their feet. He was saying, "This is who I am. This is why I have come to earth. This explains the cross. I came as a servant, to wash dirty feet, to bring you cleansing."

Jesus then drove the truth home: "Now that I, your Lord and Teacher, have washed your feet, you also should wash one another's feet. I have set you an example that you should do as I have done for you" (John 13:14-15).

This was a shocking thought because washing feet was the work of slaves. No wonder the disciples were baffled and upset. No wonder they tried to protest. After all, these are the same geniuses who just thirty minutes earlier were arguing about who would be greatest in the kingdom.

End of argument. Jesus was saying, "If you're going to be My disciples, go wash dirty feet, and let the kingdom take care of itself. If you're going to follow Me, just get down on your hands and knees and find some feet to wash. You take care of the dirty feet, and I'll decide who sits on which throne in the kingdom." That's the message. Then in verse 17 He promised, "Now that you know these things, you will be blessed if you do them."

GOOD NEWS AND BAD NEWS

I have good news, and I have bad news. The bad news is that feet stink. If you're going to wash feet, you're going to do some humbling things and some humiliating things, and you're going to be involved in some situations that aren't very nice or popular or that aren't going to be seen by the masses. You aren't necessarily going to be applauded for doing it. The good news is there is a great reward for foot washers. You're blessed if you do these things.

There are three reasons why we ought to wash dirty feet.

- Because Jesus did it.
- Because dirty feet need washing.
- Because we're blessed when we do it.

Here is the whole chapter in one sentence: *the followers of Jesus distinguish themselves through humble acts of service to those who don't expect it and are unable to repay it*. Foot washing is a distinctive mark of the followers of Jesus Christ.

GRAB A TOWEL AND GET STARTED

Only one question is left. Jesus said, "Do as I have done." My question to you is this: whose feet are you going to wash this week? It is time for us to move from theory into practice. It is time for us to move away from talk and cross over into action. Jesus didn't say, "Blessed are you if you know what I know." Jesus said, "Blessed are you if you do what I do."

How and why did Jesus do what He did?

1) He saw a need and moved to meet it.

2) He didn't wait for an invitation.

3) He took the initiative.

4) He took off His uniform of greatness and got down on His knees.

5) He didn't announce what He was going to do. He didn't stand up and say, "Well, men, I'm Jesus, and now I'm going to wash your feet."

6) He didn't wait for a thank you and didn't receive one either.

Just remember this: it all starts in the heart.

MANY WAYS TO WASH FEET

A couple of years ago my staff put together a list called "Fifty Ways to Wash Feet."[3] Here are some of them:

- Running errands for a friend.
- Baking a cake for a shut-in.
- Opening your home for international students.

- Giving twenty dollars with a note of encouragement to a single mom.
- Confronting a friend who has strayed from the Lord.
- Driving a car pool to Awana.
- Making tape recordings for the blind.
- Hugging your children every day.
- Refusing to repeat gossip.
- Sending flowers to a friend.
- Meeting a new Christian at 6:30 A.M. for discipleship.
- Picking up your own dirty underwear.
- Giving anonymously so three teenagers can go to Snow Camp.
- Intervening in a quarrel to bring two friends back together.
- Buying food for the food pantry.
- Tutoring Vietnamese immigrants.
- Helping a friend light the pilot in his heater.
- Writing your parents a love note.
- Cleaning up the kitchen so your wife can read the paper.
- Complimenting your boss.
- Keeping a secret you'd really like to share.
- Spending Saturday helping a friend move.
- Raking leaves for a senior citizen.
- Changing the oil in a friend's car.
- Making supper for a new mom.
- Forgiving a friend to save the friendship.
- Visiting a nursing home.
- Typing a term paper for a college student.
- Counseling at the Crisis Pregnancy Center.
- Inviting college students over for Sunday dinner.
- Volunteering to serve in the nursery.

- Washing windows at the church.
- Reading books to children.

These are just suggestions. The heart is what matters. The servant's heart will always find plenty of open doors for acts of kindness. If you have the right kind of heart, you will find plenty of opportunities this week to wash dirty feet.

May I suggest a simple prayer to get you started? "Lord, whose feet should I wash this week?" Don't pray for ten names. Start with just one person—your wife, one of your children, a relative, a friend, someone who lives across the street, a coworker, somebody you barely know. Ask the Lord to bring one particular name to mind.

Now write down the initials of the person the Lord has shown you. This will help you be accountable to God.

This is not that difficult if you have the right kind of heart. If you don't, it's impossible. Anyone can wash dirty feet. You can do it if you're willing to kneel down and get your hands wet. You can wash feet this week if you're willing to be a servant instead of a big shot. Jesus said, "Do as I have done for you."

Will we take His words seriously?

GOING DEEPER

1. Take a sheet of paper and write at the top "Great Servants I Have Known." Give yourself ten minutes and see how many names you can write down.
   What qualities to do these people share in common?
   Would you feel comfortable adding your own name to that list?

2. The same action can be the action of a servant or of a proud person. What difference does our motivation make as long as we are helping others?
   What happens when we do the right thing for the wrong reason?
   Have you ever received an act of kindness and wondered why the person was really doing it? How did that make you feel?

3. Read John 13:1-17.
   Why did Jesus wash the disciples' feet? Why were they so shocked?

How did Peter react?
How do you think you would react if someone you deeply respected began washing your dirty feet?

4. When Jesus said, "You also should wash one another's feet" (John 13:14), He didn't mean that literally, or did He? How can you be sure? (See 1 Timothy 5:9-10 for an interesting angle on this question.)

5. "I came as a servant, to wash dirty feet."
What light does this shed on who Jesus is? How does this affect your view of Him?
Has Jesus ever washed your dirty feet? Would you like Him to?

6. "Lord, whose feet should I wash this week?"
Whose name came to mind?
What are you going to do about it?

TAKING ACTION

This chapter contains thirty-three suggestions for practical ways you can wash dirty feet. Place a check by five that seem possible for you to do. Pick one and do it this week.

WANTED: GENTLE MEN

A Man of Honor is "gentle."
—*1 Timothy 3:3*

The scholars tell us that this word is difficult to translate because it contains so many delicate nuances.

The problem with the term *gentle* is that no English word adequately conveys the fullness of its beauty and richness. Forbearance, gentleness, magnanimous, equitable, peaceable, and gracious all help capture the full range of meaning of gentleness.[1]

This word describes a person who considers the whole picture before acting. A gentle leader protects and does not humiliate. He "guards each man's dignity and saves each man's pride." In making a decision he judges both the letter and the spirit of the law. He is willing to lose even when he is right. He is willing to yield, willing to forgive, willing to overlook. Matthew Arnold calls this quality "sweet reasonableness." You know it when you see it because the person who has it always makes you feel better when you are around him.[2]

Gentleness is an important part of God's character. Psalm 103:8 says, "The LORD is compassionate and gracious, slow to anger, abounding in love." Verse 10 tells us that "he does not treat us as our sins deserve or repay us according to our iniquities." When the Apostle Paul appealed to the Corinthians, he did so in "the meekness and gentleness of Christ" (2 Corinthians 10:1). All Christians should manifest gentleness (Philippians 4:5). It is to be the standard of all our personal relationships, especially toward those in authority over us (see Titus 3:1-2, where the Greek word is translated "considerate"). It causes us to work for peace instead of looking for ways to divide people. It is a mark of God's wisdom (see James 3:17, where the word is again translated as "considerate").

This quality is doubly important for men in positions of spiritual leadership. Shepherds lead sheep; they don't drive them, beat them, or harass them. Gentleness is important because sheep can be exasperating at times!

THE WIMPY WEASEL AND THE CREEPING CRAB

Several years ago I attended a seminar entitled "How to Handle Criticism, Conflict and Difficult People in the Church." Somebody heard that I was going and asked if I had anyone particular in mind. The answer was no, but as a pastor I've learned to adopt the Boy Scout motto: "Be prepared."

One session focused on the most common troublemakers in the church. The seminar leader gave names to each one, then explained how they act and why and how to deal with them. The list is both instructive and suggestive.

- The Charging Bull
- The Sneaky Snake
- The Roaring Lion
- The Wimpy Weasel
- The Heckling Hen
- The Tight-lipped Tiger
- Chicken Little
- The Creeping Crab
- The Emphatic Elephant
- The Pompous Panther
- The King of the Hill

Then the instructor said, "Remember, we're all difficult people some of the time." And that reminded me of a sermon I heard once called, "Is the Church Full of Weirdos?" The answer is yes, because we're all weird some of the time and some of us are weird all of the time.

GRACE-BUILDERS

Marshall Shelley wrote about the difficult people that pastors encounter. He called them "well-intentioned dragons." At the office, in the class-room, on the assembly line, living next door, and sometimes sharing the same bedroom are people who sometimes get on our nerves. Perhaps that's putting it too mildly. There are some people we just can't stand. We all have a few well-intentioned dragons around us. That's a given. It's how we deal with them that matters.

I used to think that those hard-to-live-with people were simply one more proof of universal depravity, that in a fallen world some people are going to look a bit more "fallen" than the rest of us. That's certainly true, but as the years pass, I've come to realize that God actually sends the drag-ons our way for a positive purpose. *They are grace-builders sent on a mission from God to make us better men.* Without them, life would be easier, but we would be spiritually flabby. Because of them, we are forced to grow in areas that would otherwise remain undeveloped for God.

There are four ways we are often tempted to deal with difficult people.

We Ignore Them

We do this by shutting the door, leaving the room, hanging up the phone, or telling our secretary not to let Mr. Jones know we're in the office today. Unfortunately, ignoring difficult people almost never works because dif-ficult people keep finding a way to get under our skin.

We Intimidate Them

Intimidation works when the troublesome person happens to be a wife, a brother, a sister, or a child. This is a tactic used by bosses, owners, super-visors, foremen, coaches, officers, and anyone in authority over others. Intimidators use violence and the threat of violence, indirect threats, harsh language, half-truths, body language, and a myriad of ugly facial expressions to keep people in line and to get their own way. It may involve withholding favors such as a positive review or a promotion.

We Argue with Them

I personally find this a major temptation since I love a good argument! Not long ago I came back from my daily walk and found two well-dressed visitors on my doorstep. At first they said they were visiting the neighborhood to talk about how to have a happy marriage. Then they mentioned they had come from the local Kingdom Hall. You can probably guess which religious group they were affiliated with. Soon the conversation veered into theology. What did they believe about Jesus Christ? Is He the Son of God? "Oh, yes," they said, "he's *a* Son of God." That's not what I asked. So I tried again. "Do you believe that Jesus Christ is God's one-and-only Son, fully equal with the Father in glory, majesty, dominion, and power?" Suddenly they started to backtrack.

As we talked I felt my face getting flushed, and my words began spilling out faster and faster. Soon I started raising my voice as we argued about the true meaning of John 1:1. Finally in frustration I said, "This isn't getting us anywhere." As they left, the visitors were smiling, and I was red-faced and angry. Who won that debate? Although I was right, that doesn't matter. I lost because I lost my temper and they kept theirs.

We Destroy Them

We do this through subtle means such as attacking a person behind his back, passing along bits of gossip, leaking confidential information, reporting on the moral failures of those we despise, and implying that others may have done wrong when we have no proof. A friend once told me about one of his colleagues who could "stick a knife in you and you wouldn't know it until you looked down and saw your blood on the floor."

We also destroy people by refusing to forgive them. Instead, we hold them in bondage until we think they are ready to come out of "jail." Some of us have even locked people up and thrown away the key.

POWER UNDER CONTROL

In contrast to all that, we are told that a man of God is "gentle." The word itself is translated in several different ways, including "patient," "forbearing," "genial," and "peaceable." As a father of three boys, I have many chances to put all those words to work.

Gentleness is required in dealing with children. Just a few minutes before writing this chapter my middle son came in with his report card. It was an alphabet-soup mix of grades, some good and some not so good. To make matters more confusing, he reported that one of the Bs was a "low B" and one of the Cs was a "high C." He wasn't sure how he ended up with a low grade in math because he thought he was doing okay there—"I thought I was maybe getting a B." "Do you like the teacher?" "Sure, she's great, except that she's a strict grader."

Before I go any farther with this story, I should tell you that everyone I know likes my middle son. He's friendly, he genuinely likes people, he cares deeply about his friends, and he's developing into an all-around fine young man.

I am completely sure that in his heart my son enjoys school and truly wants to do well in all his subjects. His teachers generally say they enjoy having him in class, but that his attention tends to wander and that he doesn't always apply himself as he should.

This reminds me of myself when I was in the eighth grade—trying to balance the demands of an active social life, the church youth group, hanging out with my friends, and oh, yes, doing my homework.

My middle son is hardly ever belligerent (though he can be that way when he gets angry), and I could tell as he talked that he knew he had disappointed me. When I asked him how long I should ground him for bad grades, he hung his head and said, "Three or four weeks."

After consultation, my wife and I decided to use a combination of tactics. First, we would strictly enforce the no-TV rule on school nights. We had the rule before, but it had been getting stretched out of shape lately. Second, we decided to cut down on the number of times he can hang out with his friends. Third, he had to come up with a plan (which we would approve) for raising his grades during the next nine-week grading period. Fourth, we would call the school and ask for an appointment with his math teacher. Fifth, he would bring his math book home every night without fail whether or not he had homework.

At one point I told my son that I wouldn't be so bothered by a low grade in math except that he had less-than-satisfactory grades in two other subjects. In my mind, that meant he needed to buckle down and get serious because his whole year was more or less hanging in the balance academically.

My wife and I both knew that no doubt all of this would mean that we would be spending extra time in coming weeks reviewing the U.S. Constitution, helping our middle son factor polynomials, and parsing French verbs. We also recognized that gentleness was an essential element in the equation.

Gentleness includes maintaining a steady emotional balance during times when you might prefer to fly off the handle. You can't be gentle while you are screaming, stomping your feet, and calling people names. Gentleness is power under control. It's not giving in or giving up; it's staying calm, keeping your cool, looking for alternatives, and keeping your eye on the goal.

As we deal with our lovable (and sometimes irascible) middle son, gentleness means not overreacting to a less-than-satisfactory report card. But it also means patiently finding ways to help him do what he wants to do—make better grades.[3] (By the way, his grades came up significantly during the next grading period and have continued to improve.)

When I showed my son this story and asked if I could use it in the book, he said, "That's cool. Lots of dads probably have kids like me." With an attitude like that, you have to love him. And I do.

RESTORE HIM GENTLY

Gentleness is especially required in dealing with Christians who have sinned. "Brothers, if someone is caught in a sin, you who are spiritual should restore him gently" (Galatians 6:1). There are two problems we face whenever we try to help someone else.

- Many people are slow to respond.
- Others will refuse our help altogether.

When they are slow to respond, we tend to get discouraged. When they refuse our help, we tend to get disgusted. That's what Paul is warning against.[4]

Three hundred years ago Matthew Henry wrote that when we try to help other people we

> must not be high in our expectations and demands, nor harsh in our resentments, nor hard in our impositions, but endeavor to make the best we can of everything and think the best we can of everybody.[5]

That fairly well sums it up.

"GRACE EVEN FOR PEOPLE LIKE ME"

Several years ago I received a phone call from a man I have never met. He lives a long distance from Chicago. As he told me his story, he began to weep. After many years of marriage, he foolishly committed adultery. He tried to hide it, but he couldn't live with himself. For months he hid it. For months he made excuses. For months he lived in agony. Finally he decided to come clean. His wife hadn't suspected a thing. With his voice breaking, he said, "Pastor Ray, I thought she was going to throw me out. I thought she would tell me to pack my bags and get out. I thought she would say, 'I'm through with you.' But she didn't. She told me she still loved me and wanted to save our marriage. I've never experienced anything like that in all my life." Then he went in to tell the people where he worked about what had happened. He also gave them his resignation. "They didn't condemn me. They put their arms around me and said, 'We want to help you. We want to see you restored.'"

Then his voice broke completely. "All my life I've heard about the grace of God. But I never really experienced it until this week. Now I know that God has grace even for people like me."

Indeed He does. Kent Hughes tells of an artist who submitted a painting of Niagara Falls to an exhibition but neglected to give it a title. The

curators considered the painting carefully and titled it "More to Follow."
This was fitting because Niagara Falls has been rushing and roaring with
billions of gallons of water for thousands of years, never once running
dry. All that water and still more to follow.[6]

So it is with God's grace. *There is always more to follow.* There is
saving grace, healing grace, guiding grace, enduring grace, and even
dying grace. There is grace for every problem and every need in the
Christian life.

Is there gentle grace for those moments when our patience is sorely
tested? Yes. And when faced with creeping crabs and well-intentioned
dragons, gentle grace is what we need.

> *Lord Jesus, for too long we have confused strength with intim-
> idation and have hurt those who most needed our help. Show
> us the strength of gentleness and the wisdom of kindness.
> Amen.*

GOING DEEPER

1. Many men struggle with the concept of gentleness because it doesn't
   fit our common images of manliness.
   How would you feel if you heard that someone had used the world
   "gentle" to describe you?

2. Read Exodus 34:6; Nehemiah 9:17; Psalm 86:15; 103:8; 145:8; Joel
   2:13; Jonah 4:2; Nahum 1:3.
   What do these verses teach us about God's character?
   Why is it important for us to know that God is "slow to anger"? How
   does that affect your view of God?

3. God sends "well-intentioned dragons" whether we want them or
   not. Who are some of the "grace-builders" in your life, and how is
   God using them to make you a better man?

4. This chapter lists four temptations we face in dealing with difficult
   people. Which ones are you most vulnerable to and why?

5. Read 2 Timothy 2:24-26.
   How should we respond to those who oppose us? Why is gentleness
   so important?

What should our ultimate goal be in dealing with difficult people? Why does arguing make that impossible?

6. According to Galatians 6:1, why is gentleness especially needed when restoring a sinning brother in Christ?
   What happens when we attempt to restore someone without a spirit of gentleness?

TAKING ACTION

Ask a good friend to give you a frank and honest answer to this question: "Do you consider me to be a gentle person?" Before receiving his answer, tell him that you've asked the Lord to speak through him to show you any areas of your life that do not reflect a spirit of gentleness. Use his answer as the basis for honest self-evaluation. Then ask your friend to hold you accountable to develop a gentle spirit in all your relationships.

PART III

HIS REPUTATION

NOTHING HIDDEN, NOTHING TO HIDE

A Man of Honor is "above reproach," "blameless."
—*1 Timothy 3:2; Titus 1:6-7*

P aul uses two Greek words that serve as a general summary of all the character qualities a spiritual leader should have. The first is the word translated as "above reproach" in 1 Timothy 3:2. This Greek word describes a garment without any folds. When applied to personal character, it means that the leader must be free from any secret or hidden pockets of sin. Said another way, it means that a godly leader is one whose life is such that there is nothing a detractor can grab hold of. *The Living Bible* uses the phrase, "a good man whose life cannot be spoken against." Knox translates this, "one with whom no fault can be found." It means that no charge could be brought against such a person that would contradict impartial examination.[1] Leaders are often attacked, their motives questioned, their actions criticized. While such things do happen, a leader who is truly above reproach will weather the storm because there is nothing about him about which a person could say, "Aha! I gotcha." This means no questionable conduct, no secret sins, no deliberately unresolved conflicts.[2]

The second word—usually translated as "blameless" (Titus 1:6-7)—comes from the legal realm and carries a slightly different connotation. It means "without indictment" or "unaccusable." The difference is this: "above reproach" means "one who could not be accused," while "blameless" means "one who is not accused." Taken together these two phrases establish a very high standard of personal conduct. Such a man not only has a good reputation but actually deserves it.[3]

Lest this seem too discouraging, I should point out that to be "above reproach" and "blameless" describes not perfection but a model Christian life. We should expect nothing less from our spiritual leaders.

Perhaps the word *integrity* sums up what it means to be "above reproach" and "blameless" as a man of God. The dictionary uses words such as "whole" and "complete" to describe what integrity means. To borrow a modern expression, a man with integrity has his act together. There are no loose ends that threaten his reputation. Warren Wiersbe offers this definition:

> Integrity is to personal or corporate character what health is to the body or 20/20 vision is to the eyes. A person with integrity is not divided (that's duplicity) or merely pretending (that's hypocrisy). He or she is "whole"; life is "put together," and things are working harmoniously. People with integrity have nothing to hide and nothing to fear. Their lives are open books.[4]

FORKS OF CYPRESS

Several years ago my older brother took me to visit a cemetery outside Florence, Alabama, near the remains of an antebellum mansion called Forks of Cypress. The mansion was built in the 1820s by James Jackson, an early settler of northwest Alabama. My brother and I walked among the ruins of the mansion and then crossed the country road into the dense forest on the other side. After a quarter-mile we found the Jackson family cemetery. There is no sign marking the spot—only a five-foot-high stone wall surrounding about fifty graves. Inside we found a tall marker over James Jackson's grave with a long inscription extolling his virtues, which were many.

As I walked along, my eyes fastened on the marker for one of his sons. There was a name, a date of birth and a date of death, and this simple five-word epitaph: "A man of unquestioned integrity."

Five words to sum up an entire life. Sixty-plus years distilled into five words. But, oh, what truth they tell.

"A man of unquestioned integrity." I cannot think of a better tribute.

THE ULTIMATE MAN OF INTEGRITY

There are many men of integrity in the Bible. Any list would have to include Joseph, Moses, David, Nathan, Jehoshaphat, Elijah, Hezekiah, Isaiah, Jeremiah, Daniel, Zerubbabel, Haggai, Malachi, James, Peter, Paul, John, Titus, Timothy.

These were men who stood tall above their contemporaries because they could not be bought or sold. They stand out in the biblical landscape like towering mountains rising above a flatland of unbelief, compromise, and idolatry.

But in all the Bible one man stands out above all the others as the preeminent example of integrity—Jesus Christ, our Lord and Savior.

He was the only truly blameless person who ever walked this earth. All the other great men had their weak points. But not Jesus.

No one could pin an accusation on Him and make it stick. Not even His enemies.

In this regard Matthew 22:16 is a very important verse because it tells us how His opponents sized up His character in the last few days of His life. The statement comes from the Pharisees who "laid plans to trap him in his words" (verse 15). They sent some of their well-trained disciples to trick Him with semantics. Ponder carefully their opening remarks to Him:

> "Teacher," they said, "we know you are a man of integrity and that you teach the way of God in accordance with the truth. You aren't swayed by men, because you pay no attention to who they are."

This isn't just a compliment. It's an honest evaluation of Jesus by men who intended to murder Him. Even His enemies had to admit His integrity.

What does integrity involve?

- Reputation: "We know . . ."
- Commitment to truth.

In words: "You teach the way of God.

In relationships: "You aren't swayed by men."

• Consistent lifestyle: "You pay no attention to who they are."

Even as they attempted to trip Him up, Christ's enemies had to confess that His reputation, His commitment to truth, and His consistent lifestyle made Him a man of integrity.

Why is this important? Because if His enemies had anything on Him, that would have been the time to bring it out. If Jesus had any skeletons in His closet, that was the moment to display them publicly.

But they didn't because they couldn't because Jesus was exactly what He seemed to be. His life matched His lips; His deeds matched His words; His character backed up His claims.

That's what integrity is all about.

A MAN WITHOUT GUILE

For over thirty years Dr. John Walvoord served as president of Dallas Theological Seminary. He is known around the world for his many books on theology and Bible prophecy. He is a big man with a commanding presence, and when I was a student I was always a bit intimidated by him.

One day in Greek class I heard one of my professors make an offhanded comment that stuck in my mind: "Dr. Walvoord is a man without guile. When he speaks, you don't have to wonder what he really means. What you see is what you get."

"A man without guile . . . what you see is what you get." He lived a blameless life of unquestioned integrity. I've never heard anyone else described as being "without guile."

Why are so few of us like that?

WHOSE SIDE ARE YOU ON?

A man of integrity tells the truth even when it hurts. A man going through a bitter divorce committed a moral sin that if discovered might affect the disposition of the property. Fearing that his wife had somehow found out, he vowed that even if asked, he would lie on the stand. "Don't do it," a friend said. "You can always get your money back, but you can never get your integrity back."

Truth is the heart and soul of integrity. Unfortunately, we live in a culture that has come to view truth as a disposable item; we tell the truth when it helps us, we shade the truth when we need to, and we lie if we "have to." No wonder confidence in American institutions is at an all-time low.[5]

Jesus said, "For this I came into the world, to testify to the truth. Everyone on the side of truth listens to me" (John 18:37). Jesus is on the side of truth. Whose side are you on?

THE REAL PROMISE KEEPERS

A man of integrity keeps his promises. Psalm 15:4 says that God blesses the man who "keeps his oath, even when it hurts." Ecclesiastes 5:1-7 warns against making rash and hasty vows. "It is better not to vow than to make a vow and not fulfill it" (verse 5). This has some very practical implications, such as:

- Keeping your appointments.
- Arriving at work on time.
- Paying your bills on time.
- Not overpromising just to get an order.
- Telling the truth about your product.
- Refusing to exaggerate.
- Abiding by the terms of the contract.
- Staying within your budget.
- Remembering your wife's birthday.
- Attending your son's ball game.
- Getting out of bed when the alarm goes off.
- Finishing the job.
- Giving someone the money you promised.
- Giving your employer the money you didn't spend.

Most of us intend to keep our promises. Our basic problem is overcommitment. We promise too many things to too many people with too little thought. *A man of integrity makes fewer promises but keeps the ones he makes.*

Joseph Stowell offers a helpful word for those of us plagued with the problem of overcommitment:

> I'm a classic overcommitter and have often contemplated starting Overcommitters Anonymous. I bet there would be a lot of us in the therapy sessions. We would sit around and say no. We'd say no in mad, happy, slow, and fast ways; in French, Russian, German, Japanese, Spanish, and Creole. We'd applaud and cheer when someone finally got up the courage to say no for the first time in his life, and we'd hold each other accountable. Want to join?[6]

FAITHFUL WOUNDS

A man of integrity confronts problems when it would be easier to walk away. When someone asked General Norman Schwarzkopf the secret of his success, he replied very simply, "I never walk past a problem." Another friend put it this way: "Just remember, when it comes to solving problems, the first price you pay is always the cheapest." We ignore problems, hoping they will go away, but that rarely happens. And the price of solving them goes up, not down.

Proverbs 27:6 says, "Faithful are the wounds of a friend." Better to have a friend tell you the hard truth than have somebody try to butter you up and cover up the hard things you need to hear.

Whenever I think of this principle, my dear friend Randy Miller comes to mind. One year he served as the chairman of the elders in the church I pastored in Texas. I soon learned Randy had a certain method of doing things. He was very orderly, not given to flamboyance, very much an administrator, always committed to doing things the right way.

We met almost every week to discuss the work of the church. He always carried a little pocket-sized spiral notebook with him. Over the course of a half-hour we would review the affairs of the church, checking off the items on his list one after the other. He'd go over all of his points with me, and then he would turn the page. The second page would always be about me.

He would say, "This is hard for me to say, but when you said such-and-such last week in the sermon, you didn't mean it this way, but this is how some people took it." Or, "When you didn't take time to talk to those folks, they were really hurt." Or, "I know you think we ought to do this, but I'm not sure it's the right idea." Or sometimes, "You said this, and you shouldn't have, and you need to do something about it."

Over time I discovered he was always right. He was a friend who loved me enough to tell me when I was making a mistake. You want to know how I feel about Randy Miller today? Although I haven't seen him in many years, I consider him one of my best friends. He's welcome in my home anytime.

WE'VE KNOWN ALL ALONG

We hear a lot these days about family values and the need to rediscover virtue in American society. When he compiled *The Book of Virtues* (which has sold well over a million copies) William Bennett proved that there is a deep hunger for old-fashioned character training today.[7]

But the basic building blocks of virtue are actually very simple. We've known them all along:

- Honesty.
- Perseverance.
- Faithfulness.
- Determination.
- Kindness.
- Loyalty.
- Self-control.

We've known these truths since the beginning of time. The problem isn't in the knowing—it's in the doing.

My mind wanders back to a forgotten tombstone and those five simple words: "A man of unquestioned integrity." The more you think about it, the greater it seems.

What does it mean to be "above reproach"? Let's start and end with those five words.

GOING DEEPER

1. What does the phrase "above reproach" mean to you? How do you spot a man like that? What qualities make him stand out from the crowd? Name at least five men you know whom you believe to be "above reproach." What qualities do these men have in common?

2. John Calvin (see footnote 2) makes a distinction between the "ordinary vices" found in all men and those sins that leave a "disgraceful stain" on a man's reputation. Do you agree with that distinction? What kinds of sins so stain a man that he cannot be considered "above reproach"? If a man has a "disgraceful stain" on his life because of heinous sin, can he ever again be considered "above reproach," or is he stained forever?

3. "A man of unquestioned integrity."
   Could anyone say that about you? Why or why not?
   What would need to change in your life before we could chisel those words on your tombstone?

4. The first price you pay is always the cheapest.
   If this is true, why do we so often avoid confronting problem situations?
   Can you think of a person or a situation that you've been avoiding because you hope the problem will go away? What usually happens when we avoid confronting our problems? What steps do you need to take this week to deal with problems at home or at work?

TAKING ACTION

Let's do a quick Integrity Inventory based on the material in this chapter. Rate yourself from 1 (weak in this area) to 5 (strong in this area) regarding each statement.

1. *I tell the truth even when it hurts.*	1	2	3	4	5
2. *I consistently keep my promises.*	1	2	3	4	5
3. *I have no trouble saying no.*	1	2	3	4	5
4. *People can depend on me to keep my word.*	1	2	3	4	5
5. *I confront problems the first time around.*	1	2	3	4	5

A KISS
ON THE LIPS

A Man of Honor is "respectable."
—*1 Timothy 3:2*

M ost of us have a mental image of the "respectable man." He may be the banker in town or the Congressman standing tall on Capitol Hill or the hard-working school administrator. He could be the local football coach or a greatly loved physician. In many small towns the mayor fills that role. Or it could be a pharmacist or a rancher or the chief of police. The trouble is that most of us have had our images of a "respectable man" shattered by the behavior of the banker, the Congressman, the school administrator, or the mayor. Respect is hard to come by and easily lost. How can we become respectable men in our homes, churches, and communities?

The Greek word is *kosmios*—from which we get the English word *cosmos*. Its describes a person whose life is well-ordered and well-arranged. Another word might be *dignified*. E. M. Blaiklock says this quality refers to "a certain sturdiness of character."[1] This quality is seen in a leader's outward behavior—his dress, his manners, his speech, the way he relates to the opposite sex. It touches the way he keeps his home and how he handles the various affairs of life. It basically describes a person who can keep a dozen balls in the air at one time—without dropping any and without saying, "Hey, look at me!"[2] Such a person can work through difficult problems with clear thinking. To use an old phrase that sounds sadly out-of-date, a man with this quality is a "Christian gentle-man."

Jesus used this word to describe a clean and orderly house (Matthew 12:44), a decorated grave (Matthew 23:29), and a well-trimmed lamp (Matthew 25:7). The same word is used for a bride's beautiful dress (Revelation 21:2). When the Apostle John saw the walls of the New Jerusalem studded with exquisite gemstones of every variety, he used this word to describe the perfection of colors that dazzled his eyes (Revelation 21:19).

MAKING JESUS ATTRACTIVE

Perhaps the most important use of this word is found in Titus 2:10, where Paul encourages Christian slaves to "make the teaching about God our Savior attractive." He defines this as trying to please their masters, not talking back to them, not stealing from them, but rather showing that they can be fully trusted.

A godly man lives in such a way that his life beautifies the Gospel. He makes Jesus beautiful and the Gospel attractive to outsiders.[3]

> This points the Christian man to the priority of developing his inner life, the hidden man that others cannot see. When properly developed, his outward behavior and demeanor will reflect the quality of his inner life.[4]

What steps can we take to grow into this kind of life? First, *a man must develop the right kind of foundation in his life.* In the construction world, foundations can make or break (literally!) a building. Recently I visited the Western Wall in Jerusalem and saw the massive foundation stones for Herod's Temple. Although the Roman Legion destroyed the superstructure in A.D. 70, the foundation stones have lasted 2,000 years. When we have the right foundation, the evidence of it will be seen in the outward integrity of our behavior and relationships.

A man who has integrity is attractive to others because so few men today really have it. Before a man can look well-ordered and well-arranged, he must cultivate his inner self. A man with integrity does not draw attention to himself. But when others observe someone with integrity, they immediately know that something has taken place on the inside, where it really counts.

What steps should we take to develop that kind of "respectable" life?

STEP #1:
PRACTICE HONESTY

Time magazine recently ran a cover story entitled, "Lying: Everybody's Doing It." The epidemic of dishonesty starts at the top. According to one poll, 63 percent of Americans have little or no confidence in the honesty of government leaders. Philosopher Sissela Bok warns that this perception of high-level dishonesty has seriously frayed the national fabric: "Now, there is something strange and peculiar: people take for granted that they can't trust the government."[5]

Dr. Leonard Keeler, the inventor of the lie detector, has tested 25,000 individuals and has come to the conclusion that human beings generally do not tell the truth. For those of you with kids, that's not news.

According to a fascinating book called *The Day America Told the Truth*, "Lying has become an integral part of the American culture. We lie, and don't even think about it." The authors discovered that 91 percent of Americans lie regularly:

> The majority of us find it hard to get through a week without lying. One in five can't make it through a single day—and we're talking about conscious, premeditated lies. In fact, the way some people talk about trying to do without lies, you'd think that they were smokers trying to get through a day without a cigarette.[6]

Not surprisingly, the Bible has a lot to say about the importance of honesty. Proverbs 24:26 says, "An honest answer is like a kiss on the lips." Why does the Bible use this analogy?

I think there are at least three similarities. First, for most of us, it's rare to get a kiss on the lips. Likewise, it's not often that we get an honest answer. Second, when we do kiss on the lips, it's usually deeply satisfying. Similarly, an honest answer from an honest person is gratifying. Third, when you kiss someone on the lips, you are expressing the sincerity and love that are in your heart.

Ephesians 4:25 tells us exactly what it means to be honest men: "Each of you must put off falsehood and speak truthfully to his neighbor."

STEP #2:
STOP LYING

The words "put off" in Ephesians 4:25 carry the idea of taking off a coat or a shirt and discarding it. It would be like taking the coat you have worn for years and putting it in the garbage. In the same way, God tells us to take off all falsehood. In other words, we are to stop lying.

Many of us have been wearing the coat of falsehood for a long time. God wants you to take it off and throw it away, to leave the lies behind. Like taking off a coat, this is something that you must do *deliberately*. Our problem is that instead of leaving the lies behind, we all too often put the coat of falsehood back on.

Proverbs 6:16-19 lists seven things that make God angry; two of them deal with lying. Psalm 101:7 says, "No one who practices deceit will dwell in my house; no one who speaks falsely will stand in my presence."

Since lying won't get you on God's good side, or help you win friends for that matter, it's time to come clean. Some of you have been lying for a long time, and now it's time for you to leave the lies behind. Maybe you've told a lie recently because you were afraid to tell the truth; it's time to own up to it. Have you lied to your spouse? You need to confess it. Have you lied to your boss? You need to come clean. Is there something in your past that you've never told anyone about? Maybe the hiding has gone on long enough.

Years ago I heard a man say, "You're only as sick as your secrets. If you have a lot of secrets, you're really sick." He's right. Some of us are sick because we won't come clean about our past.

STEP #3:
ADMIT YOUR MISTAKES

Although we live in a society that encourages us to make excuses, most of us don't need any encouragement. We were born knowing how to pass the buck.

It all goes back to the Garden of Eden. The serpent came to Eve and tricked her into eating the fruit. She offered some to Adam and he ate, knowing full well the consequences of his action.

At length God called out to Adam, "Where are you?" Adam answered and said, "I was afraid because I was naked; so I hid." God said, "Who told you that you were naked?" Then came the dreaded question: "Have you eaten from the tree that I commanded you not to eat from?"

Adam was cornered, caught red-handed, stripped naked of all his excuses. What would he do? He did what any man would do in the same situation. He passed the buck. His answer is a classic form of evasion: "The woman you put here with me—she gave me some fruit from the tree, and I ate it."

Did you get that? "The woman you put here with me." Adam passes the buck twice. First it was *the woman*. Then it was the woman "*you* put here." "Lord, it was her fault. She gave me the fruit, so I ate it. You know how it is when a man's wife wants him to do something. What was I supposed to do? Say no and watch her pout all night? And anyway, who put her in the Garden? You did! She wasn't my idea. I'm not complaining, Lord, because she's beautiful and cute and all that, but I didn't have this problem when it was just me and the animals."

And so it goes. The first man, the father of the human race, was also the first one to pass the buck. Make no mistake. The Bible is telling us something significant. *It is in our nature to deny our own guilt and to try to shift the blame to others.* That's what Genesis 3:8-13 is all about. It's no coincidence that the first sin led to the first cover-up. The first disobedience led to the first denial. The first trespassing led to the first buck-passing.

In all the thousands of years since then, nothing has really changed. Human nature is the same. Passing the buck is in our spiritual bloodstream. We do it now because Adam did it back then. He established the pattern:

Disobedience *leads to*
Guilt, *which leads to*
Shame, *which leads to*
Fear, *which leads to*
Hiding, *which leads to*
Blaming others.

But it is not easy to say, "I was wrong." Most of us would rather do anything than admit we were wrong. Do you remember how much trouble Fonzie had with this issue on the TV series *Happy Days*? Fonzie was too cool ever to admit he had erred. Richie Cunningham would say to him, "Go ahead, admit it, you were wrong." So Fonzie would go, "I was wr-r-r-r-r-r-." And he couldn't get the word out. He would end up saying, "I was wr-r-r-r—not right!"

But "not right" is not exactly the same as "wrong." If you're wrong, you're wrong. But if you are "not right," who knows what you really mean?

STEP #4:

START TELLING THE TRUTH

Leaving the lies behind is only part of the answer. Honesty is more complex than not telling a lie. Honesty involves our deepest motives and encompasses every area of private and public life. The Bible depicts honesty as much broader than simply abstaining from lying. Let's take a look at the second half of Ephesians 4:25:

> Each of you must put off falsehood *and speak truthfully to his neighbor.*

If you want to cultivate the character of honesty, you first need to discard the lies. Second, you must tell the truth. The Bible doesn't just tell us to stop doing something; it also tells us to begin doing something else. Stop lying—tell the truth. Scripture is clear: if we hold back on the truth, we are headed for trouble. (See Psalm 5:6; 7:14-15; Proverbs 12:17-22; 19:9.) This is especially the case in our relationships. If we resist telling the whole truth, our relationships are not going to be strong. Relationships in the family and with our friends are built on a foundation of trust. If you don't have trust—the kind that only comes from telling the truth completely—you're going to crash and burn.

TRUTH IN THE INNER PARTS

But what is a man to do if he has been living a lie for some time? One man who had been living a double life for many years finally decided to come clean about his sin. As he told the story to his friends, he spoke repeatedly of how difficult it had been to maintain a "secret relationship" while still appearing to be a spiritual leader in his local church. Because he was extremely discreet, no one ever suspected the truth. He said that during one period of his sin, he tried to make everything okay by reading J. I. Packer, R. C. Sproul, Francis Schaeffer, and Chuck Colson, hoping that by making himself better in other areas, his sin would not bother him so much. But that only made things worse because the Holy Spirit convicted him of his hypocrisy. Finally, and with great difficulty, he confessed his sin to a friend, then to the leaders of his church, then to others who needed to know the truth.

It was not easy. And restoration did not happen overnight. But for the first time in years he began to grow spiritually. Joy returned to his heart. The Bible came alive as he drank in the Word of God day by day. He discovered that his closest friends would indeed forgive him. "How could I not forgive him after the Lord has forgiven me so many times?" his wife said.

Becoming a respectable man won't happen overnight. But it will never happen as long you practice dishonesty in word or deed. Being respectable goes far deeper than having a good reputation. It touches the very core of a man's character.

When David finally came to his senses after his affair with Bathsheba, he discovered something he should have known all along— that God desires truth "in the inner parts" of a man's life (Psalm 51:6).

When will we become respectable men of God? When we start telling the truth.

GOING DEEPER

1. Think about the "respectable" men you knew as a child. Who were they, and why did you hold them in high regard?

2. Describe a time when you were deeply disappointed by the behavior of a man you highly respected. What sorts of things cause you to lose respect for another person?

3. Why is honesty such a fundamentally important part of being a "respectable" man?

4. Human beings do not generally tell the truth.
   Do you agree or disagree with that statement?
   About what kinds of things is it difficult for you to tell the truth?

5. The people we lie to the most are the people closest to us.
   What is it about men that makes us lie to those we love?
   How can we break this pattern of deception, half-truths, and
   outright lies?

6. Read Ephesians 4:20-25.
   According to verse 22, what should we do with the "old self"? How
   do we do that on a daily basis?
   According to verse 25, what is the motivation for telling the truth?
   We know that lying hurts other people, but how does telling a lie
   also hurt you? How does it hurt the Lord?

7. Why does God place such a high value on truth in our relationship
   with Him? Are there any "secret sins" in your life that need to be
   confessed and forsaken? If so, what are you going to do about it?

TAKING ACTION

Listed below are some common ways we lie to others. Check the ones that
apply to you. Share this list with a friend as a means of personal accountability.

_____ *Overstating the truth.*

_____ *Carelessness in relating details.*

_____ *Creating a false impression.*

_____ *Exaggerating my past accomplishments.*

_____ *Failing to give due credit to others.*

_____ *Flattering others to win their approval.*

_____ *Slandering others in order to hurt them.*

_____ *Giving vague answers when confronted.*

_____ *Speaking evil of others while claiming to be their friend.*

WELCOME!

A Man of Honor is "hospitable."
—*1 Timothy 3:2; Titus 1:8*

T he Apostle Paul tells us that a spiritual leader practices hospitality. The Greek word translated "hospitable" is *philoxenia*, which shows up in one form or another about ten times in the New Testament. *Philoxenia* is a compound word made up of two other Greek words: *philos*, which means "kind affection" or "love," and *xenos*, which means "stranger" or "foreigner." Literally, *philoxenia* means "one who loves strangers."[1]

SURVEYING THE BIBLICAL LANDSCAPE

What does the New Testament have to say about hospitality? Let's answer that question by taking a quick survey of some key passages. Romans 12:13 says, "Share with God's people who are in need. Practice hospitality." That is a command of Scripture.[2] It is a non-negotiable imperative given to every man who claims the name of Jesus Christ. If we are Christians, we are to earnestly practice showing love to those who are strangers to us.

A second passage is 1 Peter 4:9, "Offer hospitality to one another without grumbling." It is all too easy to open your home only to those who are your close personal friends. But Peter isn't just talking about having your pals over for a game night. That's good, and you ought to do it, but Peter isn't primarily thinking along those lines. He's thinking about those times when you show kindness to people you don't know very well. How easy it is in those cases to mumble and grumble and gripe under your breath. And when you do that, you miss the blessing God wants you to receive.[3]

We've all done that. We meet some new people and say, "Drop by anytime." So one night we're eating supper, and a knock comes at the door. Oh man! We open the door, and it's those new people—all six of them!— standing on the porch with big smiles. So what do we do? We smile right back and say, "Good to see you. Come on in." But in reality our fingers are crossed when we speak, and in our hearts we don't mean a word we said.

Of course, God knows whether we mean it or not. We aren't fooling Him a bit. That's why He said our hospitality must be done "without grumbling."

A third passage offers us a very unusual encouragement to practice hospitality. Hebrews 13:2 says, "Do not forget to entertain strangers, for by so doing some people have entertained angels without knowing it." The word translated "angels" in the New Testament simply means "messengers." It sometimes means the literal angels of God and sometimes human messengers. This particular verse is saying that the literal angels of God might come to visit us. In the back of the writer's mind is the story in Genesis 18, when Abraham welcomed three strangers who came to visit him. Without knowing their identity, he served them veal and milk and curds and fresh bread. One turned out to be the Lord Himself, and the other two turned out to be angels. The writer is suggesting that such a thing might happen to us.

HOSPITALITY ACROSS THE CENTURIES

If you read the commentaries, it soon becomes clear why there is such a strong emphasis on hospitality in the New Testament. Back then they didn't have Holiday Inns, Red Roof Inns, Executive Suites, or Hilton Hotels. When Paul came to Corinth, he couldn't check into the Airport Marriott.

The few inns they did have were ill-kept and dangerous. Many were little more than brothels and havens for brigands and robbers. So as Christians traveled from place to place across the Empire, they didn't have the option of staying in a safe place. The only way the Christian message could spread would be for Christians to open their homes to others. The only way an evangelist from Antioch could make it in Ephesus would be for a family in Ephesus to open their home to him. The only way a teacher from Caesarea could visit Cyprus would be for someone from Cyprus to open his home and say, "My brother, you are welcome to stay with us."

A TASTE OF HAITI

Does this still occur today? Or has hospitality gone out of style? Three times I have been privileged to do short-term mission work in Haiti, the poorest country in the western hemisphere. Each time I have traveled to a village called Pignon, a town of 30,000 people tucked away in the north-central region of the country. It's about as far away from modern America as you can get and still be on the same planet. There is no electricity, no running water, no radio, no TV, no air conditioning. There are no paved roads and no newspapers. The unemployment rate hovers around 90 percent. The annual per capita income in Pignon is approximately $150.

Each time I go I work with Pastor Sidoine Lucien and the Jerusalem Baptist Church. Although their church draws well over 1,000 people a week, their weekly offering is only about $200. Multiply that by 52 and you get an annual budget of around $10,000. Although they are dirt poor, somehow they have built an orphanage, six elementary schools, and a summer camp; and as I write this, they are completing the first building for a brand-new high school.

Those Christians have virtually nothing. The poorest person I know in the U.S.A. is rich compared to the richest person in the church in Pignon. What's more, the pastor and his wife have personally taken in over fifty orphans over the years and have raised them to become productive and godly men and women. In fact, many of the deacons started out as Pastor Lucien's orphans.

One day I asked Pastor Lucien how they could do so much with so little. He smiled for a moment and then in halting English said, "When I help others, God helps me." I've never heard a better statement of the Christian ethic of giving.

Hospitality is not just a theory with the Christians of Pignon; it's a way of life. And believe it or not, they don't regard our visits as a burden. To them, it's a blessing for us to come.

ROADBLOCKS TO HOSPITALITY

Having said all of that, I must admit that hospitality isn't always easy. In fact, there are some roadblocks you will have to overcome in order to begin practicing hospitality. Let me list several of the most obvious misunderstandings that prevent Christian hospitality.

ROADBLOCK # 1:
CONFUSING HOSPITALITY WITH ENTERTAINMENT

Actually, the two could not be further apart. Hospitality is at one end of the spectrum and entertainment at the other. Unfortunately, we think hospitality is what happens when we get all dressed up and invite our friends over for a party. That's nice, and it's good, but it's not hospitality.

ROADBLOCK # 2:
HOSPITALITY IS INCONVENIENT BECAUSE WE ARE TOO BUSY

This is no doubt the main reason we don't practice hospitality more than we do. At least it's *my* main reason. I confess that I use this excuse all the time. But if you are too busy to show hospitality, you are *too* busy. If you are too busy to obey the Bible, then your life (and mine) is out of order.

ROADBLOCK # 3:
YOU HAVE TO BE RICH TO BE HOSPITABLE

Fortunately, this is not true. Some of the most hospitable Christians I know live very modestly. Some are middle-income families, and some are lower-income families. In the heart of the Great Depression Al Suckow committed himself to opening his home to pastors and Christian workers who visited him in rural Montana. Although he and his wife Louie struggled to make ends meet, every Sunday they welcomed the local pastor to their table.

Sixty years later, one of Suckow's four daughters vividly remembers the visiting missionaries and evangelists who stayed in their home. "Even though we were so isolated, we met people who had been to other continents, and that introduced us to a world outside our farm in Montana."

After every Sunday worship service, Al and Louie Suckow were the last ones to leave church because they wanted to greet the visitors and invite them to Sunday dinner. "I can still hear his memorized 'grace' at the table: 'Our Father, we thank Thee for this food. Bless it to its intended use and us to Thy service. Amen.' The strange part is I really think he meant it each time he prayed it."[4]

You don't have to be rich to practice hospitality, and you don't need a fancy house. All you need is a heart big enough to include someone else around your table.

L'ABRI

Many of you recognize the name *L'Abri*. It means "shelter" in French. *L'Abri* was the name Francis and Edith Schaeffer chose for the Christian community they established in Switzerland. During the 1950s and 1960s, an amazing number of students came to L'Abri from all over the world, seeking solid answers to their deepest questions. Hundreds of those students found Jesus Christ in the process.

In his excellent book *The Church at the End of the 20th Century*, Francis Schaeffer describes what it cost to practice hospitality at L'Abri:

> In about the first three years of L'Abri all our wedding presents were wiped out. Our sheets were torn. Holes were burned in our rugs. Indeed once a whole curtain almost burned up from somebody smoking in our living room. Everybody came to our table. Blacks came to our table. Orientals came to our table. Everybody came to our table. It couldn't happen any other way. . . . You see, you don't need a big program. You don't have to convince your session or board. All you have to do is open your home and begin. And there is no place in God's world where there are no people who will come and share a home as long as it is a real home.[5]

FIRST STEPS TOWARD *PHILOXENIA*

Where should we begin? I want to give you four simple steps you can put into practice today.

STEP #1:
GO OUT OF YOUR WAY TO MEET ONE NEW PERSON THIS WEEK

Think about the people who attend or attended school with you. What about the fellow who transferred to your branch office from another state? What about your five closest neighbors? Or the new people who visit your church each Sunday? Will you take some time to meet them? You can say hello to people you've seen before but haven't met. That's a simple step, but it is so important. Hospitality begins by being willing to meet people you haven't met before.

STEP #2:
GET TO KNOW SOMEONE FROM ANOTHER COUNTRY

America has become the world's melting pot. Every metropolitan area has thousands of international students, and even the smallest towns will have people who came from other cultures. Some may be from Cambodia, some from Japan, some from Africa, some from Europe. What a marvelous opportunity to show biblical hospitality. People from other countries are truly strangers to us. We don't know them, and they don't know us. But here they are, living on our street, shopping in the same stores, working down the hall from us. We pass like ships in the night. Will you care enough to get to know someone from the other side of the world?

STEP #3:
INVITE SOMEONE TO YOUR HOME

They don't have to come today, but why don't you issue an invitation for someone to come to your home this week or the week after that. Invite them over for ice cream or for hamburgers. After all, it's biblical for Christians to eat together. (See Luke 10:6-7; Acts 2:46.)

STEP #4:
CALL SOMEONE YOU HAVEN'T TALKED TO IN A LONG, LONG TIME

It could be an old friend you haven't called in years. It may be someone who used to be a close friend, but somehow you've lost touch with each other. It might be someone you need to call in order to clear up some past misunderstandings. It could be a mother, a father, a brother or a sister, a hometown friend, or someone else whose name comes to mind.

THE ORIGINAL XENOPHILIAC

I once preached a sermon entitled "Confessions of a Xenophiliac." I began with a confession that there is no such word as *xenophiliac*. I just made it up by switching around *philoxenia*, the actual Greek word for hospitality. But I like *xenophiliac* because it sounds like it ought to be a word even if it's not.

Just before I preached the sermon, one of my staff members prayed, "O God, we thank You that You are the original xenophiliac." At first that sounded odd. And then in a flash it hit me. It's true. God is the original "lover of strangers." While we were yet sinners, Christ died for us. While we were estranged from God, He sent His Son to earth to die for us. And we who were once strangers and aliens on the earth have now been brought near to God by the blood of Jesus Christ.

We are no longer strangers, no longer aliens, no longer orphans, no longer far away from God. We are now as near to God as His own Son is, for through the blood of Jesus we are brought into God's family. Because He loved us when we were strangers, we are strangers no more.

HOSPITALITY PAYS OFF IN THE END

That same thing happens today when we show hospitality to others. We are only doing for others what God did for us. And in the end we won't be disappointed. Consider these words of Jesus:

> "'For I was hungry and you gave me something to eat, I was thirsty and you gave me something to drink, I was a stranger and you invited me in.' . . . Then the righteous will answer him, 'Lord, when did we see you hungry and feed you, or thirsty and give you something to drink? When did we see you a stranger and invite you in?' . . . The King will reply, 'I tell you the truth, whatever you did for one of the least of these brothers of mine, you did for me.'"
> —*Matthew 25:35, 37, 40*

That's the bottom line. *When you open your home to strangers, you are opening your home to the Lord Jesus.* When you welcome them, you welcome Him. No one will ever be sorry they opened their home. No one will ever be sorry they said, "Come on in and have a meal with us." No one will ever be sorry they put up with the inconvenience. No one will ever say, "I wish I hadn't helped those people."

Hospitality has its rewards, both now and in the world to come.

Who's that knocking at your door? It might be Jesus.

GOING DEEPER

1. Why was hospitality so important in the early church? What would have happened to the Christian message without the practice of hospitality? Given the vastly different cultural circumstances, how important is hospitality in today's world?

2. Many people confuse hospitality with entertainment. Take a piece of paper and list several differences. Since there is obviously some overlap (you can entertain and show hospitality at the same time), what is the essential difference?

3. In our culture hospitality is more often associated with women than with men. How do you account for that fact? Do you think hospitality comes easier for women than for men? What can you do to take initiative in this area?

4. Read Genesis 18:1-15.
   Who were Abraham's three visitors, and where did they come from? What message did they bring for Sarah, and how did she respond? How does Hebrews 13:2 apply to the twentieth century? Do you think something like this could ever happen today? Have you ever had any direct encounters with angels—actual or presumed?

5. "When I help others, God helps me."
   List any Scriptures that support this statement.
   Why are Third-World Christians much more likely to practice hospitality than those of us who live in western nations? What does that suggest about the spiritually-deadening effect of prosperity?

6. Review the Francis Schaeffer quotation given in this chapter dramatically describing the ministry he and his wife had at L'Abri.

Are you willing to experience this type of hospitality ministry? Why or why not? What would need to change in your life for this to happen?

TAKING ACTION

This chapter offers four concrete suggestions: Meet someone new this week; get to know someone from another country; invite a new person over to your home; call someone you haven't talked to in a long time. Pick one of these, and make a commitment to do it this week.

DO THE
RIGHT THING

A Man of Honor is "upright."
—*Titus 1:8*

The word *upright* means "fair, honest, just." This touches a man's business dealings, his financial affairs, how he handles his employees, how he respects his employer, what kind of deals he makes, whether he pays his bills on time, whether he keeps his promises, how he speaks about others, and whether you would trust this man with your wife and children overnight. It is a combination of goodness and honesty.

This particular quality will often be seen in the decisions made under pressure. Because an upright man has committed himself to following God's principles, he consistently makes wise choices in every situation.[1] He's the man you want by your side when the heat is on and the chips are down. He doesn't get angry or flustered in a tense circumstance because he knows the truth and acts in accordance with it. Through long years of experience he has learned what to do in the moment of crisis.

Joseph was such a man. I'm not speaking of the Joseph whose story is told in Genesis (though he too was upright), but of Joseph who was called the father of Jesus. Matthew 1:19 uses the word "righteous," a synonym for upright, to describe his reaction when he learned that his beloved Mary had suddenly become pregnant.

UP CLOSE AND PERSONAL

Let me briefly list for you the things we know about Joseph.

- His father was Jacob.

- His hometown was Bethlehem in Judea, but he lived in Nazareth in Galilee. That meant that Joseph and Mary had to travel about ninety-five miles in the dead of winter in order to register for the census.[2]

- He belonged to the royal line of David. The genealogy in Matthew 1 makes that clear.

- He was a carpenter by trade.

- He was a poor man. We know that because when he and Mary presented Jesus in the Temple, they brought birds to sacrifice. Jews only did that when they could not afford a lamb.[3]

- He was a religious man, a devout keeper of the Law, a fact we will observe more closely in just a moment.

- How old was Joseph? We don't know the answer for sure, but most writers agree that he was a young man and probably a teenager. If we said seventeen to twenty-five years old, we would probably be about right.

PLEDGED TO BE MARRIED

Matthew tells Joseph's story this way:

> This is how the birth of Jesus Christ came about. His mother Mary was pledged to be married to Joseph, but before they came together, she was found to be with child through the Holy Spirit.
> —*Matthew 1:18*

What the *New International Version* calls "pledged to be married," the older versions call "betrothed." This refers to an ancient Jewish custom in which most marriages were arranged by the parents—with or without the children's approval. The two sets of parents would meet and draw up a formal marriage contract. When the contract was signed, the man and woman were legally "pledged" to each other. This period of betrothal would last up to a year, at the end of which period they were formally married in a public wedding ceremony.[4]

That sounds like our practice of engagement, but there were some major differences. In the first place, the pledge was considered as sacred as marriage itself. During that year the couple were called husband and wife, though they did not live together. If the man died during that year, the woman would be considered a widow even though the wedding ceremony had never taken place. The only way to break the betrothal was through a legal divorce. In essence, to be "pledged" to each other was the same thing as being married, except that you could not live together or engage in sexual activity until the actual wedding ceremony transpired. The whole idea was that the one-year waiting period was meant to be a time to test commitment and faithfulness.

This is where the story gets interesting. According to Deuteronomy 22:20-21, if a woman was found to be pregnant during the betrothal, that could only mean she had been unfaithful to her husband, in which case the Law commanded that she be stoned to death.[5]

JOSEPH'S DILEMMA

When Mary turned up pregnant, Joseph only knew one thing for sure: he wasn't the father.

What words describe a man at a time like this? Anger . . . confusion . . . frustration . . . embarrassment . . . shame . . . rage . . . disappointment . . . betrayal.

What did Joseph say to Mary? What did she say to him? Did she tell him about the angel Gabriel? If she did, can you blame him for not believing her?

Did he say to her, "Mary, how could you! You were pledged to me. We were going to get married. I was going to build a little house for us in Nazareth. Mary, Mary, how could you do this? Why, Mary, why? I kept myself for you. Why couldn't you keep yourself for me?"

I would imagine that Joseph cried harder that day than he had ever cried in his life.

Put yourself in Joseph's shoes. You're a young man in love, and suddenly your girlfriend turns up pregnant. You aren't the father, but you don't know who is. What do you do? If you're like some men, you give her $200 to go get an abortion. It's easy, it's quick, it's cheap, and just like that you can make the problem go away. A half-million teenage girls take that option every year. It's the preferred solution for what people call an "unwanted pregnancy."

Thankfully, Joseph and Mary didn't have that option. Abortion was very rare in ancient Israel, and Planned Parenthood hadn't opened up a clinic in Nazareth yet.

Joseph's dilemma was of a different variety. He was an observant Jew, and under the Law he had the right to divorce Mary for unfaithfulness. In fact, the Law forbade him to marry her under those circumstances.

Here is the greatness of Joseph. *He loved her even though he thought she had been unfaithful to him. His love covered her shame.*

This is how verse 19 puts it:

> Because Joseph her husband was a righteous man [that means he wanted to do what was right in the eyes of God] and did not want to expose her to public disgrace [that means that although he thought she had been unfaithful, he still didn't want to humiliate her], he had in mind to divorce her quietly.

In those days, a man could get a divorce in two ways. First, he could get a public divorce by going before a judge at the gate of the city. That would mean the whole town would know about Mary's shame. Second, he could get a private divorce by giving her the papers in the presence of two witnesses.

It is entirely to Joseph's credit that he chose to do it privately and thus spare Mary the humiliation of a public divorce.

Having made his decision . . . he didn't do it. He had every legal and moral right to divorce Mary, but he just couldn't do it. As one writer put it, there was a "short but tragic struggle between his legal conscience and his love." He hesitated, waited, thought long and hard. Day after day he pondered the matter. Time was running out. With each passing day, it became more obvious that Mary was pregnant. Late each night he lay in bed staring into the blackness, wondering what to do.

Then one night he had a dream, a dream in which God spoke to him:

> An angel of the Lord appeared to him in a dream and said, "Joseph son of David, do not be afraid to take Mary home as your wife, because what is conceived in her is from the Holy Spirit."
>
> *—verse 20*

To us this seems strange. But not to Joseph. God often spoke to people through dreams in the Bible. It was one way He used to communicate His will to His people.[6]

Joseph needed assurance. He couldn't wed Mary until he was sure it was all right. He had to know the truth. And God met him at the point of his need at exactly the right moment. He told Joseph the one thing he most wanted to hear: "Joseph son of David, do not be afraid to take Mary home as your wife."

And the angel wasn't finished yet:

> "She will give birth to a son, and you are to give him the name Jesus, because he will save his people from their sins."
>
> *—verse 21*

The angel explained just enough and nothing more. The baby was "from the Holy Spirit" and thus not of man. Nothing more is said. We are not told precisely how the virginal conception of Jesus in the womb of Mary took place. It remains one of the great mysteries of the Christian faith. After 2,000 years of debate, we know nothing more about it than Joseph did.

But the angel did add a detail about who this baby would be. His name was to be Jesus, which means "Savior." His mission was to save His people from their sins.

That was all. It wasn't a long message, but it was enough.

JOSEPH'S FINEST HOUR

Verses 24-25 are insufficiently celebrated as great Christmas verses. They reveal Joseph's finest qualities:

> When Joseph woke up, he did what the angel of the Lord had commanded him and took Mary home as his wife. But he had no union with her until she gave birth to a son. And he gave him the name Jesus.

Every step he took testifies to his greatness.

- By *marrying her quickly* he broke all Jewish custom, but he protected Mary's reputation. She was pregnant, and he wasn't the father, but he married her anyway.

- By *keeping her a virgin until Jesus was born*, he protected the miracle of Jesus' conception by the Holy Spirit against slander by unbelievers.

- By *naming the baby* he exercised a father's prerogative and thus officially took him into his family as his own legal son.

I like Joseph. I wish I could meet him (and someday I will). He strikes me as a genuine Man of Honor.

TOUGH AND TENDER

We usually give more attention to Mary than to Joseph, and rightly so. But Joseph deserves credit too. He is a model of the man of faith—struggling with his doubts, persuaded to believe what God said, and ultimately acting upon what he knew was right.

In these days of confusion, Joseph is a wonderful model of what a godly man looks like:

- He was tough when he could have been weak.
- He was tender when he could have been harsh.
- He was thoughtful when he could have been hasty.
- He was trusting when he could have doubted.
- He was temperate when he could have indulged himself.

Could we use those same words to describe our lives?

- Are you tough-minded, determined to do what is right no matter what it costs?
- Are you tender with your wife and with your children?
- Are you thoughtful, taking your time to make important decisions, or are you quick to jump to conclusions and quick to say things you later regret?
- Are you trusting even when you think you could figure out a better way to do things?

- Are you temperate and considerate of your wife and her special needs, or do you pressure your wife and children to perform up to your standard of perfection?

There is one other line of proof about the kind of man Joseph was. When Jesus grew up and began His ministry, He chose one word above all others to describe what God is like. He called Him "Father."

Where did Jesus learn about fathers? Humanly speaking, from Joseph.

Men, *the way your children respond to God depends largely on the kind of father you are*. You teach them something about God every day just by the way you live in front of them.

A LITTLE BOY NEVER FORGETS

Doing the right thing often isn't easy.

When a good friend of mine, Frank Lustrea, heard that his wife's parents needed a place to stay, he didn't hesitate to offer his own home. Not everyone thought it was a good idea, but that didn't matter to Frank. To him, the word *family* means that you take care of each other no matter what.

For twelve years he and Eleanor cared for John and Constance Lazar. His father-in-law had Parkinson's disease, which utterly humiliates its victims. Slowly the once good-looking vibrant man became a shell of his former self. In his younger days he had played his tuba in the brass band at the First Romanian Baptist Church in Chicago. Sunday afternoons he marched with the band down the street, drawing a crowd so the pastor could preach the Gospel.

But those days were long gone by the time he and his wife moved in with Frank and Eleanor Lustrea. Now the man could barely walk because his body was so contorted by the disease. When he fell, his young grandson Bob would help him back up. It could have been embarrassing, but his grandson doesn't remember it that way.

> The clearest picture I have in my mind of my grandpa is of him in his pajamas, hunched over his rocking chair because he couldn't sit up straight. He was bent over so badly that his head angled directly toward the floor. Directly beneath his head there

was a stool and on that stool was his opened Romanian Bible.
This was his regular practice. The picture is burned into my con-
sciousness. Never was such an eloquent message delivered.[7]

When Frank Lustrea invited his wife's parents to live with him, he didn't
think about the impact it would have on his young son. But Bob saw his
father do the right thing, and in his own words, "his decision of thirty-
plus years ago is still paying dividends in my life."

Good fathers make it easy for their children to believe in God.

GOING DEEPER

1. The whole concept of betrothal is very foreign to our thinking.
   What godly purpose was upheld by this ancient practice?

2. Many engaged couples sleep together before their marriage,
   reasoning that it doesn't matter since they are going to be married
   later anyway. What biblical principles are violated by this practice?
   What positive things are gained by waiting until marriage?

3. What emotions ran through Joseph's heart when he first heard that
   Mary was pregnant? How did he feel? How would you feel in the
   same situation? Would you have believed Mary's story?

4. His love covered her shame.
   What does this statement mean? What does it reveal about Joseph's
   character?
   Why didn't Joseph divorce Mary publicly? What risk did he take by
   divorcing her privately? Why did he take that risk?

5. God met him at the point of his need.
   How did God do this?
   Does God still do this today? Can you remember a moment of crisis
   when God supplied your need so directly that it could only have
   come from Him? How did this come about?

6. Good fathers make it easy for their children to believe in God.
   What impact did your father have on your view of God? Was it
   positive, negative, or basically neutral?
   Name three specific ways in which fathers can encourage their
   children to believe in God.

TAKING ACTION

Think of the various areas of your life—professional, personal, home, financial, family, church, relationships, spiritual, and physical. What is the single toughest problem you face in each area? Write down the area, the problem, and beside each one a reason why you believe God is sufficient to meet your need in that area. Review your list daily, using it as a basis for your commitment to be God's man in each area no matter what it costs.

MY FATHER'S NAME

A Man of Honor has "a good reputation."
—1 Timothy 3:7

H ere is another quality that is often overlooked. The phrase "good reputation" is literally "good witness." What kind of witness do you have with the people outside the church? All too often we neglect to consider a man's reputation in the community. But the voice of the people is sometimes the same as the voice of God. This touches a man's reputation with his neighbors, his friends, his coworkers, and his non-Christian buddies. The godly leader ought to be admired by those outside the church. Although they will not always understand why, unbelievers are quick to spot a difference. "You're different somehow. I just can't put my finger on it."[1]

How can we live in such a way that our reputation enhances our Christian testimony and doesn't detract from it?

HONOR YOUR PARENTS

Most of us know the Fifth Commandment by heart: "Honor your father and your mother, so that you may live long in the land the LORD your God is giving you" (Exodus 20:12). Most of us also understand that this commandment applies to our children—that is, they should honor us. For too long we have relegated this commandment to young children and sometimes even used it as a club over their heads. But God never intended that this commandment be aimed primarily at young children. After all, how many young children were present at Mount Sinai? Most of the people who received the Ten Commandments were adults.

This commandment is primarily for grown-up children. It is God's way of telling us how to treat our parents.

What we don't understand is that our parents are part of our family as long as we live. First Timothy 5:8 warns us that "if anyone does not provide for his relatives, and especially for his immediate family, he has denied the faith and is worse than an unbeliever." Paul means to say that since even unbelievers take care of their own, if we fail to do that, we are doing even less than the pagans do.

Therefore, we are on perfectly biblical grounds in saying that one way to maintain a good reputation is to honor our parents.

REMEMBER WHO YOU ARE

On maybe the third or fourth day of a ministry trip in Russia I noticed something unusual about the way the men addressed one another. They would say each other's first name and then they would add a middle name that always ended with "ovich." John Sergey, for instance, was always addressed as "Ivan Mikhailovich Sergei." When I asked John about it, he said Russians always use the patronymic. *Patronymic* is a word that means "the name of my father." The "ovich" ending in Russian literally means "son of." Therefore, "Ivan Mikhailovich" literally means "John son of Michael." It's a way of recognizing your family lineage. Every son bears his father's name.

When John asked me my father's name, I told him my dad was named Tyrus Pritchard, after the great baseball player Ty Cobb. His full name was Tyrus Raymond Pritchard. My older brother took his first name, and I took his middle name. John thought for a moment and then said that in Russian my name would be "Ray Tyrusovich"——"Ray son of Tyrus."

That pleased me when I heard it because I've always been proud of my father. The thought of being called by my father's name is one of the greatest honors I could imagine. I think he would be proud and pleased too.

In the small town in Alabama where I grew up, my father was a well-known and greatly loved physician. There were four of us Pritchard boys who grew up in that small town. Outside of our circle of friends, we were known as "Dr. Pritchard's sons." In those days that meant a certain responsibility was laid on our shoulders. We had to live up to the good name our father had established. And we knew—boy, did we know!—that if we ever got into trouble, our misbehavior would reflect badly on our father.

My father died twenty-two years ago. But when I go back to visit that small town, someone always recognizes me as "Dr. Pritchard's son." Such is the power of a good name; such is the enduring relationship that lasts long after a father has died. To be truthful, the most wonderful compliment anyone can ever pay to me is to say, "Your father would be proud of you." That thought brings tears to my eyes even as I write these words.

I am still my father's son though he is dead and gone. I will always be my father's son. That relationship will never change, and the burden to honor his name will never be lifted from my shoulders. It is a heavy burden, but a sweet one, and I would never want to be freed from that sacred obligation.

But a part of him lives on in me and in my three brothers. If I can be permitted to paraphrase the words of Jesus, if you have seen me, you have seen my father—however imperfectly, however incompletely, however mixed in with other influences on my life. My dad is in me—in my face, in my voice, in my actions, in my habits. I even see him in my three sons—fainter still, but the influence is there. My sons are like me in many ways, but I am like my father in some ways, and so his influence passes on to the third generation.[2]

That's what it means to bear my father's name. It is far more than having the same last name. His character and personality was in some small way passed on to me. And even though he has been gone for twenty-two years, I have a sacred responsibility to hallow his name—to live up to the things he taught me, to try to be as good a man as he was, to live in such a way that people who never knew him will look at me and say, "His father must have been a good man" and that the people who knew my dad will say, "He's a credit to his father's name."

LET YOUR LIGHT SHINE

But that is not the only name I bear. I have another patronymic attached to my name. As a Christian, I bear the name of my heavenly Father. I have an even more sacred obligation to honor His name and to increase His reputation in the world. When I do that well, people who don't know God will look at my life and say, "He must have a great God," and God will look down from heaven and say, "That's my boy!"

Jesus said, "Let your light shine before men, that they may see your good deeds and praise your Father in heaven" (Matthew 5:16). Notice that Jesus didn't say that men would listen to your pious words. The men of the world have heard all the "religious" talk they want to hear. Most of them instinctively distrust Christians who do nothing but talk about their faith. Talk is cheap, but the men of the world recognize and appreciate someone who walks his talk.

What are the "good deeds" Christ had in mind that would shine in the darkness? Let's just focus on deeds of practical kindness. I have a friend who has been burdened for one of his neighbors, an elderly lady from the Ukraine who lives several doors down the street. But how could he build a bridge of friendship to someone from a completely different culture? The key turned out to be a thatching machine. One day as he was de-thatching his lawn, he happened to strike up a conversation with his neighbor. That same day he walked over and offered to de-thatch her lawn for her for free. Naturally she was thrilled and amazed that anyone would do something like that. It took him several hours to finish the job, but the payoff has been an open door for his entire family to befriend a lonely woman. His girls have become good friends with the woman, and she loves to bring over Ukrainian specialties for the family to try.

That's the whole story, so far. But the story isn't over. The door is wide-open for a conversation about Jesus Christ. Who knows where it will lead?

COURAGE IN SUFFERING

Sometimes the "good reputation" urged in 1 Timothy 3 is earned through suffering.

My friend Peter Blakemore, pastor of Harrison Street Bible Church in Oak Park, Illinois, died not long ago. I saw him for the last time when I attended a pastors' prayer meeting in connection with the National Day of Prayer. I came a few minutes late and found the men gathered in a circle ready to pray. As I walked in, I recognized most of the pastors immediately, all except for one man in a wheelchair, whom I did not recognize from the rear. He had two teenage boys by his side.

When I sat down, I realized the man in the wheelchair was Peter Blakemore. Peter was about forty years old, married, with seven wonderful children. He lived in Oak Park all his life, the only exception being a few years when he went to college and graduate school. His father pastored the Harrison Street Bible Church for over thirty years, and Peter took up the ministry in his father's stead.

My friend's trial started when he noticed a strange pain in his pelvic area. When it wouldn't go away, he sought medical help, but the doctors couldn't pinpoint the source of the trouble. Eventually they found a tumor, performed a biopsy, and sent it off for analysis. It took a long time to get a correct answer, but eventually a lab on the West Coast reported that Peter had contracted a very rare form of cancer. He began chemotherapy in a desperate attempt to eradicate the cancer.

Nothing they tried seemed to work. At one point he traveled to Dallas to investigate several specialized treatments. Those didn't work either.

When I saw Peter at that prayer meeting, he was bent over a bit but smiling as he sat in the wheelchair. As we prayed, I heard a rubbing noise coming from my left. It was Peter's oldest son, massaging his Dad's back because the pain was so intense.

I think Peter was the last one to pray. He said something like this: "Lord, when I discovered I had cancer, the only thing I asked was that You might use this to honor and glorify Your name. I thank You, Lord, that You have abundantly answered my prayer. If I make it, I will stand up and give You praise. But if I don't, I'll give You honor and glory till the very end."

As soon as the prayer meeting broke up, I sat down beside Peter and asked him how he was doing. The news was not good. A tumor had developed in his right lung, growing to the point that it had shattered several of his ribs. That's why he was doubled over in pain.

Peter told me that the doctors did not know for sure what kind of cancer this new tumor was. They told him that it could be one of two different kinds. "If it is one kind," he said, "I have two or three weeks to live. If it's the other kind, I have one or two months."

He said it calmly, without fear or panic. In fact, he was smiling as he said it. As I looked at him, his face was radiant with the glory of God. Like Moses of old, my friend Peter had seen the Lord, and now nothing else mattered.

He told me that he had preached the previous Sunday for the first time in seven weeks. They had to prop him up in his wheelchair, but he somehow found the strength to preach for an hour from Romans 11:33, "How unsearchable his judgments, and his paths beyond tracing out!" That text means that you can't tell where God has come from or where He is going. All you know is that He is with you, even in the midst of your pain.

The room was empty; all the other pastors were gone. Peter's last words to me were, "All my life I've been speaking about God's grace and trying to get people to listen. Now they listen when I speak, because I've discovered that through it all, God's grace is sufficient."

With that his sons began to wheel him out of the room. Though bent over with pain, he smiled and waved at me as he left.

The words of the Apostle Paul came to my mind: "Though outwardly we are wasting away, yet inwardly we are being renewed day by day" (2 Corinthians 4:16).

After Peter died, the local paper printed an extensive obituary. A columnist wrote a tribute based on a testimony Peter had given at an outdoor worship rally a few months before his death. The columnist did not go to Peter's church and in fact had never met him. He spoke of Peter's quiet, unassuming manner, how he talked about his illness and how his faith helped him deal with it. He mentioned that Peter spoke of the need for courage. It was "a remarkable little speech, remarkable for its lack of hyperbole or self-pity or sentiment or melodrama. Without ever raising his voice, he spoke with considerable authority." The writer noted that the Harrison Street Bible Church was a small congregation but very close-knit, "in no small part due to the efforts of their pastor."

Maybe Peter Blakemore wasn't talking about himself when he spoke of courage that day at Mills Park in Oak Park, Illinois. Maybe he was talking about the rest of us—those who must go on living without those who have tried so hard to show us how.[3]

That's what it means to have a "good reputation with outsiders." It comes from living such an authentic Christian life that others notice the difference.

WHY SHOULD I BE AFRAID?

Several months after his death, someone in the community wrote a letter describing Peter's impact on her family. She described how he and her husband served as coaches for a T-Ball team, how Peter was a "noticeably kind, gentle man," how he loved children and cared for all people. She noted that he refused to schedule practices or games on Sunday because that was "our Lord's Day." She spoke of how he took time out to get to know all the parents of the children on his team. "There was no favoritism with Peter, no preferences for friends and acquaintances. We were all God's children and treated by Peter as a valuable gift from God."

One night when he was ill, this friend stayed with Peter so his wife and children could go to his sister's wedding rehearsal.

> The Lord led me to Peter's side that night. Oh my, but he was ill. And in such pain that he couldn't speak, but he wrote me notes about times he had ministered to others. I sat quietly beside him and read the Bible while he rested. At one point that evening, he coughed up quite a bit of blood. When the doctor came in, he asked Peter, "Are you scared?" Obviously, they felt Peter was desperately ill. "No, I'm not scared. Why should I be?" he calmly replied. As they worked with him, I walked into the hall and said, "Oh my dear Lord, please let Peter live here longer to touch many lives. He has so much to give."[4]

Although God did not answer that prayer in the way she prayed it, He did answer it in another way—through the legacy left behind by this Man of Honor for God.

When will we learn that it's not how long we live that matters, but what we do with the years we are given? Some people live eighty years but fritter them away on things that don't really matter. Others die at forty-two, but their influence for Jesus Christ goes on and on and on.

GOING DEEPER

1. The voice of the people may be the voice of God. Do you think God could ever speak through unbelievers to reveal His will?
   Under what circumstances might the voice of the people not be the voice of God? How can we tell the difference?

2. Some men may not take this quality seriously. "After all, Jesus said we should expect trouble in the world. Why should we be concerned about what unbelievers think about us?" That's a fair question. How would you answer it?

3. How do you distinguish between maintaining a good reputation and merely currying favor with unbelievers? What are the character traits that unchurched people generally respect? At what point does building bridges with the unchurched become a form of spiritual compromise? What are the danger signs of this?

4. Read 1 Timothy 5:8.
   What action makes a Christian "worse than an unbeliever"?
   Name several ways a man can adequately "provide" for his own family. How does this apply to our extended family—parents, grandparents, uncles, aunts?
   According to Matthew 15:3-9, what did Jesus call religious people who used their religion as an excuse not to care for their parents? Could Jesus say this about you?

5. List several ways adult children can honor their parents. How does the Fifth Commandment apply to children whose parents mistreated or abandoned them? How can we honor our parents even after they are dead?

6. Think about the people in your own neighborhood. How many do you know by name? How many of them know you are a Christian? In what ways are you letting your light shine before them?

7. How would your unchurched friends feel if they learned you had been elected to a position of spiritual leadership? Would they be surprised or pleased?

TAKING ACTION

Here's a challenging project. Ask an unchurched friend to evaluate your reputation as a husband, a father, a friend, and a colleague at work. Tell him that you value his opinion and that he should be frank in sharing both your strong and weak points. Ask him to imagine that he is giving an anonymous character reference because you are being considered for the position of elder in your local church. Use his response as part of your self-evaluation to determine areas in your life that need attention.

PART IV

HIS SPIRITUAL LIFE

EXPERIENCE NEEDED

A Man of Honor takes time to grow.
—*1 Timothy 3:6*

He must not be a recent convert, or he may become conceited and fall under the same judgment as the devil." The word translated "recent convert" is *neofuton*, from which we get the English word *neophyte*. It literally means "new plant."[1] New plants need nurturing, they need fertilizer, they need someone to pull the weeds and make sure they get enough water and light. New plants need lots of tender, loving care. What they don't need is the pressure of having to be leaders. Remember, even a mighty oak tree was a new plant once. Given time and careful attention, that new plant will someday become strong enough to stand on its own. Until then, keep it in the hothouse.

But note the warning: "He may become conceited and fall under the same judgment as the devil." The literal Greek here is very picturesque: "He may be wrapped up in smoke." That is, by elevating a man too soon to leadership, he may begin to blow smoke and eventually be blinded by his own arrogance.[2]

The danger here is that new believers simply haven't been properly trained or tested yet. They lack the maturity, wisdom, and experience that only come from knowing the Lord for many years. Martin Luther said three things were necessary for the making of a minister: prayer, meditation, and temptation (resisted and conquered). Only when a man has been around the block a few times is he ready for leadership.

This applies to every level of spiritual leadership. Don't put a new believer in a key position! Don't be quick to elevate someone new to your congregation. Give them time to get acclimated. If they are worthy, they will demonstrate that fact over time. Don't rush. Take your time. It takes a lifetime to grow a good leader. Don't spoil the process by elevating someone too soon.

IT'S OKAY NOT TO KNOW

So much of what we need to know can't be learned quickly. Nor can it be learned in a classroom. The things that really matter are discovered only in the laboratory of life.

Finding God's will is often like that. After writing a book on the topic[3] and doing interviews around the country, I discovered that almost every question dealt with the subject of certainty. "How can I know in advance whether or not I should _____?" You can fill in the blank a dozen different ways—"move to Miami," "sell my house," "ask Rosa to marry me," "sell my stocks," "apply for a new job." The answer is always the same: in seeking God's will, you normally won't know in advance how things are going to work out.

Sometimes you will make the decision and everything works out just fine. Other times you will decide and then your world begins to fall apart. Most of our decisions end up somewhere between "just fine" and "total catastrophe," but you normally won't know in advance precisely where.

ABRAHAM DIDN'T KNOW

It takes time to learn these truths. In reality, *God often uses uncertainty to humble us to the point where we are forced to be totally dependent on Him.*

Consider Abraham, perhaps the greatest man of faith in all the Bible. Hebrews 11:8 explicitly says that "By faith Abraham, when called to go to a place he would later receive as an inheritance, obeyed and went, even though *he did not know where he was going*." That last phrase is a truly amazing statement. He didn't know where he was going when he left Ur of the Chaldees or how long it would take or how he would know when he got there. In fact, you could fairly say that what he didn't know was much greater than what he did know at that point. But he still made the journey because God called him and he obeyed.

Discovering God's will is often like that. If you are looking for a formula that will provide you with a complete road map before you start the journey, forget it. God doesn't work that way. Often He simply says, "Follow Me." At that point you have the choice of staying or following. But if you decide to follow God, please understand that you may feel like Abraham leaving Ur—"he did not know where he was going."

NO OVERNIGHT OAK TREES

Several of my good friends seem to be going through the same thing right now. I'm thinking of someone who is agonizing about a major move away from Chicago. Partly he is driven by business concerns and partly by the need to find a warmer climate and partly because he feels that his family needs to make a new start. He and I have spent many hours together over the last five years laughing, crying, talking, sharing, joking, discussing, praying, and playing together. Suddenly he has decided to move far away, to a part of the country he really knows very little about, to a city he's visited once, to start all over again. We have some mutual friends who live in that faraway city, which helps, but only slightly, because my friend doesn't know anyone else there. And to make matters worse, he doesn't have a job in the new city. To top it all off, he's a native Chicagoan from the day of his birth, and so is his wife.

As I think about this, I can't quite put all the pieces of the puzzle together. What exactly does God have in mind for my friend? Is this just another midlife crisis in which a man decides to chuck the old life and start all over again? If so, moving is better than having an affair or some of the other wild options men choose.

The truth is, I don't know why this is happening, and neither does my friend. But deep in his heart he believes God has opened the door and he must go through it. Do I have some fears for him? Absolutely. Especially since he is moving to a new area without the promise of a new job. But I comfort myself with two bits of information. First, he truly is a godly man who wants to do what is right. Second, he won't be the first person to make a long cross-country move with no secure future. Abraham already holds that honor. So I am supporting my friend even while scratching my head over the whole thing. Sometimes (often!) God's will is inscrutable even to those who are attempting to follow it.

But you don't learn these truths overnight. Some lessons can only be mastered through hard experience in the laboratory of daily life.

That's why becoming a spiritual leader can't happen quickly. Dandelions pop up in a few days, but it takes decades to grow a mighty oak tree.

A STUDENT, NOT A VICTIM

Hard times provide some of the most important lessons of spiritual growth. Several years ago Jim Warren, host of *Primetime America* on the Moody Broadcasting Network, the nationwide ministry of Moody Bible Institute, shared a statement that revolutionized my thinking in this area. It is deceptively simple: "When hard times come, be a student, not a victim." The more I ponder those words, the more profound they seem. Many people go through life as professional victims, always talking about how unfair life is.

> A victim says, "Why did this happen to me?" A student says, "What can I learn from this?"
>
> A victim blames others for his problems. A student asks, "How much of this did I bring on myself?"
>
> A victim looks at everyone else and cries out, "Life isn't fair." A student looks at life and says, "What happened to me could have happened to anybody."
>
> A victim believes hard times have come because God is trying to punish him. A student understands that God allows hard times in order to help him grow.
>
> A victim would rather complain than find a solution. A student has no time to complain because he is busy making the best of his situation.

A victim believes the deck of life is forever stacked against him. A student believes God is able to reshuffle the deck anytime He wants to.

A victim feels so sorry for himself that he has no time for others. A student so focuses on helping others that he has no time to feel sorry for himself.

A victim begs God to remove all the problems of life so he can be happy. A student has learned through the problems of life that God alone is the source of true happiness.

Many things happen to us beyond our control. In that sense we are all victims of unexpected circumstances. Unfortunately, some people never rise above the victim mode. But it doesn't have to be that way. We have the opportunity to choose the way we respond to the things that happen to us. By the grace of God, we can decide to become students, not victims, as we face the trials of life.

FOLLOW THE LEADER

We can also grow spiritually by learning from those who are farther along the road. A book like this can serve as a road map, but you also need a personal guide who knows every curve, every detour, every shortcut, and every dead-end.

Howard Hendricks says that every man needs a Paul, a Barnabas, and a Timothy. You need an older man to show you the ropes, a friend to hold you accountable, and a younger man who is watching your example. That means that every Christian man should be a follower and a leader. Since most men are older than some and younger than others, everyone will have opportunities both to learn from and to teach others.[4]

A Message for Younger Men

Let's concentrate on learning from older men for a moment. Psalm 145:4 tells us, "One generation will commend your works to another; they will tell of your mighty acts." Hebrews 13:7 says, "Remember your leaders, who spoke the word of God to you. Consider their way of life and imitate their faith." *Listening to older men of God is a primary way that younger men become godly*. Older Christians tell us of the "mighty acts" of God in their generation. They build our confidence as we discover what God has done in the past. They provide a model for us to follow. From them we learn how to pray, how to listen to God, how to walk in faith, how to handle our problems in a Christlike fashion, how to be godly businessmen, how to be loving husbands and godly fathers, how to face tough times without falling apart.

Psalm 92:12-15 says that the righteous are blessed with long life and good health and fruitfulness even into old age. They don't dry up and wither away, but they stay fresh until the end. '

But note how the righteous end their life: they leave this world praising God all the way. They proclaim, "The LORD is upright; he is my Rock, and there is no wickedness in him" (verse 15). Only those who have seen life in all its fullness can say that with conviction. Here is a fundamental difference between the old and the young. The young know the words to the song; the old know the composer.

A Message for Older Men

The really important lessons of life are learned only through hard experience. Only those who have known suffering and hardship can say with deep conviction, "The Lord is upright. All that He does is good. He makes no mistakes, and He made no mistakes in my life." It is only looking back that the testimony of the righteous is seen in its full power.

Some blessings are given to the young—to marry, give birth, and raise children for the glory of God; to set out to conquer the world; to find a mountain and climb it; to have a career, to rise in your chosen profession; to make a mark with your life. These things occupy the early decades of adult life.

But the old have a different calling. All these things they have already done, persevering through years of struggle and long nights of prayer, seeing their children grow up, go off to school, find a mate, get married, and get started in life. They have seen their children and their grandchildren and perhaps even their great-grandchildren. Some of them have lived so long that they have outlived their friends. Perhaps they buried a wife along the way.

The old, those in the sunset years, are given a privilege that only comes to those who last that long. At the age of forty-three I can only testify to my life so far. But older men have lived far longer, and they know from experience things I have not yet discovered.

Here is a worthy goal for those who have lived to see the crowning years of life. Do not be silent. Do not let these precious days go by quietly. Speak up for the Lord. You have things to say that only you can say. If the Lord is your Rock, say it. If He has held you up through some hard times, let the rest of us know about it. The younger generation needs to hear this from you personally. Was He strong enough for you? Did He hold you up in the darkest moments of life? Did the Rock tremble, or did His foundation remain firm beneath your shaking feet?

This word is for those men who have reached the sunset years of life. We need your testimony, your years of experience. Most of all, we need you to tell us, and tell us again, that the Lord is a Saviour upon whom we can all depend. Tell us, and we will listen. We who are younger will someday be where you are now. Help us build our lives on the only Rock that will not be moved. Show us the way, and one day we will thank you by sharing with our children what you shared with us.

ARE YOU WILLING TO PAY THE PRICE?

What if you are a new convert—one of those new plants that Paul talked about? My advice to you is twofold. First, find some godly older men who can show you the ropes of the Christian life. It doesn't have to be a formal arrangement. Just ask God to show you some godly men and then follow their example. Second, don't be in a hurry to take on a position of spiritual responsibility. Give God time to develop some depth and maturity in your life. Focus on becoming a man of God in every area of your life. If you are married, make loving your wife and your children a top priority. Learn to be a godly example where you work. Put your roots down deep into the Word of God. Pray for opportunities to share Christ with others. Serve behind the scenes quietly, and if God chooses, He can give you a bigger place to serve. In the meantime, wait on the Lord and you will not be disappointed.

Spiritual growth isn't that difficult, but it won't happen overnight.

Would you like to become a man of God? You can if you want to, but you have to be willing to pay the price.

GOING DEEPER

1. Why does Paul warn against putting a new convert into a position of spiritual leadership? What happens when this command is ignored?

2. What positive traits do new converts bring to the Lord's work? What traits will they typically be lacking? Name some positive ways you can encourage new believers without putting them into positions of leadership too quickly.

3. How does this principle apply to just-married men who suddenly find themselves the spiritual leaders in their own homes? What practical help can churches give so that these men don't crumble under the pressure?

4. God often uses uncertainty to humble us.
   Why is uncertainty so humbling? Has God ever used a time of uncertainty as a humbling factor in your own life? Looking back, do you regard it as a positive or negative experience?
   If you could ask God to make one thing clear to you right now, what would it be?

5. We are all victims of unexpected circumstances.
   Name an unexpected circumstance in the last five years that has changed your life. How?
   Why do some people become victims while others become students? What makes the difference?

6. Becoming a spiritual leader won't happen overnight.
   Why does it take years to develop true spiritual leadership?
   Does this mean young Christians can never be spiritual leaders?
   In your opinion, how long should it take for a new Christian to grow into maturity? Explain your answer. What are the major factors that either help or hinder rapid spiritual growth?

7. Read Titus 2:2.
   Name the six qualities older men should exhibit. Why are these qualities particularly relevant? Think of three older men whose lives reflect these qualities. What life experiences do they share in common? How long have they been believers?

TAKING ACTION

Let's call this the "Paul and Timothy project." Make a list of the godly older men you know. Consider approaching one of those men with a view to meeting together on a regular basis for prayer and mutual encouragement. Then think about the men your age or younger who need your encouragement. Begin to pray for three younger men by name every day. Commit yourself to giving a word of encouragement to at least one of those men each week.

JESUS PEOPLE

A Man of Honor is "holy."
—*Titus 1:8*

The particular word Paul uses in the above verse refers to personal piety. It is the quality of life that causes a leader to conform to that which pleases God.[1] A holy person is someone who brings you into the presence of God simply by walking into the room. It doesn't refer to fake piety or to a holier-than-thou mentality. In fact, that's the opposite of what this word means. *A holy man makes it easy to believe in Jesus.* Such a man simply exudes the presence of God by the sheer force of his goodness and godliness.

In this sense, the "holy" man is the exact opposite of the worldly man. It isn't just that one man goes to church and the other doesn't. After all, plenty of worldly men go to church every Sunday. And you really can't pin down one particular outward act that distinguishes the holy man. Rather, the holy man lives in an atmosphere saturated with God's presence.

Recently two people referred to Dr. Hudson Armerding, past president of Wheaton College, in those terms. One friend told me that whenever you were around him you felt you were in the presence of a holy man. Another said that whenever Dr. Armerding spoke, he made you feel as if God were speaking directly to you.

LARRY KING AND BILLY GRAHAM

Larry King interviewed Billy Graham on the day of President Clinton's inauguration. At one point he asked Mr. Graham, "Are you afraid to die?" "No, I'm not afraid to die. I know that I'm going to heaven." King asked him, "You know you're going to heaven?" King repeated the words slowly as if to make sure he had heard Dr. Graham correctly. "Oh yes, I'm certain of that," Graham replied. "I've put my trust in Jesus Christ to take me to heaven. I'm not worried at all about dying. In fact, I'm looking forward to it."

At that moment the camera switched to Larry King, who said nothing for a long moment. The look on his face told the whole story. You might call it baffled amazement. Larry King—who has an answer for everything—had no answer when brought face to face with a holy man.

How can we develop this quality of practical holiness? *We must begin with the observation that holiness stems from who we are, not from what we do.* To be holy means to be set apart for God's use.[2] That's why we call the Bible the *Holy* Bible; it is a book set apart for God. Colossians 3:12 tells us that all believers in Christ are "holy and dearly loved." First Peter 2:9 calls us a "holy nation, a people belonging to God."

To be holy means to live in such a way that people know you belong to God. Therefore, the starting point in seeking holiness is to recognize that since God has already declared us His holy children, we are to so live that everyone knows we do in fact belong to Him.[3]

This leads to a fundamental question: if an unbiased observer were to watch my life, would he conclude that I belong to God? Or would he conclude that I am just like everyone else?

Every Christian man must make three important decisions regarding his relationship to God. These decisions go to the very core of what it means to be holy as opposed to being worldly.

DECISION # 1:
I MUST GIVE GOD THE RIGHT TO BE GOD IN MY LIFE
WHETHER I LIKE IT OR NOT

This is the question of ultimate authority. Does God have the right to be God in your life? You say, "Of course He does." Yes, but have you told Him so? Or do you feel the need to fight with God about His plans for you? Franklin Graham wrote a moving biography of Bob Pierce, the founder of World Vision. In the foreword Richard Halverson recounts a prayer he often heard Bob Pierce pray: "Lord, I give You license to interfere in my life and plans at any time, in any way, at any cost." What a great way to approach life. "Lord, You're in charge. I've got my plans, my dreams, my personal agenda. But if You want to change things, go right ahead . . . and You don't have to tell me in advance."[4]

That's what I mean by giving God the right to be God. We must not say, "Lord, You can do such-and-such, but only if I agree to it in advance." In the first place, God won't agree to that stipulation; in the second place, if He did agree to inform us in advance, He wouldn't be God anymore.

- He has the right to direct your life any way He sees fit.
- He has the right to answer your prayers as He sees fit.
- He has the right to bless you as He sees fit.
- He has the right to include sickness as part of His plan for you.
- He has the right to change your plans in midstream.
- He has the right to answer some prayers but not others.
- He has the right to lead you through deep waters.
- He has the right to allow sorrow to come your way.

He's God! He can do whatever He wants in your life. Have you ever acknowledged that fact?

DECISION # 2:
I MUST NOT JUDGE GOD BY HIS ABILITY
TO FULFILL ALL MY DESIRES

This is the question of ultimate satisfaction. This one is tricky because God does indeed have the ability to fulfill all my desires. Yet it is rarely His will to do that. More often than not, some of my deepest desires will never be fulfilled.

- I may want fame,
  but God may choose not to give it to me.
- I may want healthy children,
  but God may allow muscular dystrophy.
- I may want to be married,
  but God may not lead in that direction.
- I may want financial security,
  but God may allow poverty.
- I may want many friends,
  but God may not give them to me.
- I may have my heart set on a certain career,
  but the door may not open to me.
- I may think that I should write a book,
  but the publishers may not agree with me.
- I may hope for a long life,
  but God may take me home before I'm forty-five.

Who knows what God will do? I have my dreams, but God has His will. "The lot is cast into the lap, but its every decision is from the LORD" (Proverbs 16:33). You might paraphrase that verse this way: "Life is like a roll of the dice, but God is in charge of how the numbers come up."

Let me turn this truth around so we can see it from the other side: God doesn't owe you anything.

- Not fame.
- Not fortune.
- Not happiness.
- Not health.
- Not career advancement.
- Not long life.
- Not a wonderful marriage.

He doesn't owe you anything!

But (and this is the biggest but in history) *God has promised to be with you*. He has promised that He will never leave you. He has said He will walk with you through the most difficult experiences of life. He has said, "I will never leave you" (Hebrews 13:5).

That much is certain.

God has said, "Most of the things you dream about will never come true . . . at least not in the way you envision them. But here's one thing you can count on: once you come to know Me through My Son Jesus Christ, I will never leave you. Never."

- No matter what happens.
- No matter where you go.
- No matter what you do.
- No matter what mistakes you make.

I am learning that is enough. If God walks with me, then the rest of my dreams and lofty plans don't really matter.

DECISION # 3:
I MUST CONSTANTLY EVALUATE MY PRIORITIES
IN LIGHT OF MATTHEW 6:33

This is the question of ultimate priority. Jesus Himself laid down the great principle of life when He said, "But seek first his kingdom and his righteousness, and all these things will be given to you as well."

- God's kingdom must come first.
- God's plans must get top priority.
- God's cause on the earth must be my first concern.
- God's reputation must come before mine.

Why? Because God *must* come first! Period. End of discussion. But notice the promise in Matthew 6:33. When I put God first, "all these things" will be given to me.

What are "these things"? Let's start with the basic stuff of life. Food. Clothing. Shelter. Friends. Meaningful work. God says, "If you take care of My business, I'll take care of yours." Simple as that. How would you like the Almighty to say, "Stop worrying about your rent. I'll take care of it"? Sound bizarre? But that's exactly what Jesus is saying.

Put God first and "all these things" we worry about will fall into place. Not without difficulty, not without pain, not without a struggle, but they will fall into place.

Our trouble is, we want to reverse that promise. "Lord, once I take care of 'all these things,' I'll put You first." No deal. God doesn't work that way.

Do you know what to call a person who puts "all these things" ahead of God? An idolater. After all, idolatry is nothing more than wanting anything too much—more than God. Think about it—uncontrolled desire soon leads to idolatry because it reverses the ultimate priorities of life.

HOLDING ON TOO HARD

A friend of mine once came to me with a sobering message: "Ray, you're holding on too hard. You've got to let go." When she said that, I mumbled something spiritual, but I didn't believe her. It took me a year or more to see the truth of her words.

My friend was right. I didn't want to let go. That thing I was holding on meant everything to me. It was my baby, my dream, my future. I held on to it because I was deathly afraid to let go.

That particular thing in my life—a good thing in itself—had become an idol to me. But I couldn't see it because I knew it was a good thing.

My friend was right. I was holding on too hard. That thing had become a controlling obsession in my life.

God eventually had to take it away from me. Oh, that was painful. I fought and argued and wept. But God paid no attention to my anger. He slowly and carefully pried my fingers away one by one. When He got down to the thumb, I fought Him with all my strength but to no avail. In the end He took back that which had always belonged to Him. As I look back on that ordeal, I am grateful to God for His severe mercy in taking the idol from my hands.

BREAKING IDOLS ONE BY ONE

The idol was destroyed but at a terrible cost. In one of her books Elisabeth Elliot comments that the Christian life is a process in which God breaks our idols one by one. I have learned the hard way how true that is. God loves us too much to let anything come between us and Him. As we grow older, God pulls our fingers away from the things we value the most. In the end there is nothing left but God.

Have you ever thought how strange life is? You are born, grow up, get married, get a job, have children, raise your kids, take a vacation, retire, and then die. And your children—what do they do? The same thing. And their children? The same thing.

You are going to live sixty or seventy or eighty years. For some of us, most of that time is already gone. Truly we are here today and gone tomorrow. Take the whole span of human history. Where does your life show up on the screen? It's just a microscopic blip.[5]

You have two choices. You can spend your life chasing idols your hands have made. (But when you die, your idols die with you.) Or you can spend your life doing God's will. Then when you die it's not over. Life has just begun!

THE DIFFERENCE A GODLY MAN CAN MAKE

Most of us know that the sins of the fathers reap bitter consequences, even to the third and fourth generations (Exodus 20:5). Perhaps you have experienced the bitter result of past mistakes made by your father or grandfather or even your great-grandfather. But it doesn't have to be that way. You can break the chain of negative consequences by committing yourself to a life of holiness. Exodus 20:6 promises that God will show love to a thousand generations of those who love Him and keep His commandments. Consider the following testimony:

> My grandfather died just a few years ago and my dad had the challenge of delivering the eulogy. He said 1) his dad loved his wife, 2) he loved his children, and 3) he loved his God. My dad went on to describe details and instances of each of those points. *He loved his wife*; he described how when his dad would come

home each night from work he would hug and kiss his wife a million times in front of the kids no matter how mad she got. Well, I thought, that's him—my dad.

He said *he loved his children*. He talked about how his dad would wrestle around with the kids and play with them whenever he could—kissing and hugging them and showing his love for them. Well, I thought, that's him—he has done that and still does—my dad.

He said *Grampa loved his God* and the fact that his children and his grandchildren are following after the Lord is a testimony to the legacy he left. Well, I thought, that's him—my dad.

When my father dies I will deliver the same eulogy. Except I'll tell them that he surpassed my grandfather in all areas, especially his love for God and for the Lord Jesus Christ. The Lord radically changed my dad when I was around seven years old and from a man driven by the world and striving for corporate success, he became a man who sought after the things of God. He graduated from an evening school Bible course and became devout in studying and applying the Bible and is now a respected Bible teacher at church. Every time I see him he's studying the Bible.

He has led a life that has contributed to all of the children going into full-time Christian ministry. He hasn't given up loving Mom or loving the kids or grandkids. As a matter of fact he loves them more. He is able to live for the Lord before the watching world, giving testimony to the fact of God's grace and bearing testimony to the legacy left by his dad.

If I can carry on that legacy, I will consider myself blessed. My dad told me recently that his grandfather (his dad's dad) was exactly the same and that he had a great influence on his life as well. One life lived for God can infect and affect generations to come—it is the truth. I love my dad greatly, and God has blessed me immensely with such a good example to follow.[6]

That's four generations of faithfulness, with another one on the way. It is happening exactly as God promised.

Even if you don't come from a godly heritage, you can establish one so that generations to come will follow the Lord as you have done. That can happen if you are willing to become a holy man of God.

GOING DEEPER

1. When you read the phrase "a holy man of God," what images come to your mind? Name three men who seem to fit your mental image. What qualities do they share in common? If you could, would you like to become that kind of man?

2. Holiness stems from who we are, not from what we do.

   Does that statement surprise you? Why do many people connect holiness with certain outward activities? Is it possible to read the Bible and pray and not be holy? Explain. What's keeping you from totally surrendering to Christ right now? Do you have the courage to admit it out loud? Tell someone this week what it is.

3. A holy man makes it easy to believe in Jesus.
   How does this happen?
   What would need to change in your life for non-Christians to see Jesus in you?
   What's the first step you need to take to move in that direction?

4. God must have the right to be God in your life.
   What does that statement mean? If God is God, doesn't He already have that right?
   Why does God demand the right to change your personal agenda without informing you in advance? What happens when you refuse to yield your personal agenda to Him?

5. Read Romans 5:1-5.
   List some of the things God has given His children.
   According to verse 5, what has God already poured out into our hearts? How does that fact encourage you?

6. God's kingdom must come first.
   In a practical sense, what does this mean? Can you think of a situation in which you would have to set aside your career plans in order to serve God? How does this apply, for example, to gifted physicians who leave a lucrative practice in America to serve in Nigeria?

TAKING ACTION

What idols are in your life? Before answering that question, remember that an idol is anything good that becomes *too* important to us. Your wife,

your children, your family, your career, your home, your material possessions, your closest friendships, your plans for the future, your
dreams—any or all of these can become idols to you. When any created
thing has become our source of ultimate satisfaction, that created
thing—as good as it might be—has become an idol. With that in mind,
make a list of potential idols, writing down everything that might have
gained too high a priority in your life. For the next five days review your
list every morning, releasing those items one by one to God. Although this
process is painful, in the end you will experience a feeling of enormous
relief as God takes back that which always belonged to Him in the first
place.

MEN OF THE WORD

A Man of Honor knows the truth.
—*Titus 1:9*

This verse is worth quoting in full: "He must hold firmly to the trustworthy message as it has been taught, so that he can encourage others by sound doctrine and refute those who oppose it." Every word here is important. "Hold firmly" means "constantly holding on to and not letting go." "The trustworthy message" refers to the essential truths of the Christian faith—the fundamentals that must not be compromised. "Sound doctrine" is literally "healthy doctrine" or "wholesome teaching," referring to the well-balanced teaching of God's Word that produces healthy Christian living. To "refute" is to correct or convince those who contradict the truth.[1]

This presupposes:

- A settled body of Christian truth.
- A knowledge of that truth.
- A willingness to proclaim that truth.
- A willingness to defend that truth.

The Christian message has never been universally popular; some have always opposed it. We need Men of Honor who are so well grounded in the truth of the Bible that they can accurately teach it to others and courageously defend the truth when it is attacked.

OBSERVATIONS FROM THE BIBLE

Very early in the life of the church a need arose to clarify basic Christian beliefs. Acts 2:42 speaks of "the apostles' teaching." Jude 3 speaks of "the faith that was once for all entrusted to the saints." Second Thessalonians 2:13 speaks of "belief in the truth." Romans 6:17 speaks of "the form of teaching to which you were entrusted."

When these passages (and many others like them) are taken together, they establish that even in the earliest days of the church the apostles found it necessary to stress the importance of believing sound doctrine. It must be "held," "guarded," and "kept" because it is "truth" that was "entrusted" to the saints of God. Think of it as a sacred deposit passed along from generation to generation. God first entrusted the truth to the apostles, who under the inspiration of the Holy Spirit wrote it down so future believers would have a reliable source from which to draw. That sacred truth must be guarded carefully because there are many people who will oppose it and seek to silence or destroy it.

Beware of Wolves!

In fact, the New Testament contains many warnings against false teachers. They are called "wolves in sheep's clothing," "savage wolves," "false prophets," "heretics," and "those whose condemnation is sure." Paul even says that "the time will come when men will not put up with sound doctrine. Instead, to suit their own desires, they will gather around them a great number of teachers to say what their itching ears want to hear" (2 Timothy 4:3). Because that danger is always with us, the church in general and each local church in particular must continually restate its basic Christian beliefs.

First Timothy 3:16 offers a very basic statement of faith. Consider how many different doctrinal truths are implied in this one verse: "Beyond all question, the mystery of godliness is great: He [Christ] appeared in a body [the Incarnation], was vindicated by the Spirit [crucifixion and resurrection; the Holy Spirit], was seen by angels [doctrine of angels], was preached among the nations [evangelism, world missions], was believed on in the world [salvation], was taken up in glory [ascension of Christ, heaven]."

Hebrews 6:1-2 functions in much the same way when it lists the "elementary teachings": "repentance from acts that lead to death, and of faith in God [salvation], instruction about baptisms [water baptism], the laying on of hands [church leadership; spiritual gifts], the resurrection of the dead [resurrection], and eternal judgment [eschatology; heaven and hell; the Second Coming of Christ]."

In those two passages—which go back to the earliest days of the church—you already have the basic doctrines of the faith laid out in seed form.

OBSERVATIONS FROM CHURCH HISTORY

But eventually the apostles died, and within a few years all those who knew the apostles died. As the generations rolled on, there arose new challenges to the Christian faith—attacks on the Deity of Jesus Christ, attacks on the canon of Scripture, attacks on the doctrine of the Trinity. In fact, a glance at church history reveals that the early church faced a long series of spiritual counterfeits. Pick up a history book and you find names like the Docetics, the Gnostics, the Cerinthians, the Arians, the Nicolaitans, the Marcionites, the Nestorians, the Ebionites, and the Sabellians. Those are just dusty names to us, but to the early Christians they were flesh-and-blood heretics who tried to peddle a distorted version of Christianity.

From one point of view, the first 450 years of the church is a story of missionary expansion and continual doctrinal clarification. Over time the church fathers began to write down their basic beliefs. These written statements were called "creeds," from the Latin *credo*, which means "I believe." Three of these creeds have survived across the centuries and are still in use today—the Apostles' Creed, the Nicene Creed, and the Athanasian Creed.

During and after the Protestant Reformation all the major leaders felt it important to state their beliefs in a succinct fashion. They did this not only to help their followers, but also to distinguish their beliefs from those they opposed. Some examples would be the *Sixty-Seven Articles of Zurich* (1523), Martin Luther's *Small Catechism* (1529), the *Augsburg*

Confession (1530), the *Heidelberg Catechism* (1563), the *Second Helvetic Confession* (1566), and, several generations later, the *Westminster Confession of Faith* (1646). Mark Noll has a helpful word about the purpose of these Reformation confessions of faith:

> The great outpouring of confessions in the first century and a half of Protestantism performed a multitude of functions. Authoritative statements of belief enshrined the new ideas of the theologians, but in forms that could also provide regular instruction for the common faithful. They lifted a standard around which a local community could rally and which could make plain the differences with opponents. They made possible a regathering of belief and practice in the interests of unity, even as they established a norm for disciplining the erring.[2]

In the centuries since the Reformation, Protestants have never stopped writing confessions of faith. Every denomination has its own statement, and so do most local churches.

While there are always dangers in writing down your doctrine, Christians across the centuries have felt that the advantages far outweighed the dangers. Geoffrey Bromiley summarizes the case for a written statement of faith:

> The dangers of creed-making are obvious. Creeds can become formal, complex, and abstract. They can be almost illimitably expanded. They can be superimposed on Scripture. Properly handled, however, they facilitate public confession, form a succinct basis of teaching, safeguard pure doctrine, and constitute an appropriate focus for the church's fellowship in faith.[3]

Those words strike me as both wise and convincing.

"If It Works for You"

We live in a confused generation. Once we lost the concept of absolute truth in the Bible, it was only a short step to opening the door to universalism. Lacking any solid foundation for truth, most unchurched people have adopted a kind of "anything goes" mentality. "If it works for you, it must be okay."

The majestic words of Jesus stand in stark contrast: "I am the way and the truth and the life. No one comes to the Father except through me" (John 14:6). When Jesus said, "I am the truth," He was making an utterly exclusive claim about Himself. But how can we engage in effective evangelism in a post-Christian society that rejects any concept of absolute truth? We must understand that many people have shifted from being *agnostic* to *ignostic*. An agnostic says, "I don't know if God exists." The ignostic says, "I don't know what you mean." We're now dealing with people who don't know who God is or who Jesus is or what the Gospel is or what salvation is all about. That means we have to start at the very beginning. We can't assume that people know the basics about God. Most of them don't. We've got to go back to the ABCs.[4]

No Fuzzy Thinking

If we're going to reach this generation, we're going to have to study apologetics—the art of explaining the Christian faith to those who don't believe it. We have to be able to answer questions and give a rational explanation for what we believe and why we believe it. Fuzzy-headed Christianity won't cut it because the people of the world are already fuzzy about God. Believers are going to be put on the spot—at work, at the neighborhood block party, at the Rotary Club, at the local high school, in the coffee shop, at the grocery store, and in the car pool. We won't be able to get by with pat answers. We have to get serious about our Christian faith.

WHAT CAN WE DO TO EQUIP OURSELVES AND OUR FAMILIES?

Unless we see the danger, we will do nothing. If we say, "I'm strong, my family is strong, those people will never affect me," we are setting ourselves up for a fall. In light of the many warnings in the New Testament, we ought to take this matter very seriously.

Make Sure of Your Own Relationship with Jesus Christ

It all begins here. Jesus said, "Not everyone who says to me, 'Lord, Lord,' will enter the kingdom of heaven" (Matthew 7:21). It is very possible to talk about Jesus and not be a Christian. It's also possible to be a church member and not be saved. It is possible to be a church member and know all the right answers and still be lost because you have never personally made the decision to trust Jesus Christ—and Him alone—for your salvation.

Ground Yourself and Your Family in the Word of God

The cults prey on church members who don't know what they really believe. That's why when the cults use terms like "salvation" and "born again," the untaught Christian gets confused and thinks they mean the same thing we do, when they really don't.

Also, we must face the fact that our children are being subtly influenced by New Age mystical teaching. It's going to get worse in the days ahead. New Age teaching is coming into the public schools under the guise of meditation and visualization.[5] If we don't give our children something to believe, there are people out there who will. Parents are sadly mistaken if they think sports and hobbies will protect their children as long as a little Sunday religion is thrown in for good measure. That won't work. Our kids are in a battle the moment they walk out the front door. The best thing we can do is to make sure our homes reflect genuine spiritual reality. That means grounding our children daily in the Word of God.

Learn to Listen with Discernment

Don't be a sucker. Don't believe everything you hear. Don't assume the music you hear is okay just because you can't understand the lyrics. Don't buy into the lie that it doesn't matter what you believe as long as you are sincere. We need more Christians who will listen carefully and then search the Scriptures to see if what was said lines up with the Bible.[6] And we need more believers who will obey 1 Thessalonians 5:21-22: "Test everything. Hold on to the good. Avoid every kind of evil."

A while back a friend and I were talking about how so much that is spiritually counterfeit has penetrated the movies, television, the Internet, modern music, and the best-seller lists. My friend said, "Pretty soon we won't be able to do anything." Thankfully, we're not there yet. There are a great many good and wholesome and pure things left in the world. But there is also a great deal that is evil. And when we are faced with evil—in whatever form—our job is to just say no and take a stand for Jesus Christ.

Realize That There Is a Great Spiritual Hunger in Our Generation

That's why Hinduism is on the rise in America. It also explains why New Age gurus draw thousands to their seminars and why the Mormon church is growing so fast. People who ought to know better are being led astray by the make-believe stories of false teachers.

If the people of this generation do not find God's truth, they will believe Satan's lies. After all, a starving dog will eat whatever you put in front of him. Something has to fill the void within.

It is at precisely this point that we have a great opportunity. We have to do more than simply protect our children. It's not enough to learn what is true and what is false. We have an obligation that goes beyond our own family. God has made us debtors to the whole world. It won't be enough in the Last Day to say, "But, Lord, I took care of my own family. We all made it. See, we're all here." The Lord will say back to us, "My child, what did you do for your friends and neighbors? What about that man who came to your door? What about your sister, your daddy, your boss, your pals at work? What about them? Why aren't they here with you? Did you even try to tell them about Me?"

The Darker the Night, the Brighter the Light

We live in the greatest days of human history. It may well be that we are the final generation before the return of Christ. That would explain why Satan has made such an energetic effort to spread his lies. But where sin abounds, grace super-abounds. The very fact that we live in such spiritual darkness means that when the light shines, *it really shines*. Let us not be discouraged by the difficulty of the task. Let us instead be encouraged by the opportunities of the hour. The people of this generation are eating out of the devil's trough when they could be feasting at the Father's table. Let us go out into the highways and byways and in Jesus' name invite them to the banquet that never ends.

ADDITIONAL RESOURCES

Listed on the next page are several recently published books that will equip you to answer questions from non-Christians.

E. Calvin Beisner, *Answers For Atheists, Agnostics, and Other Thoughtful Skeptics* (Wheaton, Ill.: Crossway Books, 1993).

Wilfried Corduan, *Reasonable Faith* (Nashville: Broadman and Holman, 1993).

Norman Geisler and Ron Brooks, *When Skeptics Ask* (Wheaton, Ill.: Victor Books, 1989).

Phillip E. Johnson, *Darwin on Trial* (Downers Grove, Ill.: InterVarsity Press, 1991).

_____ *Reason in the Balance* (Downers Grove, Ill.: InterVarsity Press, 1995).

Cliffe Knechtle, *Give Me an Answer* (Downers Grove, Ill.: InterVarsity Press, 1986).

Peter Kreeft and Ronald K. Tacelli, *Handbook of Christian Apologetics* (Downers Grove, Ill.: InterVarsity Press, 1994).

Ravi Zacharias, *Can Man Live Without God?* (Dallas: Word Books, 1994).

GOING DEEPER

1. The dangers of creed-making are obvious.
   Name some of those dangers.
   Name some of the positive benefits of creed-making.
   In your mind, do the dangers outweigh the benefits, or do the benefits outweigh the dangers? Explain.

2. Why does the New Testament contain so many warnings against false teachers? What does that tell us about Satan's overall strategy?

3. What major false doctrines threaten the church today?

4. Under what circumstances would you confront a brother about his doctrinal teachings? How do you distinguish between the non-negotiable doctrines of the faith and the secondary matters about which genuine Christians legitimately disagree? Give examples in each category.

5. At what point would you personally leave a church or a denomination because of false teaching? How do you relate to true believers who attend liberal churches?

6. How do you personally balance the need for doctrinal purity with the call to Christian unity? What steps should believers take to "speak the truth in love" (Ephesians 4:15)?

7. Why is the study of apologetics especially important in our generation?

8. Our kids are in a battle the moment they walk out the front door. Do you agree with that statement? Do you think the pressure on children is greater today than in previous generations? Explain your answer.
   What practical steps can we take to ground our children in the Word of God? If you have children, what are you doing in this area? How effective is it?

TAKING ACTION

Commit to reading one of the books from the Additional Resources list. Or ask your pastor to recommend a good book in the area of apologetics.

THE TEACHER'S REWARD

A Man of Honor can "teach" others.
—1 Timothy 3:2

he phrase "able to teach" translates one Greek word meaning both "having a teachable spirit" and "able to teach others."[1] This presupposes:

- A teachable spirit—eagerness to learn.
- A good working knowledge of the Bible.
- A willingness to share spiritual truth with others.
- A willingness to confront false teaching when necessary.

Spiritual leaders must love the Word, must cling to the Word, must know the Word. No wavering, no doubting, no compromising. John Calvin noted that this qualification does not mean that every man must be unusually gifted in public speaking. Some are, some aren't. And many men who can speak well in public may not be good teachers of spiritual truth. Rather, it refers to "wisdom in applying the word of God" so that others grow spiritually.[2]

Since teaching is also a spiritual gift that not all believers possess, how can this requirement be met by those not having that spiritual gift? The answer is not hard to find. Though not all of God's children have the spiritual gift of teaching, and though spiritual leaders are not equally gifted in teaching, all can and must teach. Some will flourish in front of a class; others will do better leading a small group or in one-on-one discipleship. Not all will teach in the same way, but all must be able to do it in some way.

The church of Jesus Christ is built on the Word of God. Therefore, men of God must be men of the Word. This is non-negotiable.

A YOUNG MAN AT THE CROSSROADS

Just before World War II a young man from North Carolina traveled to Florida to study at a small Bible college. After graduating, he attended Wheaton College. Everyone recognized his gifts as a preacher of the Gospel. However, after several years in the ministry he faced inner doubts about the truth of the Bible. The turning point came early in 1949 at Forest Home Conference Center in Southern California. That week a battle raged in his soul: "Is the Bible the Word of God or not? Can I believe it or not?"

Finally the night came when he knew he had to make a decision. He skipped the evening meeting to pray by himself. He talked to his friend J. Edwin Orr early that evening and laid out the great dilemma of his heart. Orr said, "You'd better go off and pray and get the matter settled." So off he went into the woods to settle the matter once and for all. Finally he realized that he would never have all the answers. So he knelt down and began to pray. In his own words:

> I dueled with my doubts, and my soul seemed to be caught in the crossfire. Finally, in desperation, I surrendered my will to the living God revealed in Scripture. I knelt before the open Bible, and said, "Lord, many things in this Book I do not understand. But Thou hast said, 'The just shall live by faith.' All I have received from Thee, I have taken by faith. Here and now, by faith, I accept the Bible as Thy Word. That which I cannot understand, I will reserve judgment on until I receive more light. If this pleases Thee, give me authority as I proclaim Thy Word, and through that authority convict men of sin and turn sinners to the Savior."

That was the turning point for Billy Graham. Six weeks later a crusade began at the Canvas Cathedral in downtown Los Angeles, a meeting that would change the course of American history. The crusade was extended for weeks because so many thousands of people were coming to Christ. You may have heard the story of how William Randolph Hearst instructed all the newspapers in his chain to "puff Graham," and soon the word about Billy Graham was spread from coast to coast.

By his own admission, everything that has happened in Billy Graham's life goes back to that night at Forest Home when he put the Bible down and knelt before God and said, "Oh, God, I do not understand it all, but I am willing to believe it and willing to obey it."[3]

What happened to Billy Graham must happen to all of us if we are to be men of God. We will never impact others if we have doubts about the Word of God. If we don't believe it is true, we have nothing worth teaching to others.

A RABBI NAMED JESUS

What word would you use to describe Jesus Christ? For most of us, words like Savior, Redeemer, and Lord come to mind. But the gospel writers used one word more than any other to describe Christ. More than sixty times in the Gospels Jesus is called a teacher.[4] He taught by the seashore, on the mountains, on the plain, in a boat, in the synagogue, and in the Temple. He taught large crowds, small groups, and individuals who came with questions. He taught whenever He had an opportunity and whenever He found anyone who would listen. We don't think of Jesus as a rabbi, but that's what people called Him—"Rabbi" or "Teacher." Luke says in Acts 1:1 that the Gospel of Luke is a record of "all that Jesus began to do and to teach."

TWO CRUCIAL POINTS

As a beginning point, I would like to lay down two simple but crucial points.

First, *there is a sense in which all Christians are to be teachers.* In the Great Commission Jesus told His followers to "go and make disciples of all nations." Part of that commission was: "teaching them to obey everything I have commanded you" (Matthew 28:20). Paul picked up on that idea in Colossians 3:16 when he said, "Let the word of Christ dwell in you richly as you teach and admonish one another with all wisdom."

The writer to the Hebrews gave that same idea a different twist. Writing to believers who had not progressed past spiritual infancy he said, "Though by this time you ought to be teachers, you need someone to teach you the elementary truths of God's word all over again. You need milk, not solid food!" (5:12).

What a rebuke and what a challenge to all of us. Where are you along the spectrum of Christian growth? Are you still drinking from the bottle and trying to learn your spiritual ABCs? Or have you moved on to solid food? If the answer to the last question is yes, then you ought to be a teacher.

Every believer ought to be involved in teaching on at least two levels. First, we are all to be involved in teaching new converts the basic principles of the Christian faith. To put it another way, every Christian ought to be either learning his ABCs or teaching them to someone else. Here it is in concrete terms: you ought to be able to teach a new believer how to find assurance of salvation, what the Gospel is all about, how to pray, how to read the Bible, how to have a quiet time, how to handle temptation, how to be filled with the Spirit, and how to lead someone else to Christ. Second, we are all to teach each other the things we have learned from the Word. Doing this demands that you be growing yourself through personal Bible study, group study, worship attendance, reading good Christian books, and serving in the local church.[5]

Second, *there is a spiritual gift of teaching that some Christians possess.* This gift was obviously very important to God because it is mentioned in four different passages of Scripture—Romans 12, 1 Corinthians 12, Ephesians 4, and 1 Peter 4. Romans 12:7 says, "If it [your spiritual gift] is teaching, let him teach." That's plain and simple. Teachers are to teach. That's to be their specialty, and they shouldn't get bogged down in other ministries. Find the teachers, turn them loose, and let them teach God's Word to the congregation.

The gift of teaching is one of the most important gifts of the Holy Spirit. It is far more important than any of the so-called sign gifts. People with sign gifts may attract a lot of attention, but they don't do as much good as those gifted teachers who simply go about their work day after day, week after week, explaining the truths of the Bible to little children, teenagers, and adults. In God's economy, the teachers come far ahead of the miracle-workers.[6]

A RELIGION BUILT UPON TEACHING

I say that because Christianity, at its heart, is a teaching religion. Unlike the eastern religions and the various New Age cults that bypass the mind, Christianity is built upon definite intellectual content. That's why the Bible says, "Love the Lord your God with all your heart and with all your soul and with all your mind" (Matthew 22:37). And that's why Romans 12:2 calls us to be "transformed by the renewing of your mind." Anyone who takes away the intellectual content of the Christian faith has in reality taken away Christianity itself.

We tend to downplay the importance of teaching today. The anti-intellectual spirit of the day has even infected the church. The me-generation stresses feelings and emotions over facts and ideas. Even when we come to church, we judge the effectiveness of the service by how it makes us feel. If we feel good, the service was good; if we don't, it wasn't. Experience is in, and doctrine is out. How-to sermons are in; expository preaching is out.

We have zeal without knowledge, faith without facts, emotion without understanding, and consequently big programs and small doctrine. We would rather feel good than study hard.

The inevitable result is an empty faith that must constantly be whipped up by an appeal to the emotions. Such a faith will not stand the test of time. Experience without truth leads to mindless Christianity.

Ours is a reasoning faith. *It cannot survive apart from a body of truth*. In that sense teaching is what the Christian faith is all about.

WAYS WE CAN TEACH OTHERS

There are an unlimited number, but let me suggest five.

By Writing to Prisoners

Chuck Colson and Prison Fellowship, as well as other trusted Christian ministries, have helped open our eyes to the unseen multitudes behind prison bars. Many inmates have come to Christ, and many others are searching for spiritual truth. When you write to a prisoner, you are actually engaging in evangelism, discipleship, encouragement, and teaching.

By Teaching in a Public School

We often think the public schools are totally closed to the Gospel, but it isn't necessarily so. The law clearly permits the teaching of the Bible as history and literature and as part of western culture. You can't preach or pray out loud, but you can find ways to show how the truth of the Bible is relevant to all of life.

By Ministering to Engaged Couples

An increasing number of churches stress the importance of proper marriage preparation. This usually involves premarital counseling but often includes a class led by several specially trained married couples. This offers an excellent way for husbands and wives to serve the Lord together.

By Teaching Persons with Handicaps

The handicapped represent one of the hidden mission fields right where we live. There are things we can do, people we can reach, lives we can touch for the Savior, if only we step forward willing to spearhead a ministry to men, women, and children with disabilities.

By Teaching Overseas

This is one of the most exciting opportunities available today. I remember listening to Dr. Charles Ryrie tell us about a fourth-year student who asked if he knew of any teaching opportunities. When Ryrie said yes, the young man asked where. When Dr. Ryrie said they were overseas, the young man said he wasn't interested. But the gift of teaching is not the gift of teaching only Americans. You can use it anywhere.

These suggestions are just the tip of the iceberg. You can teach children, teenagers, singles, young couples, and older adults. You can teach one-on-one, in small groups, in big groups, or in huge gatherings. Your willingness to teach others can be used at home, at church, at school, on the mission field, in music, in drama, on TV, on radio, and in a million other ways that are limited only by your imagination, your initiative, and your willingness to serve the Lord.[7]

SOWING, WATERING, REAPING

It's often hard to measure your effectiveness by what you are doing today. Sometimes you are just sowing seeds, sometimes you are watering; and it may seem like the harvest will never come. Teaching is like that. You plant a lot of seeds, you water, you pray a lot, and you sit back and wait. Not all the seeds will come up, but some will.

And here's the good news: you don't have to be famous or brilliant to teach. You don't have to be highly educated. You don't have to be clever or witty or unusually attractive. You don't have to be anything but willing. It won't cost you anything but your life. If you don't mind being a sower, you can be a teacher. There are hungry minds and open hearts all around us. The door of opportunity is wide open.

Most of us know so much. The lack of knowledge is not our problem. If anything, we know too much. We are biblically well-educated. The question is not, "What do you know?" but rather "What are you doing with what you know?" Look at all that seed God has given you. Enough for you and enough for your family, with plenty left over. Isn't it about time you planted some of it?

GOING DEEPER

1. Who was your favorite elementary school teacher? Your favorite junior high teacher? Your favorite high school teacher? Your favorite college teacher? Pinpoint the positive qualities you remember from each person. Then focus on the qualities all these favorite teachers share.

2. Why is it absolutely essential that spiritual leaders have a firm faith in the Word of God? What happens when doubts begin to creep into this area? Are you sure the Bible really is the Word of God? How do you know? What practical steps are you taking to grow in your knowledge of the Bible?

3. In what sense are all Christians to be teachers? What Scriptures teach this truth? How well are you personally obeying this command?

4. You ought to be able to teach a new believer how to find assurance
   of salvation, what the Gospel is all about, how to pray, how to read
   the Bible, how to have a quiet time, how to handle temptation, how
   to be filled with the Spirit, and how to lead someone else to Christ.
   How well do you understand each of these topics?
   When was the last time you tried to teach any of these things to
   another person?
   What else would you add to this list of the ABCs that every Christian
   should know?

5. In God's economy, the teachers come far ahead of the miracle-
   workers.
   Do you agree with this statement? If it is true, why do some people
   put such a big emphasis on the sign gifts?
   Would you rather have the gift of teaching or the gift of miracles?
   Explain your answer.

6. Many people are frightened by the thought of public speaking or
   standing in front of a crowd. Name at least five ways you can teach
   others outside of a classroom setting.

TAKING ACTION

Every church—no matter how large or small—always has opportunities for men who are willing to teach others. Investigate the openings in
your own church by talking with your pastor, a staff member, or one of
the lay leaders. If your church offers a teacher training program, be sure
to take the course. One hint: remember that teaching is more than standing in front of a classroom. You can teach through evangelism, discipleship training, or one-on-one counseling.

PART V

HIS FAMILY LIFE

A ONE-WOMAN
MAN

A Man of Honor is a one-woman man.
1 Timothy 3:2; Titus 1:6

In the best of circumstances marriage isn't easy. Anytime you put two sinners together in close quarters, they are bound to rub each other the wrong way from time to time. Adding to the burden is the reality of one or two full-time jobs, raising children, financial pressures, and overcommitment. Our culture doesn't help by glorifying promiscuity, publicizing celebrity affairs, and making it relatively simple (though not entirely painless) to get a divorce.

No wonder so many marriages are in trouble. No wonder divorce has invaded the Christian church. No wonder we aren't surprised to hear that our friends have decided to split up and go their separate ways. While attending a retreat recently, I heard of several clergy couples who had gotten divorced or were on the verge of taking that step. Upon reflection, I realized that the news was hardly news at all, which saddened me greatly.

WHAT IS A ONE-WOMAN MAN?

First Timothy 3:2 and Titus 1:6 say a spiritual leader must be "the husband of but one wife." Unfortunately, this qualification has been so wrapped up in controversy that we have missed its essential teaching. In Greek the phrase literally reads "a one-woman man." What does that mean? There are several possibilities:

- Only one wife at a time.
- Never divorced or remarried.
- Never remarried even after the death of the wife.
- Marital faithfulness.

Everyone agrees that #1 is included. This standard clearly excludes polygamy and bigamy. There are good arguments for and against #2. I doubt that #3 is intended since it seems to contradict what Paul says in 1 Corinthians 7 about the advisability of remarriage.[1]

The fourth option suggests that Paul has in mind marital faithfulness as a character quality of a godly leader. A spiritual leader is "not a flirtatious man but one who is content with his wife."[2] Why is that important? Because if a man is not faithful to his wife, how can he be trusted to be faithful to his obligations elsewhere? If a man cheats on his wife, where else will he cheat?

Here are some questions we ought to ask about potential leaders:

- Is he a flirt? Does he have roving eyes?
- Are his affections centered on his wife?
- Does he demonstrate affection for and loyalty to her in ways others can see?
- Is his marriage a model for others to follow?
- Is he above reproach in his dealings with the opposite sex?
- Is his life free from pornography in every form?

Many Christian men who have never been divorced would have trouble answering those questions acceptably. That's why I regard this as a higher standard than simply asking, "Has he ever been divorced?" The real question is, "What kind of marriage does this man have?"

To be a one-woman man means to put your wife first in your affections, to center your thoughts around her. She must be first—and there can be no number two. I understand the phrase "the husband of but one wife" to teach that a godly man must have an exclusive relationship with one woman and one woman only. It's a positive statement about loyalty and faithfulness. Seen in this light, to be "the husband of but one wife" is a moral qualification, not simply a marital one. *The issue is the quality of the marriage, not simply the legal state of the marriage.*

LETTERS FROM THE PAST

What does it mean to be a "one-woman man"? Let me suggest five practical anwers to that question.

Being a one-woman man means, for one thing, letting go of past relationships. I learned this truth early in my marriage. I think Marlene and I had only been married for two years when I happened to find a bag of letters written to me by different girls during my high school and college days. None of the letters were questionable or X-rated, and all of them had been written long before I met Marlene. Some were friendship letters, others were more romantic in nature, but none of them contained material I would have been ashamed for my wife to see. When we got married, I simply threw those letters in a big sack along with other correspondence I had saved over the years. Looking back, I kept those letters because they seemed like an important part of my past that was gone forever.

Marlene never mentioned the letters to me. I presume she knew I had them, but if they bothered her, she never said a word about it. And I don't remember having a great moral dilemma about whether or not to keep the letters. I had them, I kept them, I never looked at them, I never even thought about them.

Until one day when I suddenly realized I had to throw those letters away. Even though twenty years have passed since that moment, I still find it hard to explain why I felt as I did. As far as I can recall, the letters posed no particular moral problem and were not a source of irritation to my wife. But one day I realized that as a married man I had to throw those letters away. Without consulting my wife I grabbed the letters and threw them in a big, black, plastic trash bag and tossed it in the garbage can. When I told Marlene, she smiled and said nothing.

In some ways I think my marriage began that day. Or perhaps I should say that's when I stopped being a teenager and became a man. I'm not sure if my marriage improved, but that's not the point. Something happened that day when I threw those letters away. By that simple act I was saying to myself, "Ray, you belong to Marlene and only to her. What happened before doesn't matter. Those old letters belong to another place, another time, another life, another person. From this day forward your future belongs with your wife."

Would it have been wrong for me to keep the letters? For me at least, the answer is yes. First Corinthians 13:11 tells us that growing up means putting away childish things. And Philippians 3:13-14 challenges us to forget what lies behind and to press on toward the goal of the high calling of God in Jesus Christ. That goal includes many things, not the least of which is unswerving loyalty to one woman and only one woman.

"MY WIFE WAS MORE IMPORTANT TO ME THAN FOOTBALL"

Being a one-woman man also means putting your wife above your career. For twenty years Gary Olson was a high school football coach in Oak Park, Illinois—twelve years as an assistant, eight years as the head coach. His teams won and won often, enjoying one winning season after another. Almost every year they made it to the state playoffs. More than that, Gary had a reputation as a tough but fair coach who gave everything he had to the young men who played ball for him. More than a few went on to play college football, but most finished their careers when they graduated from high school. But that wasn't the end. Coach Olson gave his home phone number to his players so they could call him any time they were in trouble. Many of them continued to call him long after they graduated.

Then his wife was involved in a terrible accident that almost took her life. She was riding a bicycle when a panel truck hit her at an intersection. After a long hospital stay followed by numerous surgeries, she began the long, difficult road toward recovery.

According to Gary's own testimony, football wasn't as important to him anymore. Suddenly the thing that had been the passion of his life since he was in junior high school just didn't matter. He realized that his wife, Dawn, would need his help and support more than ever before. It really came down to a simple equation: someone else could coach the football team; no one else could take his place at his wife's side.

So at the age of forty-four he made what seemed like a disastrous career move. He gave up football. He just walked away from it. "I took a good look at my life, and I realized that my family needed me right now. I couldn't give all I had to football and to my wife. It wasn't a hard decision. My wife was more important to me than football."

Six years have passed since he made that decision. Looking back, he says he did the right thing and would do it again. Now that Dawn has recovered, he has returned to coaching again. But when Gary Olson says, "My wife comes first," you know he means it. More importantly, Dawn knows it too.

"UNCLE OSIE"

Being a one-woman man also means loving your wife when she can't love you back. Oftentimes the true test of a man's love for his wife comes in the later years. Osian Anderson was a barber on the north side of Chicago. When his wife, Ruth, developed Alzheimer's disease, he cared for her as long as he could; but eventually they had to move into a nursing home. He lived in one wing, while she lived in the other wing strapped in a wheelchair, completely unaware of her surroundings. The disease had not only taken her mind, it had also taken away her ability to care for her most basic needs. She couldn't even feed herself.

Uncle Osie was always cheerful, except when he spoke of his wife. He spent as much time with her as he could every day. Once he asked the chaplain why God didn't take Ruth home, but the chaplain had no answer.

Davis Duggins would occasionally come with his wife and two daughters to visit Uncle Osie. Once when they couldn't find him in his room, they asked directions to Ruth's room and made their way to the other wing. Davis tells in his own words what they saw there:

> For some reason I stopped before we entered the room. I could see Uncle Osie in front of the window, sitting by his wife's wheelchair. He had something in his lap. It took me a second to figure out what it was—a box of chocolate candy.
>
> While we watched unnoticed from the doorway, I saw him reach into the box, take a chocolate, and break off a small piece. Then he leaned over, opened his wife's mouth, placed the choco-

late on her tongue, and let it dissolve. The whole time she just sat there, staring blankly. He was whispering something, but I couldn't hear.

We didn't stand there long. Uncle Osie noticed us and stood up, looking a little embarrassed. "I was just giving her some chocolate," he said. "I remember she used to enjoy it so much."[3]

That's what it means to be a one-woman man. You stay with your wife, you keep your vows, and you do whatever you have to do to take care of her.

THE STRIPPER

Being a one-woman man means leaning on your friends to help you stay faithful. "I've got to go. He's one of my best friends. I can't skip it." My friend was referring to a birthday party he felt he just had to attend. But you see, some friends of a friend were throwing the party, and one of their surprises for the birthday boy was . . . a stripper.

What do you do then? How do you remain true to your Christian commitment while not unnecessarily offending your friend on his birthday? The key word is "unnecessarily." Sometimes standing up for the Lord will put you in some uncomfortable (and unpopular) positions.

The man took his question to a group of Christian men. "What do I do when the stripper comes out?" The men offered several answers but mostly told him that they had great confidence in him and that they knew he would make a wise decision. They also told him later they would ask him how he handled it, and they offered to pray for him.

Off he went to the birthday party. When the stripper came out, he left the room. Others left with him. No confrontation, no ugly scene, no compromise.

End of story? Not quite. One of the men in the Christian group had the same thing happen later in a completely different setting. "Let's go see a stripper," someone suggested. "No thanks. My wife's a queen, and I don't want to dishonor her by doing something like that," my friend responded. One fellow in particular ragged on him. Silence. Then a voice came from across the room. "Hey, are you a Christian?" "Yes, I am."

Later that night the fellow who had ragged on him said, "I really admire you for what you did."

My friend responded that way because his friend had asked for advice about the birthday party. So it is that one man helps another, we hold each other accountable, and we stand together shoulder to shoulder and back to back. It's easier to stand tall when you're not standing alone.

"I WILL NEVER LEAVE YOU"

Being a one-woman man means divorce simply isn't an option. Anything less and you are not really glued together. As long as you harbor divorce in the back of your mind even as a theoretical option, there will be a little space between you and your wife, a tiny wedge that you can use against your mate when the going gets tough.

Several years ago I went to Louisiana to speak at a couples retreat. While I was there, my friend Ron Lambe talked to me about his marriage. "Ray, from time to time I sit down with Patricia and I say to her, 'Sweetheart, there is nothing you can do that will ever cause me to divorce you.'" Then he added, "She needs that security." What a wonderful step it would be if you sat down with your wife this week and said that to her—maybe even in front of the children.

This chapter has two applications. For single men, being a one-woman man means developing the qualities now that will make you a good husband later if God opens the door to marriage. In any case, God has called you to a high standard of moral purity. Live in such a way that your purity and integrity will be seen by all who know you.

For married men, the challenge is simple: live so that no one will be surprised to know you are married and everyone will know without asking that your wife is first in your heart.

GOING DEEPER

1. Why is being a one-woman man an important qualification for spiritual leadership? What happens when this qualification is ignored when choosing leaders?

2. Since this is a moral qualification and not just a statement about marital status, how might a remarried man meet this qualification

while a married might man might fail it? What extra difficulties
might a divorced and remarried man have in being a truly one-
woman man?

3. She must be first and there can be no number two.
   What things are ruled out by this high standard?
   What positive steps could you take to demonstrate to your wife
   that she is first in your affections?

4. How do men and women differ in their sexual needs, feelings, and
   attitudes? What practical steps can husbands and wives take to help
   each other in this area?

5. Why is it important that a married man make a clean break with
   any past relationships? What happens when this principle is
   ignored? Any there any such relationships in your life that need to
   be broken for the good of your marriage? What do you plan to do
   about it?

6. Many Christian men struggle to balance their careers and
   marriages. Few will be faced with the dramatic choice Gary Olson
   faced. But we all must make the decision to put our wives first. Short
   of giving up your career, how can you show your wife that she is
   more important to you than your job?

7. How does the use of pornography dishonor your wife and hurt your
   marriage? Explain.

8. "There is nothing you can do that will ever cause me to divorce
   you." Have you ever said that to your wife?

Will you commit to doing it this week? If not this week, then when? If
you don't want to say it, what is holding you back, and what will it take
for you to say those words?

TAKING ACTION

Would you like a project that could change your marriage this week?
Take a 3 x 5 card and write down five things you appreciate about your
wife. They can be small things, and they don't have to be related to you
personally—for example, "I appreciate the way she makes our home
beautiful," or "I appreciate the way my wife gets excited watching our son
play T-Ball," or "I like the way my wife smiles when she sees me coming

through the door at night," or "I appreciate the fact that she encourages me in my dreams." Write down five each day. By the end of the week, you will have thirty-five new reasons to respect your mate.

WHERE MEN OF HONOR SHINE

A Man of Honor manages his household well.
—1 Timothy 3:4-5

S uppose you had three minutes to live, and your loved ones were gathered around you waiting to hear your last words. What would you tell them?

Perhaps you are in the hospital dying of some terrible disease. You know the end is near. As you search your mind for the right things to say, a thousand thoughts flood your mind. What can you say in your dying moments that will sum up your life? How do you compress sixty or seventy or eighty years of living into just a few sentences?

Or what if you don't have three minutes? What if you're involved in a terrible accident while traveling on the interstate? What if you have only thirty seconds? What would you say to your loved ones?

Some questions are always theoretical . . . until the moment comes and you really do have only thirty seconds to live. Before that, it's a question you kick around with some friends late at night over a cup of coffee.

If you had thirty seconds to live, how would you summarize the things that are most important to you?

DYING FAITH

There is such a thing as dying faith—vibrant trust in the Lord that manifests itself in the final moments of life on earth. I suppose all of us are planning to live a long time, but these days you can never be sure. The stray bullet, the out-of-control driver, the renegade gang member—who knows? Any of us could be struck down at any moment.

Suppose you knew you were going to die in the next twenty-four hours. What would you do? Where would you go? What would you say to the people you love?

A few months ago I thought about this, and I decided that if I had only thirty seconds to live, I would gather my boys around me and tell them four things:

- Take care of your mother.
- Love each other.
- Marry a Christian girl.
- Serve Jesus Christ forever.

That's it. Thirty seconds and I'm gone. Those four things summarize everything I would want my boys to know. After that, I would be ready to go.

GETTING YOUR AFFAIRS IN ORDER

First Timothy 3:4 tells us that a spiritual leader "must manage his own family well." The word *manage* means "to stand before and lead." The word *well* means "in an orderly fashion." *Spiritual leaders are men who handle their families in an orderly fashion.*[1]

But why does Paul bring up the family? Because the home is the best training ground for leadership. Spiritual leadership begins at home! *The family is like a church in miniature, and the father is the pastor of his own family.* To me, the whole concept of the father as the head of his home means that as the spiritual leader the father feels a deep sense of personal responsibility for those God has entrusted to his care. Being the head doesn't mean giving orders and demanding obedience. Far from it. It really means shouldering the awesome burden of raising a family that will bring glory to God.

Notice the penetrating question Paul asks: "If anyone does not know how to manage his own family, how can he take care of God's church?" The word translated "take care of" is the same verb used for the Good Samaritan who "took care of" the poor man he found on the road.[2] It means to "assume personal responsibility for the care of another person." That's what a father is to do for his family. As the head of the home, God holds him responsible for his wife and children. He will answer to God someday for what happens to them.

So the home is the church in miniature and the birthplace of budding spiritual leaders. Habits formed there last forever. Principles imparted there are never forgotten. Eternal truth is hammered out on the anvil of daily life.

Managing involves many things, including the following:

- Setting priorities.
- Planning for the future.
- Providing what is needed.
- Handling crisis situations.

By the way, when is management best seen? In a crisis. Anyone can lead a business when things are going well. Good managers shine when the business is in trouble. *The same is true at home. Family problems should not automatically disqualify a man from spiritual leadership. It's not what happens but how he responds that makes all the difference.* Some men rise to the occasion; others cut and run. The men who rise in a crisis are the leaders you want.

YOU CAN'T WALK AWAY

How do you respond when your daughter turns up pregnant? What do you do when your son turns to drugs? What will you say when you have to file for bankruptcy? How will you react when you suddenly lose your job? What if your oldest son flunks out of college? What if your wife needs hospitalization? What if your marriage is in trouble? Will you face the problem, or will you try to avoid it? A good manager never walks away from a problem. He faces life head-on and deals with it honestly.

He Helps His Family in a Time of Crisis

I've always believed that the best way to handle problems is head-on, which is exactly how our new van hit the tree at 1 A.M.

It happened like this: on Monday afternoon Marlene and I (and our two younger boys) left for a few days of vacation in Michigan. Our oldest son stayed behind because he had a job working at a local grocery store. We asked an adult friend to stay with him while we were gone. That night various circumstances kept her from getting to our house until late in the evening. Meanwhile, our oldest son had asked two friends to come over and spend the night. That was okay with us as long as an adult was around. Since she was late getting home, the boys had a big time—playing music, watching TV, eating, laughing, and shooting off fireworks in the sewer (fun, though illegal and dangerous).

About 12:30 A.M. the boys asked our friend if she would let them drive her car (none of them had their driver's license yet). Somehow the boys talked her into saying yes, and somehow they ended up driving our van instead of her car. At 12:45 A.M. the joyride began. Two of the boys drove the van around the block without incident. When the third boy got behind the wheel, he accelerated too fast, then turned too sharply around a corner. The van jumped the curb, nearly hit a house, and sideswiped a fence. When someone shouted at him to stop, he panicked and hit the gas pedal by mistake, catapulting the van across the street and into a tree at approximately 50 mph.

"It was like a scene from the end of the world," someone said later. There was screaming, sudden impact, silence, broken glass, blood, darkness, fear, shock, pain. The police came, then the paramedics. The four of them were taken to four different hospitals. The injuries included a lacerated forehead, facial cuts, a shattered wrist (later requiring surgery), a broken right kneecap (requiring three surgeries), severe lacerations, and a deep puncture on the left shin. Our son ended up with a broken left ankle and three broken bones in his right foot.

When the call came at 2:30 A.M. Michigan time, it was every parent's worst nightmare come true. "Your son has been in a serious automobile accident and has been taken to the hospital." The next two days were a sleepless blur of phone calls, hospital visits, unending explanations, lots of "what ifs," and many moments of anger and deep frustration. My oldest son nearly lost his life. So did two of his best friends. So did our adult friend.

But through it all we experienced the grace of God. This whole awful event was a wake-up call to our family, to the three boys, to our adult friend, and to our neighbors (the accident took place less than one block from our home). I have learned again how precious life is, how thin is the margin that separates the living and the dead, how quickly we go from joy to sorrow, and how totally unimportant money is compared with the value of just one human life. I can always write another book or find another church to pastor, but I could never get my son back again.

God spared my son, humbled me, and caused our entire family to look to Him in a brand-new way. The van was totaled, and we ended up losing our insurance. The others involved have mostly recovered from their injuries. Our neighbors have been gracious, saying over and over, "Don't worry about the grass or the fence or the tree. We're just glad the boys are alive."

For me, helping my family through a crisis meant many different things: 1) Assuring my son of my love for him in spite of the wreck. 2) Going that morning to visit my neighbors one by one. 3) Visiting the four people in the hospital. 4) Dealing with the insurance company. 5) Informing the elders of my church about the accident. 6) Telling my congregation on Sunday morning. 7) Finding temporary transportation. 8) Patiently explaining what happened to everyone who asked. 9) Meeting with my son, his two friends (and their parents), and our adult friend to talk openly about what happened and why. 10) Asking my friends for advice and also for their prayers. 11) Talking together as a family about the things we have learned from this crisis.

There are really no rules to follow in dealing with crisis situations except the most basic one, which is to believe that since God is in control, He will give you the strength to deal with whatever comes your way. With that confidence, you can handle your family problems one step at a time. And I am more convinced than ever that hiding your problems never works. When you try to protect your reputation, it only makes you look worse when the truth surfaces, which it usually does.

Being open and honest about your family crises serves three good purposes: First, it enlarges the circle of support. Second, it encourages others to be open about their difficulties. Third, it teaches your own children how a godly man deals with unexpected problems.

He Protects Them from Danger

In some ways this might be the father's biggest responsibility. Nothing is more truly noble than the notion that a man is called by God to protect his wife and children from harm. Protecting those you love is a large part of what it means to be a man.

Many years ago when I was growing up in northwest Alabama, my family would travel to Oxford, Mississippi, to spend a few days at the farm where my father grew up. Since my father was a surgeon, his work at the hospital often meant we would go over early and he would follow us a day or so later. But we would always travel back home together.

There was always a certain routine we would follow. My mom would drive the first car along with two of the boys. Then the other two boys would ride with my father. We took the same route every time—from Oxford to New Albany to Tupelo to Fulton. From Fulton we drove along a deserted country road across the state line to Red Bay, and from Red Bay we traveled to my home in Russellville, Alabama.

Whenever we traveled in two cars, my dad always made sure that Mom drove the first car. My father would always say, "Hon, you go first." I saw him do it dozen of times. It took me years to figure out why he made her go first. Dad wanted to make sure that if she had car trouble he would be right behind her so she wouldn't be left stranded on the road.

It is a small point, infinitely small in the great scheme of things, but when I thought about a man protecting his family, the memory of my father following my mom home across those deserted country roads floated back into my mind. It is a husband's honor to protect his wife; it is the wife's privilege to be protected by her husband.

He Serves His Family by Praying for Them

When John Tahl retired from Moody Bible Institute after more than thirty years, I was invited to attend his retirement dinner. Afterwards a variety of people gave testimony to John's sterling Christian character and his radiant Christian faith. Then the host asked his daughter Carole to say something about her father. She talked about what a good man he was and how he had loved his children. "I remember that early in the morning I would get up and go downstairs. I would see my father on his knees praying for me and my sisters." As she began to cry she added, "I've never forgotten the sight of my father praying for me."

A friend of mine, Tom Phillips, wrote about the impact of his father's prayers for him during his high school years:

> For about 5 years I threw 140 copies of the *Chattanooga Times* every morning. I would get up about 4:00 A.M., pick up my papers at 4:30 A.M., throw them until about 6:00 A.M., and then come home and get back in bed. Every morning at 5:30 A.M., when I passed our house, I would notice my dad's bedroom light on. One day when we were playing golf I asked him why he got up so early. "When you throw the papers on Anderson Avenue behind our house, all the dogs bark and they wake me up. When I hear the dogs, I know you're out there throwing papers, and I always get up and pray for you until you return home."

Tom added one sentence to this story: "What a fantastic example to me of a man who prayed and had a burden for his son."[3]

Men, have you prayed for your family today? Husbands, have you prayed for your wives? Dads, have you prayed for your children? Have you taken the role as the priest that God has called you to be—to serve your family through prayer? Men, if you want to see God work in your family, it has to start with you! It has to start in the home, and it has to start with husbands who truly love their wives and with fathers who truly love their children—who will put their family first, who will protect them, and who will pray for them.

Everything God wants to do in families is possible if husbands will love their wives and if fathers will love their children. It all begins right there.

GOING DEEPER

1. The father is the pastor of his own family.
   Do you believe that? How does it make you feel?
   How well did your father pastor your family while growing up? How well are you doing with the family God has given you?

2. Much debate swirls around the concept of the husband as the *head* of the home. Some people focus on authority, others on responsibility, still others on serving. As a man, do you believe that God has called you to be the head of your home? How would your wife answer that question? How can that headship be expressed in partnership with your wife?

3. Good managers shine when the business is in trouble.
Why is this statement true?
How does a crisis reveal the reality of our faith in God? In what ways can we glorify God even in the midst of a difficult family crisis?

4. What principles should we follow in order to help a friend during a family crisis without adding undue pressure or complicating the situation?

5. Think back to a crisis in the last two years involving you or your family. How did you handle it? What, if anything, would you do differently? How did your Christian friends either help or hinder the situation?

6. Why is it better to deal with a personal or family crisis openly and honestly? Since we can't involve the whole world in our problems, what guidelines should we follow in this area? List the negative results that come from hiding our problems.

7. Have you prayed for your wife and children today? Take a moment and pray for them right now.

8. If you are single, this chapter still applies to you. How well are you managing your own personal affairs? Has God given you a circle of close friends (or adult siblings or other relatives) who have become like a family to you? In what ways can you as a single man appropriately show your concern for them?

TAKING ACTION

Suppose you had thirty seconds to live. With your wife and children (and grandchildren) gathered around you, what would you say? How would you sum up the deepest values of your life in a few sentences? (If you are single, apply this question to your closest friends and family members.) Think about that question, and write out your answer. Then gather your family and read it as your personal gift to them. If your family is scattered, consider writing it in a letter. By all means, record your answer somewhere so that succeeding generations will know the things you valued the most.

IS THERE A FATHER IN THE HOUSE?

A Man of Honor is a good father.
—*1 Timothy 3:4; Titus 1:6*

Not long ago I ran across a report called "One Day in the Lives of America's Children."[1] Here is part of what it said: Every day in the USA:

- 2,795 teens get pregnant.

- 372 teens miscarry.

- 1,106 teens have abortions.

- 1,295 teens give birth.

- 27 children die from poverty.

- 10 children are killed by guns.

- 30 children are wounded by guns.

- 6 teenagers commit suicide.

- 135,000 children bring a gun to school.

- 7,742 teenagers become sexually active.

- 623 teenagers get syphilis or gonorrhea.

- 211 children are arrested for drug abuse.

- 437 children are arrested for drinking or for drunken driving.

- 1,512 teens drop out of school.

- 1,849 children are abused or neglected.
- 3,288 children run away from home.
- 1,629 children are in adult jails.
- 2,556 children are born out of wedlock.
- 2,989 children see their parents divorced.

We have the form today, but we don't have the substance. We're good at big weddings; we're lousy at good marriages. We know how to make babies; we don't have a clue about raising them.

And our children pay the price.

CHILDREN WHO BELIEVE

A Man of Honor must be a good father. This particular qualification is stated two different ways. First Timothy 3:4 says a spiritual leader must "see that his children obey him with proper respect." Titus 1:6 adds that he must be "a man whose children believe and are not open to the charge of being wild and disobedient." These verses are frighteningly specific. I say that in full view of the fact that I have three boys living at home—two teenagers and one almost there. The challenge today is to raise godly children in a world that constantly pulls in the opposite direction. We aren't told how the father is to do this, but we are told what the results will look like:

- Children who "believe" (or it may mean they are faithful to the parents).[2]
- Children who "obey."
- Children who show "proper respect."
- Children who are not "wild."
- Children who are not "disobedient."

SO FAR, SO GOOD

One or two points deserve special mention. Paul is probably not speaking of young children, and possibly not even of teenagers.[3] He may be envisioning grown children who have already left the home and have gone out on their own. Certainly that is the only way to get a long-range view of how the children have turned out. I look at my own three boys and say, "So far, so good. But we've got a long way to go."

The word *wild* is literally "unsaved." It means to live an "unsaved" lifestyle. It refers to a wild, indulgent, immoral, and debauched way of life—one that is typical of the surrounding pagan community. More than that, the word speaks of excessive lewdness as a pattern of life. Children make many mistakes in the course of life, but those raised in a godly home will be inclined toward righteousness. Some will try drugs, many will rebel, many will be trapped by immorality, some will seek abortions, others will break the law; but the seeds of a godly heritage will eventually bear fruit along the way.[4]

THE IDEAL PICTURE

To summarize:

- A spiritual leader should be a model father.
  (That doesn't mean "perfect.")

- No one can raise "perfect" children who never
  make mistakes.

- The godly man never gives up on his children.

- Wild and disobedient children reflect badly on a father's
  ability to guide others.

- How a father responds to a crisis in his family reveals much
  about his ability to handle a crisis in the church and on the
  job.

A godly leader takes great care with his children, knowing they are his single greatest contribution to the world. One writer describes the ideal father this way:

> "His firmness makes it advisable for the child to obey."
> "His wisdom makes it natural for the child to obey."
> "His love makes it a pleasure for the child to obey."[5]

Do your children respect you enough to submit to your leadership? In asking that question, the issue is not their response but the quality of life you live before them. Some fathers *demand* respect and wonder why they don't get it; others *command* respect by the combination of love and godliness that they model.

The ideal leader has a family that is committed to Jesus Christ—a family in which the husband loves his wife, and the wife is dedicated to her husband's spiritual leadership, and the grown children love Jesus Christ and love and respect their father and their mother too. That's the picture! It takes time to build a family like this, and it takes a father with the discipline and desire to see it happen. But it's worth it in the end.

FROM HERE TO THERE

Having said that, the question becomes, how do you get from here to there? Some men reading this book may be so far from the ideal that they feel it isn't worth striving for. Let me share some practical steps you can take that will make a difference at home.

STEP #1:
PRAY FOR YOUR CHILDREN

Dad, when was the last time you prayed by name for each of your children? If you have to stop and think, it's been too long!

I know a man who started praying for his children almost twenty-five years ago. Each night he went into their bedrooms and prayed over them after they had fallen asleep. He kept up this practice night after night as long as his children were at home. Several years ago his children came home from college for a few days. One morning when the father mentioned that he had prayed for them the night before, his daughter said, "I know, Dad. I saw the footprints in the carpet."[6]

Footprints in the carpet. What wonderful evidence of a father's concern.

Several months ago a friend suggested to my wife that Psalm 20 offers a wonderful guide to praying for your children. Since then, we have used it to pray for each other and for our three boys.

Psalm 20 is a prayer by the people of Israel on behalf of their king. It catches exactly the right tone of prayer for those we know the best and love the most. Do we not already pray for God to help our children when they are in trouble? Do we not already ask God to bless them? Do we not ask God to grant all their requests and to make all their plans succeed? The Psalm also reminds us that true success in life comes only to those who "trust in the name of the LORD our God" (verse 7). I suggest that you use Psalm 20 as a guide to praying for *your* children. Pray it over them in their presence. Help them memorize verse 7. Use it to celebrate their victories and to console them in their defeats.

STEP #2:
PRAISE YOUR CHILDREN

When was the last time you hugged your children? When was the last time you said, "I'm so proud of you"? When was the last time you bragged about them in their presence? Nothing can take the place of praising your children. It's hard enough to be a kid in this world. They need all the support they can get—especially from home. *It's especially important for you to praise them to someone else in their hearing. That simple act builds their self-confidence as nothing else can do.*

Some of you will recognize the name Henrietta Mears. For many years she was the director of Christian education at the Hollywood Presbyterian Church. She was also the inspiration for a whole generation of Christian leaders. Henrietta Mears was a wonderful student of human nature. These are her words: "Whenever I meet a new person, I imagine them wearing a sign across their chest which reads, 'My name is _____. Please help me feel important.'"

This week, instead of constantly criticizing your children for messing up, try praising them. It may do so much good that you'll never get around to the criticism.

STEP #3:
LISTEN TO YOUR CHILDREN

Most of us fathers fail miserably in this area. Our children talk, but we don't listen. We're too busy reading the paper or watching TV. Usually we expend so much energy on the job that we have nothing left for our children.

It's amazing how much wisdom we will discover in our children if only we'll stop to listen to them. All you have to do is ask. Your children will be delighted to tell you what they think.

STEP #4:
SET LIMITS AND SAY NO

Bishop Fulton Sheen said it well: "Every child needs a pat on the back so long as you give it low enough and hard enough." As we have already noted, praising your children is absolutely crucial. But just as crucial is the determination to say no when necessary. Even more important is the determination to back up your words with appropriate action.

STEP #5:
SHOW THEM THE POWER OF FAITH IN GOD

Psalm 145:4 tells us, "One generation will commend your works to another; they will tell of your mighty acts." It is the privilege of parents and grandparents to pass along the stories of God's faithfulness so that children and grandchildren will know that the God of the Bible is alive today.

My friend Allan MacLeod-Smith has often spoken about his grandfather who served as a missionary in South America for almost fifty years. He recounted for me an amazing story that took place during a visit to the United States en route to their home in New Zealand:

> My grandfather was a man of faith who lived the walk of absolute dependence on God's provision and providence. Of the many wonderful stories I heard while growing up, the following is one of the most remarkable. Soon after my parents were married, my mother suffered a ruptured appendix when she was six months pregnant with my sister Elizabeth. During the procedure they delivered Liz premature, and my mother contracted malaria from an infected blood transfusion. During the worst of things, the hospital told my father, "Your wife will be dead by morning. Make sure you come in tomorrow and pay your bills." My grandfather was visiting with my grandmother from the mission field in South America. My father went home despondent and my grandfather prayed for my mother all night by her hospital bed.

My grandfather said she looked just like a corpse, lying there shaking from malaria, The next morning my mother was completely healed and never had another malaria attack.

Here is the most interesting part of the story. My grandfather gave my dad nearly all the money he had to help pay the huge medical bills. My grandfather told no one that he had given the money for his trip to New Zealand where they would spend a year on home leave. No one knew of this except God. He had tickets for the train ride to San Francisco, but nothing else. He and my grandmother left by train for California as though nothing was unusual. When they arrived, my grandparents left the train station looking for a cab to take them to the shipyard, still with no tickets or any idea of how they were going to pay for their fare. A man approached my grandfather, pressed an envelope into his hand, said, "I don't know why, but the Lord told me to give this to you," then disappeared into the crowd. When my grandfather looked into the bag, he found the exact amount of money they needed for their tickets to New Zealand. My grandfather never saw the man again.[7]

That true story, which happened many years ago, has been told and retold by the children and the grandchildren as a reminder of how God cares for His own.

Has God answered your prayers? Tell your children. Did He rescue you from danger? Tell your children. Did you discover His faithfulness when all hope was lost? Tell your children. Was your marriage an answer to prayer? Tell your children.

If your God is alive, make sure and tell your children so they can share your faith in that same God and someday pass the faith along to the next generation.

STEP #6:
MODEL THE RIGHT KIND OF LIFE

Our children copy everything we do. This is one of the most terrifying truths of parenthood. I discovered this years ago when someone saw Joshua and me walking down the street together. Although he couldn't have been more than five years old, he walked with one hand in his pocket and his shoulders slightly bent, just as I do. "He looked like a carbon copy walking beside you," a friend said.

The power of example!

One of my childhood friends used to say, "I'm not sure the world is ready for a bunch of Ray Juniors walking around with big feet and thick glasses." But that's what I'm producing, whether the world is ready or not.

Several years ago our lunch included seedless white grapes. For some reason I decided to show the boys how I could throw a grape into the air and catch it in my mouth. After a couple of successes and a couple of misses, Mark and Nicholas decided to try it. Then they decided to practice throwing grapes to each other. Then they decided to throw grapes *at* each other. Then we had an all-out grape war right at the table. Marlene came in and said, "Look what you started." Joshua grinned and said, "Yeah, Dad, you're a great role model."

The power of example!

I'll never forget the night I attended an open house at our junior high school. There on the wall was a picture of my oldest son and underneath it a series of questions he had answered. One of them read: "My hero is . . . my dad because he's a great father, and I want to be like him when I grow up." I cannot begin to say how I felt when I read those words. Joy, amazement, and fear—fear lest I should somehow fail my son. I'm his hero. Is there any greater reward in this world? Is there any greater obligation?

A DAD-SHAPED VACUUM

We started this chapter by saying that kids today are in trouble. So many of their problems can be traced to absentee fathers. When Dad doesn't care enough to come home and spend time with his children, we shouldn't be surprised if the kids turn to drugs, alcohol, gangs, violence, and every sort of antisocial behavior to cover their pain.

No one—not even a mother—can replace a father in a child's life. To paraphrase a famous quote, there is a "dad-shaped vacuum" inside your child's heart, and no one can fill the void except you.

I don't know any way you can guarantee how your children will turn out because kids have a mind of their own. However, God has shown us what we can do to tip the scales in our favor. I can sum up the application to fathers in a single sentence: *make it easy for your children to obey*. If you want your children to honor you, you must live a life worthy of their honor. If you want your children to trust you, you must be trustworthy. If you want your children to love you, all you have to do is love them first.

It's not that our children don't want to honor us. The problem lies within us. If we do our part, our children will do the rest.

GOING DEEPER

1. The statistics at the beginning of this chapter should alarm every thinking adult. How do you respond to the people who say we shouldn't bring children into a world like that?

2. Read Psalms 127 and 128.
   In what sense are children a "reward" from the Lord (127:3)? Why is the man blessed whose "quiver" is full (verse 5)? Is this an argument in favor of larger families? How can a man know when his quiver is indeed full?
   In what sense is a godly wife like "a fruitful vine" (128:3)?
   According to Psalm 128:1, what condition must be met for a father to enjoy the blessing of a happy family? How well are you meeting that condition right now?

3. A spiritual leader must be a model father.
   What does that phrase suggest in your mind? Think of three or four fathers who fit that phrase. What qualities do they share in common?
   Why is it important that a father never give up on his children? What happens when he does?
   Suppose a man has failed in this area, and his children have now left home and have gone out on their own. What practical steps can he take to rebuild his relationship with them?

4. The seeds of a godly heritage will eventually bear fruit along the way. Do you agree with this statement? What qualifiers would you put on it?
   Why do some children raised in an apparently godly home seem to rebel against God and never return to the Lord? Whose fault is it?

What does Proverbs 22:6 really mean? Why is it important to take the "long view" in raising our children?

5. Some fathers *demand* respect; other fathers *command* it by their love and godly life.
Which kind of father did you have? Did you fear your father? Did you respect him? Did you love him? Looking back, how close did he come to being a model father?
What impact has his example had on your own fathering?
How would your children answer this question about you?

6. When was the last time you praised your children for a specific accomplishment or positive attitude? How did they respond? Would your children say you are more likely to praise them or correct them?

7. Why is it important for parents to set clear limits? What happens when we are negligent or arbitrary in this area? Why does Colossians 3:21 warn fathers not to embitter their children? What kinds of things are likely to embitter or exasperate our children?

8. How can a noncustodial parent apply the teaching of this chapter? What special challenges will he face in being a godly father? How will these truths apply to a father in a blended family?

TAKING ACTION

What do your children like to do for fun? (If you don't know the answer, ask them. You may be surprised at their answers.) Make a list of at least five things you know they would enjoy doing with you. Set aside time to do at least one of those things with your children this week. If your children have grown up and moved away, give them a call this week. If you have no children, consider volunteering to work in the children's ministry of your local church.

PART VI

HIS PERSONAL HABITS

THE BEAST IN THE BOTTLE

A Man of Honor is not a habitual drinker.
—*1 Timothy 3:3; Titus 1:7*

The particular phrase Paul uses literally means "not lingering over wine." It is variously translated as "not a lover of wine," "not addicted to strong drink," "not a drunkard," "not a hard drinker," "not excessive in his use of wine."[1] I might add that the word also includes the thought of not frequenting places where wine is misused. It means not using wine as a way of life. John MacArthur explains that such a man "does not have a reputation as a drinker. He doesn't frequent bars or involve himself in the scenes associated with drinking."[2]

While this does not demand total abstinence, it does make clear that a lover of wine cannot be a leader of God's people. Godly leaders must be above reproach in the use of alcohol.

Over the eighteen years I have served as a pastor, the subject of drinking has come up again and again. The week before I preached on this subject a few years ago, I came into my office and found a brown bag on my desk. It was labeled, "For your sermon on drinking." Inside was an empty Schlitz Malt Liquor bottle. I started my sermon by holding up the bottle and saying, "I have only one question: why was it empty when it got to me?"

We had a good laugh about the empty bottle, but it points out our basic problem in this area. The evangelical consensus against social drinking has largely evaporated in the last few years. A generation ago it was a given that if you belonged to an evangelical church, you didn't drink. Period. End of discussion. Drinking was something that other people did. We didn't want any part of it.

NEEDED: A PERSONAL CHOICE

Times have changed. I think it is useful to revisit the subject of the Christian and social drinking. After all, the Bible does have a great deal to say about the use and abuse of alcohol. From time to time it is good to remind ourselves about the biblical teaching so that we can make wise decisions in this area.

While the Bible has a great deal to say about intoxicating beverages and the danger of abuse, it does not lay down a binding rule about drinking per se. Therefore, a personal choice is necessary.

There are a great many references to wine, strong drink, and drunkenness scattered throughout the Bible. The earliest reference is in Genesis, the last in Revelation. The total number of verses would run up into the hundreds. However, there is not a binding rule—"Thou shalt not drink." In one place the Bible says, "Do not get drunk on wine" (Ephesians 5:18). In another place the Bible speaks of "wine that gladdens the heart of man" (Psalm 104:15). In one place Paul says no drunkard shall inherit the kingdom of God (1 Corinthians 6:10). In another place he advises Timothy to "use a little wine because of your stomach and your frequent illnesses" (1 Timothy 5:23).

Because there is no universal rule, each believer must make his own decision guided by the larger teachings of Scripture, his own situation, the counsel of others, and common sense.

THINK BEFORE YOU DRINK

However, to put the matter that way does not exactly settle the issue, does it? A quick check of the concordance under the word "wine" shows that many of the references warn the reader of the negative effects of alcohol. Consider the following examples:

- Proverbs 20:1—"Wine is a mocker and beer a brawler."
- Isaiah 24:9—"The beer is bitter to its drinkers."
- Ephesians 5:18—"Do not get drunk on wine."

- Galatians 5:19-21—"The acts of the sinful nature are obvious . . . drunkenness."

- 1 Peter 4:3—"For you have spent enough time in the past doing what pagans choose to do—living in debauchery, lust, drunkenness, orgies, carousing and detestable idolatry."

One of the passages influential in my thinking is found in Genesis 9. It tells the strange, sad story of Noah's drunkenness. The Bible says that he was "a man of the soil." He planted the first vineyard, made the first wine, and ended up the first man to get drunkin the Bible. From that drunkenness came the shameful episode where Ham saw his father's nakedness, which led to the breakup of a family and the fragmentation of the whole human race. That story stands as a warning to all who would minimize the dangers of alcohol.

The Bible warns us repeatedly of the dangers of alcohol. Let's look at one other passage, Proverbs 23:29-35.

> Who has woe? Who has sorrow? Who has strife? Who has complaints? Who has needless bruises? Who has bloodshot eyes? Those who linger over wine, who go to sample bowls of mixed wine. Do not gaze at wine when it is red, when it sparkles in the cup, when it goes down smoothly! In the end it bites like a snake and poisons like a viper. Your eyes will see strange sights and your mind imagine confusing things. You will be like one sleeping on the high seas, lying on top of the rigging. "They hit me," you will say, "but I'm not hurt! They beat me, but I don't feel it! When will I wake up so I can find another drink?"

What is the Bible telling us? That we cannot drink? No. That it's a sin to take a drink? Not necessarily. It's telling us there's danger ahead. Think twice before you take the first drink.

FAMILY MATTERS

Suppose you are traveling through the mountains and come to a fork in the road. One fork has a sign that says, "Safe for all travelers." The other is labeled, "Dangerous road. Watch out for falling rocks. Soft shoulders. Landslides possible. Sharp curves, with no guard rails. Travel at your own risk." Both roads are open, both offer scenic views, and you see cars going both ways. Which way are you going to go? I suppose it depends on how ready you are to risk your own life. Either way, you've got a choice to make.

Most of us know the terrible toll that alcohol exacts on our society.[3] What you may not know is how bad the problem has become for our children.

- So bad that there are three million teenage alcoholics.

- So bad that 60 percent of all teenage deaths are caused by alcohol abuse.

- So bad that 70 percent of all teenagers twelve to seventeen drink at least occasionally.

- So bad that 6,000 teenagers are killed by drunk drivers each year.

- So bad that every day 1,000 teenagers begin drinking alcohol for the first time.

- So bad that the average teenager begins to drink between the ages of thirteen and fourteen.

- So bad that 40 percent of teenage suicides are drunk at the time of death.[4]

There are so many things we can't completely protect our children from—worldly advertising, peer pressure, the negative examples of some of their rock music heroes. When they hit junior high, they will enter a world in which many of their friends drink on a regular basis. How can we help them? How can we give them the inner strength to say no? The experts say we can do three things. 1) Exercise, firm, loving discipline. 2) Provide a strong spiritual foundation. 3) Make sure there is no alcohol in the home.

Dad, your own example is the best weapon you have to protect your child from alcohol abuse.

MY BROTHER'S KEEPER

Consider the words of the Apostle Paul in Romans 14:13: "Make up your mind not to put any stumbling block or obstacle in your brother's way." It's never enough to say, "It doesn't hurt me" or "I don't see anything wrong with it." Your Christian responsibility doesn't end there. If the Christian faith means anything, it means that I must love my neighbor as myself.

Look at what Paul says next: "As one who is in the Lord Jesus, I am fully convinced that no food is unclean in itself" (verse 14). Meaning, I can eat anything I want. I can eat steak, lobster, ice cream, pizza, or even Jimmy Dean Pure Pork Sausage. No law against it. But that's not the end of the story.

He goes on to say, "If your brother is distressed because of what you eat, you are no longer acting in love. Do not by your eating destroy your brother for whom Christ died" (verse 15). The principle is: You have freedom to eat and drink, but it is never right to use your freedom in such a way that it injures other people.

The conclusion comes in verse 20: "All food is clean." I can eat what I want and drink what I want. "But it is wrong to eat anything that causes someone else to stumble." I am free, Paul says, but not free to do what I please without regard to my brother. Here's the bottom line: "It is better not to eat meat or drink wine or to do anything else that will cause your brother to fall" (verse 21).

Let me offer four key points to think about:

- In the area of food and drink, all things are permissible or clean.

- I have liberty to partake. I have liberty not to partake.

- I must be mindful that my choices have consequences for other people. I must be fully aware of those consequences and act accordingly.

- Especially, I must limit my liberty in those areas that could harm another person.

A long time ago a man asked the question, "Am I my brother's keeper?" For the Christian, the answer is always yes.

WHAT IF I JUST SAID NO?

What would happen if you just said no? What if you decided that you would not drink alcohol? What would that mean for you personally?

It's easier to say what it wouldn't mean. For instance, you wouldn't necessarily have to:

- Give up all your friends.
- Make a big scene when you are offered a drink.
- Become a blue-nosed prude.

It also wouldn't mean that you . . .

- Couldn't laugh at funny beer commercials.
- Could never go to a place where they serve liquor.
  (If you know how to say no, you can go wherever you want.)
- Could never have any fun for the rest of your life.

If you decide to say no, it would simply mean that you choose—for good and sufficient reasons, for your own sake and for the sake of others—to voluntarily abstain from alcoholic beverages.

THE LAWYER WHO MET JESUS

Some years ago in Saint Louis a Christian businessman said to his lawyer, "I've been wanting to ask you a question, but I've been a coward."

The lawyer said, "I've never known you to be a coward about anything. What's the question?"

"Why are you not a Christian?" asked the businessman.

The lawyer looked downward and said, "Isn't there something in the Bible that says no drunkard shall have any part in the kingdom of God? You know my weakness."

"That isn't the question. I asked why you aren't a Christian."

"Well, I can't recall that anyone ever asked me if I was a Christian, and I'm sure nobody ever told me how to become one."

The Christian opened his Bible and explained that Jesus Christ could forgive his sins and give him a brand-new life. Then he said, "Let's pray together." The lawyer prayed a simple prayer, expressing his faith in Jesus Christ and asking God to break the power of alcohol in his life.

Later, speaking of his deliverance from alcohol, the newly born-again lawyer said, "Put it down big, put it down plain, that God broke that power immediately."

That man was later called into the ministry and became famous for an edition of the Bible with helpful notes at the bottom. Millions of copies have been sold. The lawyer's name was C. I. Scofield, and his Bible is called the *Scofield Reference Bible*. There's a church in Dallas named after him—the Scofield Memorial Church. His faith in Christ set him free from alcohol.[5]

Deliverance from alcohol will not always happen as dramatically or as instantaneously as that. But the power of the Gospel of Christ can deliver a man from the chains of addiction.

THE DECISION IS YOURS

I want to say it again and say it clearly: where the Bible makes no binding rule, we must not either. Therefore, my appeal is to your heart and to your mind. In some ways the question of drinking is only a peripheral issue—a minor point among many things more pressing. In other ways it is of paramount importance. The pressure is on all of us to give in to our culture. Hardly a night passes that those seductively funny TV commercials do not enter our living rooms. We constantly face the temptation to drink—at work, at a nice restaurant, with our friends, when we visit family. It is easy and very acceptable to become a social drinker. In fact, it is easy to slide into that position by default—a drink here, a glass of wine there, and suddenly we've changed our minds altogether.

Make up your mind now. Don't be sucked into a compromise by peer pressure and the deception of advertising. If you are free to drink, you are also free not to drink.

Which will it be for you?

GOING DEEPER

1. Why do you think the Bible includes this particular qualification for spiritual leaders? Why is the use or non-use of alcohol an important spiritual issue?

2. Godly leaders must be above reproach in their use of wine.

Does this statement demand total abstinence? Why or why not? Give some contemporary uses of alcohol that in your mind would be clearly prohibited by this standard.

3. Read Proverbs 23:29-35.
Answer the six questions posed by verse 29.
List the physical results of intoxication in verses 33-35. Have you known anyone whose life was hurt by alcohol abuse? What impact has that person's experience had on you?

4. What contrast is made in Ephesians 5:18? What does this tell us about the essential impact of alcohol on the human body?

5. Why doesn't the Bible simply come out and say, "Thou shalt not drink"? What advantage can you see from the fact that each believer must make a personal decision in this area?

6. Read Romans 14.
As you read through this chapter, what are some of the "disputable matters" Paul mentions in verse 1? Can you give some contemporary examples of these same kinds of issues?
According to verse 10, how should we *not* respond to believers who have different convictions regarding these controversial areas?
According to verse 21, when is it better not to drink wine? Name a situation in which that prohibition might apply in your own life.

7. Would you want your own children to follow your example in the use or non-use of alcohol? Why or why not?

TAKING ACTION

Taking responsibility for your own life involves learning what the Bible actually says about alcohol. Using a concordance or a Bible dictionary, look up every reference to "wine," "strong drink," and "beer." What does the Bible really say on the subject? Summarize your findings in one paragraph. Then write another paragraph that summarizes your own personal decision regarding the use or non-use of alcohol.

GIVERS AND TAKERS

A Man of Honor does not love money.
—1 Timothy 3:3

Not long ago a friend who lives in another state called to say hello. A number of months ago his company closed down. Then he did consulting work for four months. Then he was unemployed for four months. Now he has found work at a new company—for a much lower salary. He also has a second job, and his wife holds down two part-time jobs. "We just wave at each other in passing," he said. They're thinking about selling their home in order to stay solvent. When I asked how I could be praying for him, he answered in one word: "Finances."

The pressure to have more affects all of us. We need a CD player and we need it now! We need a new car and we need it now! The kids need a new wardrobe and they need it now! Once the decision is made that you need more, your choices are relatively limited. Most couples analyze the matter this way: "Either we save money (that's too hard and it takes too long), or the wife goes to work (a good choice if the children are in school), or we borrow money (the best choice because we can have it now and pay for it later)." If you haven't got it, borrow it, charge it, steal it, or take a second job to pay for it. That's the credo of this generation.

DOWNSIZING AT HOME

This is a common problem—particularly among baby boomers. Men especially try to replace themselves with things, a practice that leads to all kinds of bad behavior. You constantly have to buy something new—a house, a car, a diamond ring. So you work two or three jobs and are gone all day and into the night. You end up tired, cranky, and deeper in debt.

The answer is simple. *We have to learn to live with less.* It is possible. I heard an encouraging story from a man whose income probably stretches into the low six figures. They live in a very comfortable lifestyle in a fashionable subdivision in a major city known for its preoccupation with the visible signs of wealth. As I listened, I realized they were wealthier than I thought, because he mentioned having a butler and a maid. He said that he and his wife had just sat down with their kids and asked what they thought about the way the family lived. The man said, "I was amazed to find our kids don't like it. The house is too big for them, so they feel embarrassed to invite their friends over, and they don't like it when the chauffeur comes to pick them up at school."

His wife spoke up and said, "It's wonderful to hear them talk that way. Now we're looking for a way to get into a smaller house, one that will enable us to open our home to those in need." That's a telling story, isn't it? We tend to think that having more is the answer. Sometimes having more is the problem.

This issue touches how a man views his whole life. *The godly leader must not make money the goal of his life. He must not be absorbed with the goal of increasing his net worth.* In 1 Timothy 6:17-19 Paul has some strong words for the rich. They are tempted to be "arrogant" and to put their trust in their wealth. Instead they should learn to trust God and then focus on becoming "rich in good deeds." This, the apostle says, will lay up "a firm foundation" for the future.

Being a "lover of money" (1 Timothy 3:3) doesn't imply anything dishonest or wrong. It simply means that you have wrongly made money (and the things money can buy) the measure of your life. How foolish and how sad.

HOW TO GIVE LIKE A CHRISTIAN

There is only one answer to the tyranny of money. *We must learn to give it away.* The sooner we learn how to do that, the happier we will be. And the more we give away, the greater will be our freedom from selfish greed.

Second Corinthians 9:7 explains the basic principle of Christian giving: "Each man should give what he has decided in his heart to give, not reluctantly or under compulsion, for God loves a cheerful giver." This verse tells us four things about our giving.

It Should Be Personal

"Each man should give what he has decided." Giving is an individual decision between you and the Lord. It doesn't matter what anyone else gives—how much or how little. You aren't even to worry about that. Since giving is always personal, you can't pass this responsibility off on other people.

It Should Be Deliberate

"What he has decided in his own heart." No one ever becomes a generous giver by accident. It's not something you slide into; it's a choice you make. Giving is like farming: the seed doesn't plant itself. You'll never learn to give as you should until you decide to start moving in that direction. It doesn't happen any other way.

When Lyle and Jean Leland were married in 1959, they committed themselves to give generously to support the Lord's work. As time went on, that wasn't easy because the Lord blessed them with six children and the Lelands were never rich. But over the years they gave faithfully to their local church, to Christian organizations, and to missionaries scattered around the world. After Mr. Leland died in early 1995, his wife wrote this testimony to his generosity:

> The only time the IRS audited him was when they couldn't believe that a man with that-sized family and that much income could or would possibly give as much as he did. But his orderly records soon proved that God was top priority in our home.[1]

It Should Be Free-will

"Not reluctantly or under compulsion." Here is where so many of us stumble. Too many people give to God but wish they didn't have to. Perhaps you've heard the story of the miserly man who mistakenly dropped twenty dollars into the offering plate when he actually intended to give only five dollars. After the service, when he noticed that the twenty was gone from his wallet, he said to his wife, "At least I get credit for giving twenty dollars." "No, dear, the Lord knows your heart. You only get credit for giving five dollars," his wife replied. She was right, of course. What you give grudgingly is the same as if you never gave it at all. Seed planted under pressure from the pulpit will never yield a fruitful harvest.

It Should Be Cheerful

"For God loves a cheerful giver." The Greek word for "cheerful" here is *hilaros*. We get the English word *hilarious* from it. The word means "cheerful, glad, or happy." It means to give with "joyful eagerness." Here is a great truth: it is not only how much you give, but *how* you give that matters to God. Keep it in balance. How much you give is important, but how you give—your heart attitude—is also important.

HELEN KELLER'S TESTIMONY

So many times we walk through life saying, "What have You done for me lately, Lord?" And the Lord answers back from heaven, "If only you knew."

Helen Keller was born in Tuscumbia, Alabama, not far from where I grew up. If you've seen the marvelous film *The Miracle Worker*, you remember that Helen Keller was born deaf, blind, and unable to speak. Eventually she learned to speak and to write, blessing millions with her story of courage in the face of incredible difficulty. Helen Keller was a fervent Christian with a dynamic outlook on life. She stated, "I thank God for my handicaps. Through them I have found myself, my work, and my God."

I rest my case on those words. A truly healthy person has a deep sense of gratitude for all of God's blessings.

THE FOUNTAIN OF GOD'S GOODNESS

Sometimes we wonder, "How can we learn to give gladly, freely, from our hearts, of all that we have?"

Here is the answer: *when we truly come to grips with the goodness of God, we are able to give.*

Everything in the Christian life flows from this mighty fountain. When I realize the goodness of God—not in the abstract or in the theoretical, but personally—not in general, but what God has done for *me*, then (and only then) am I free to go, to pray, to tell. I do not need to be coerced. I do not need to be pressured.

> *When finally we look and see what God has done …*
> *When finally we count our many blessings*
> *   and name them one by one …*
> *When finally we understand that God*
> *   is the Ultimate Giver …*
> *When finally we see that life itself comes*
> *   gift-wrapped from on high …*
> *When we know—really know—*
> *   that all of life is a grace …*
> *Then we begin to praise.*
> *Then we begin to give.*
> *Then we begin to sing.*
> *Then we begin to tell.*
> *Then we begin to serve.*
> *Then we begin to enter into the Abundant Life.*
> *When finally we see what Jesus has done for us …*
> *When it finally breaks through that only by*
> *   the grace of God do we have anything valuable …*
> *Only then does life really begin to change!*

At that point, wonderful things begin to happen to us.

- What was duty is now privilege.
- What was law is now grace.
- What was demanded is now volunteered.
- What was forced is now free.
- What was drudgery is now joy.
- What was taken for granted is now offered up in praise to God.

Giving is no problem when we finally see what God has done for us.

GOD OWNS IT ALL

Everything you have belongs to God. In the truest sense, you don't own a thing because God owns it all. He simply loans you certain possessions that you are to manage on His behalf. You came into this world with nothing, and you will leave with nothing. An Italian proverb says, "The last robe has no pockets."[2]

Sometimes when a man dies, we ask, "How much did he leave?" The answer is always the same—he left it all. Billy Graham has commented that he's never seen a Brinks truck following a hearse. The truth is, all you have worked for will be left behind after you are gone. The great issue of life is not, how much did you make? but, what did you do with what you were given?

Here are three principles to consider regarding your resources:

- *Reduce*: Consider downsizing. Could you live on 20 percent less than you do now?

- *Reuse*: Enjoy what you already have. Contentment is wanting what you have, not having what you want.

- *Recycle*: Give back to God, so He can recycle the blessing to others.[3]

MY PERSONAL TESTIMONY

When Marlene and I got married twenty-two years ago we decided to tithe.[4] Back then we making just a few hundred dollars a month. Things were tight. I was in seminary, and Marlene was working to help put me through school. Over the years we've had some difficult times financially and physically and in every other way. But we have tithed through every part of our marriage, and I'm so glad we have. If you brought a wheelbarrow full of cash and said, "Here is all the money you've given over the years," I'd say, "Take it away. That's not my money. I gave that to God years ago."

When I shared that truth with my congregation, Dr. and Mrs. Gustav Hemwall came up afterwards to speak to me. Mrs. Hemwall shook my hand and said, "I'm so glad we learned about tithing before we got married." Then Dr. Hemwall said, "Pastor, I learned what you were preaching over sixty years ago. I am so glad I learned it back then. I've been tithing ever since, and God has always taken care of us."

"I ONLY LOST WHAT I KEPT FOR MYSELF"

That reminds me of a wonderful story about Maxey Jarman, who as a Christian businessman supported many worthy causes, including Billy Graham crusades. He freely gave his money to benefit God's work around the world.

But the day came when his company collapsed and with it his personal fortune. Someone asked him, "Mr. Jarman, don't you regret giving all that money away? Think what a difference it would make if you had it all back." To which he replied, "Oh no, I don't regret any of the money I have given away. After all, I only lost what I kept for myself."

What a fantastic perspective on life. "I only lost what I kept for myself."

Sadly, it is only after a tragedy that many people discover that truth. It is only when we lose it all that we realize it was never ours to begin with.

Happy is the man who discovers that the best thing you can do with money is give it away.

GOING DEEPER

1. Men especially try to replace themselves with things.
   Do you agree with this statement?
   Have you ever tried to do that? What happened?
   Why doesn't it work?

2. How much do you owe on your credit cards? Have you ever been in trouble because of too much credit-card debt? How did that impact your marriage? What did you do about it?

3. We have to learn to live with less.
   That may sound good, but how do you do that on a practical basis? What would happen if you voluntarily chose to live on 60 percent of your current income? What changes would you have to make? How would you explain it to your friends? Do you think your marriage could survive such a change?

4. Read 1 Timothy 6:17-19.

What is the great danger facing the wealthy? How does money cause us to lose our trust in God?
What command does God give in verse 18? What promise does He make in verse 19?

5. Why is it important that our giving be done cheerfully? What happens to your spiritual life when you give out of pressure or a guilty conscience?

6. What is tithing, and how does it apply to Christian giving? Do you tithe? If so, how has your experience compared with the author's? Would you recommend tithing as a basic standard for others to follow? Why or why not?

7. Why is it so important that we grasp the goodness of God in relation to our giving? What does the author mean when he says that "all of life is a grace"? Name three specific ways in which you have experienced the goodness of God in the last twelve months.

8. What is your personal giving plan? What percentage of your money do you give to your local church (and other Christian causes) each year? What does this say about your personal priorities?

TAKING ACTION

Let's do a "checkbook checkup." Look at your check stubs for the last three months. How have you been spending your money? How much are you keeping for yourself? How much are you giving away? Would you be glad or embarrassed if your closest friends knew how you spent your money? What (if anything) needs to change in this area? List three practical steps you can take to become a generous giver.

NO FUNNY MONEY

A Man of Honor is not a crook.

—*Titus 1:7*

P aul tells us that the spiritual leader must "not pursue dishonest gain." This phrase implies deliberate dishonesty. It is sometimes translated "not addicted to dishonest gain" or "to questionable money-making." The *New English Bible* uses the colorful phrase "no money grubber." Moffatt says that a godly man must not be "addicted to pilfering." Put simply, he must not be money-hungry. *The godly leader must not be an embezzler, a thief, a crook, or a cheat. His financial dealings must be above reproach. There cannot be the slightest ques tion about the way he handles his money.*[1] If there is, if he has a reputation as a "sharpie" who cuts a hard deal, if he is known as a man who plays fast and loose in his business affairs, if he laughs and says, "Everyone does it," don't make that man a leader![2]

In the last chapter we considered the warning against being a "lover of money." In this chapter we're looking at another warning: "not pursuing dishonest gain." The difference is this: loving money is honest but wrong, while pursuing dishonest gain is wrong *period*. Both are condemned as inappropriate for spiritual leaders.

THIRTY PIECES OF SILVER

The New Testament offers several vivid examples of men who loved dishonest gain. For instance, Jesus condemned the Pharisees for turning God's house into "a den of robbers" (Mark 11:15-17). Evidently they were offering to exchange currency at an exorbitant rate and were charging outrageous prices for the animals needed for sacrifice.[3] Thus they took advantage of travelers coming to Jerusalem to worship God in the Temple. This abuse of power so enraged Jesus that He overturned the tables of the money changers and drove them away.

And what about Judas, who betrayed our Lord for thirty pieces of silver? Think of it! Selling out Jesus for a handful of coins!

Over and over again the New Testament warns against certain false teachers who crept in unawares. Not only did they teach falsehood, but they did it for the money. Such false teachers are "experts in greed" (2 Peter 2:14). Jude called them "shepherds who feed only themselves" (verse 12) and "flatter others for their own advantage" (verse 16) and "follow their own ungodly desires" (verse 18). Such men deserve "the punishment of eternal fire" (verse 7); for them "blackest darkness has been reserved forever" (verse 13).

YOUR MONEY = YOUR LIFE

It may surprise you to learn that the Bible speaks of money (and the things that money can buy) in over 1,000 verses of Scripture. As a matter of fact, Jesus spoke more about money than He did about heaven and hell combined. Sixteen of His thirty-eight parables deal with money. The Bible is a book filled with practical advice and solemn warnings concerning the awesome power of money.

Why? *Because your money is your life.* Take a look at your next paycheck. It represents a portion of your life you'll never get back. It stands for one week or two weeks or a month of your life, time spent working and now gone forever. It takes your life to make money, and when your life is over, your money will be gone. You'll leave for some other place, and your money will go to someone else.

Consider this: when you give someone a gift worth $75, you are really giving them that portion of your life it took to earn $75. You're not just giving a gift worth such-and-such an amount of money—you're giving the part of your life that it took to make that much money.

Your money *is* your life. It costs your life to earn it. No wonder the Bible says so much about it.

LIFESTYLES OF THE RICH AND FRUSTRATED

But there is a larger lesson to be learned. People who think money will make them happier are deceived. There is no intrinsic relationship between money and happiness. The Bible warns us that "the love of money is a root of all kinds of evil" (1 Timothy 6:10). In Ecclesiastes 5:10-12 Solomon gives us a penetrating analysis of the rich man and his special problems.

He Is Perpetually Dissatisfied with What He Has

"Whoever loves money never has money enough; whoever loves wealth is never satisfied with his income. This too is meaningless" (verse 10). It's like the story of the man who asked the millionaire, "When are you going to stop working and start taking it easy?" Answer: "When I make enough money." "How much is enough?" "Just one more dollar." Money has a way of doing that to you. The love of money is a narcotic. The more you have, the more you want.

He Amasses a Great Fortune Only to See Others Consume His Wealth

"As goods increase, so do those who consume them. And what benefit are they to the owner except to feast his eye on them?" (verse 11). Nobody keeps his money forever. Even the man who corners the market in soybeans will eventually have to sell his soybeans or see them rot in the warehouse. After all, you can only wear one pair of pants at a time. You can only eat one meal at a time. You can only drive one car at a time. The rest is just for show.

He Loses Sleep Worrying Over His Vast Empire

"The sleep of a laborer is sweet, whether he eats little or much, but the abundance of a rich man permits him no sleep" (verse 12). Here is the picture of the classic Type A personality. Hard-driving, demanding of himself and everyone around him—a workaholic. Up early. In bed late. Stressed out. Worried about protecting his investments. Doesn't exercise because it's a waste of time. Doesn't eat right because he doesn't have time. Doesn't spend much time with the kids because he's got a business to run. His wife? Which one? His first? His second? His third? Or his mistress? Call 911. The guy is on the A Train heading toward Heart Attack City. He's living on the edge with a time bomb ticking inside his chest.

And do you know the worst of it? He can't sleep. The poor fellow tosses and turns, adjusts the pillows, lies awake staring into space worrying about his investments and whether he can fight off that hostile takeover. This man eats, sleeps, and drinks his work. Which is why he doesn't eat righ⁺ ʃleep right, or drink right. He's a mess, and his marriage is probably a wreck.

Meanwhile, the employee who runs his computer system for him is sleeping just fine. And why not? He doesn't have his boss's problems. His wife sleeps beside him. She works to help make ends meet. Between them they do just fine. It's a good life, made better by the fact that they aren't driven by the fear of losing all they have.

Lest we be tempted to take this warning lightly, God has given us many examples of "dishonest gain." Here are a few of them: using rigged scales (Proverbs 22:23; Hosea 12:7), taking bribes (Deuteronomy 16:19), cheating widows (Matthew 12:4), charging too much interest on loans (Proverbs 28:8), extorting money (Ezekiel 22:29), stealing from the poor (Amos 5:7), paying unfair wages (Deuteronomy 24:14-15), taking advantage of single-parent families (Zechariah 7:10; Malachi 3:5), trafficking in stolen goods (Psalm 62:10), chasing after get-rich-quick schemes (Proverbs 28:20, 22; cf. 20:21; 23:4-5), using religion as a scheme to make money (1 Thessalonians 2:5; 1 Timothy 6:5), refusing to work and expecting to be paid anyway (2 Thessalonians 3:6-13), and making money through evil partnerships (Psalm 50:18). Christian men will face all these temptations and many more. Will we have the courage to say no?

EASY MONEY

I grew up in a "dry" county in Alabama. That statement won't make much sense to some people, but it means that it was illegal to sell alcoholic beverages in my home county. I can remember the hot controversy that surrounded the "wet-dry" elections. On one side the churches and the bootleggers joined in a strange alliance against the business owners who hoped to profit from taverns and liquor stores. In the last few days before the election there was a blizzard of competing letters to the editor, full-page ads listing the upstanding citizens on both sides of the issue, thunderous sermons warning against the entrance of Demon Rum, and the promises of rivers of cash flowing into our depressed economy.

In the years since I left home, the county has gone "wet." But when I was a boy it always voted "dry." That meant, among other things, that thirsty patrons had to drive to the county line or had to visit one of the local bootleggers. (That term did not refer to men who actually brewed illegal whiskey in some Rube Goldberg contraption out in the country, but rather to enterprising types who purchased wine, beer, and whiskey somewhere else and brought it into our county to resell it illegally.)

Now I'll have to be up-front and say that my knowledge of this is all secondhand since I never visited a bootlegger personally. But many of my friends and acquaintances knew where to go and what to say in order to procure whatever they wanted. I was told that if you knew the right people, you could usually get all the alcohol you wanted. It's not that the local police were blind to all this, but like law enforcement everywhere, they had better things to do than trying to shut down the bootleggers entirely. So within the confines of our "dry" county there existed a "wet" culture. Not everyone liked this arrangement, of course, but for many years it worked very well as a kind of unspoken political compromise.

One of the things I didn't understand then was how much money could be made by selling illegal liquor in a "dry" county. After all, someone had to go to the risk of importing the stuff from Nashville or Birmingham or Atlanta or who knows where. If caught, the importers faced a possible prison sentence and certain public humiliation. So anyone willing to take the risk stood to make a ton of money.

Which brings me to one particular Sunday morning. I must have been about twelve or thirteen years old, one of a group of perhaps nine boys in the class. In my mind's eye I can still visualize our little class sitting on metal folding chairs in a small, dreary, sterile, pale green, nondescript Sunday school room in the corner on the second floor of the Educational Building. We came not because we loved Sunday school but partly out of habit, partly because our parents made us, and partly because our teacher told great stories.

Among his other exploits, our teacher was a private pilot—the only one I knew as a child. He flew little two- and four-seater planes all across the South—usually on vacation, but sometimes on business trips.

His story that Sunday was actually quite simple. Not long ago he had received a phone call from a man asking a question on behalf of someone else. He represented certain "outside interests" who knew that our teacher was a pilot. Would he be interested in doing some flying for these "outside interests"? That depends. What would he be flying? Small silence, then a clearing of the throat, and the answer: "Liquor." The people who supplied the bootleggers needed someone to fly their booze into our county. He wouldn't have to sell it or drink it or do anything else—just hop in the plane and fly the stuff from wherever it was to the airstrip outside our small town. The "outside interests" would take care of the rest.

Looking back, I am a bit surprised that he told us the story. But we were riveted to our seats. Our teacher had been asked to do something illegal! It was the most exciting thing we had ever heard. But the story wasn't over yet.

The man on the phone said that in exchange for flying the liquor in, our teacher would receive hundreds of dollars each time he did it. Thirty years ago that meant the equivalent of thousands of dollars today.

What about the police? Either they would be "taken care of" or they would simply never know about it. It was a good deal, easy money, a way to become rich with virtually no downside.

Except, of course, the downside of a guilty conscience. Above everything else, our teacher was a Christian. All of us loved his class because we knew that his faith in Christ was genuine.

What would he do? As he told the story, he paused at this point, as if waiting for the answer to come to him. Once the offer was on the table, he had to respond. When it came, it was simple and direct. "I just told him no." Five words. No excuses. No "let me think about it and get back to you." No pressing for extra details. No lingering over the money he could make.

"I just told him no." The words hung in the air that Sunday morning.

Over thirty years have passed, but that moment is etched forever on my memory. One man, one phone call, a tempting offer, and five simple words.

I cannot begin to describe the impact that story had on my life. Here was a man I admired who had the courage to say no to temptation. He could have said yes, and I would never have known about it. In fact, he probably lost thousands of dollars that could have helped put his children through college and helped set up a retirement fund.

But he just said no. I'm sure the "outside interests" found someone else who would take their money. That's not the point. Evildoers will usually find someone to join them in their schemes.

MAY HIS TRIBE INCREASE

Here and there the Lord has his Men of Honor who just say no to temptation even if means giving up a chance to make more money.

I'm sure we must have had a regular lesson from the Sunday school quarterly that day, but if we did, I have long since forgotten it. But the story he told has stayed with me for thirty years.

In the words of the Bible, he did not pursue dishonest gain. Across the decades I rise to salute him. May his tribe increase.

GOING DEEPER

1. What is the essential difference between loving money and pursuing dishonest gain? How can you tell the difference? At what point does the line get blurry between those two categories?

2. List some contemporary examples of "pursuing dishonest gain." Consider your own job or profession. What would someone in your position do if he chose to pursue dishonest gain? Have you ever known anyone who did these things? What happened to him? How easy or difficult is it to cover up this type of activity? Do you consider underpaying your income tax an example of "pursuing dishonest gain"? Explain.

3. Jesus spoke more about money than He did about heaven or hell. What does that fact tell you about the importance of money in the Christian life?
   Is money more important than heaven or hell? If not, why did Jesus talk about it so much?

4. Your money is your life.
   What does that statement really mean? Do you agree with it?

If you had to place a monetary value on your life right now, what would it be?

To what extent does the need for money control your life? What can you do to change the situation?

5. Read Proverbs 27:23-27.
   According to verse 24, what happens to riches? Why is it important to know the condition of your flocks (verse 23)? What does that mean in terms of your present job?

   What promise is made regarding your family in verse 27?

6. Consider the Sunday school teacher mentioned in this chapter. Have you ever received a similar offer? Were you strongly tempted to say yes? How did you respond? Do you have any regrets about your decision?

TAKING ACTION

Let's do some self-evaluation. Answer the following questions honestly. If you are married, discuss them with your wife.

- How much money would it take to pay all your bills right now?
- How much money would it take to make you really happy?
- How much pressure do you feel from financial need on a day-to-day basis?
- What is the greatest temptation you face regarding money?
- What impact does all this have on your spiritual life?
- What (if anything) needs to change in this area?

CHOOSING THE BEST

A Man of Honor "loves what is good."

—*Titus 1:8*

W e now come to the final characteristic. This quality sums up the entire list and holds it all together. "Loving what is good" means to support good people, good causes, and good ideas. It reaches to the motivation of a leader's life. What excites him? What hobbies does he cultivate? What brings a smile to his face?

Some people are excited by trifles and trivia, others by outright evil. Few truly love what is good in life. When we find such people, we ought to follow them, for they understand the difference between the good, the near-good, and the not-so-good. One commentator calls this quality "the unwearying activity of love."[1]

The word *good* describes that which is positive, uplifting, beneficial, upright, honorable, and healthy, as opposed to that which is evil, depraved, ugly, useless, and degrading. To love good requires that you also hate evil.[2] It demands a personal choice that influences every part of your life. Paul's words in Philippians 4:8 flesh out the concept of loving what is good: "Finally, brothers, whatever is true, whatever is noble, whatever is right, whatever is pure, whatever is lovely, whatever is admirable—if anything is excellent or praiseworthy—think about such things."

GIGO

Almost a generation ago, when the computer revolution had just begun, not many people knew how to operate a computer, and those who did made many mistakes. Sometimes neophyte experts entered the wrong data only to discover a universal truth: what you put into a computer determines what comes out. If the raw data is bad, the computer can't do anything good with it. But if you put the right data in, the right answers come out.

In order to express that truth, the pioneers in the field coined a brand-new word that describes in four letters both the cause and consequences of putting the wrong data into the computer. Most computer buffs know what word I'm talking about. The word is GIGO. It stands for Garbage In, Garbage Out.

What is true of computers is also true of the human mind. That comparison is apt because the human mind has often been compared to a computer. In fact, the human mind is far more complex than the most advanced computer ever designed. But the basic principle of GIGO is still true: Garbage In, Garbage Out.

What you put into your mind determines what you get out.

10,000 THOUGHTS A DAY

Did you know that the average person has 10,000 separate thoughts each day? That works out to be 3.5 million thoughts a year. If you live to be seventy-five, you will have over 26 million different thoughts.[3]

You have probably had over 5,000 separate thoughts since you got out of bed this morning. You'll probably have another 5,000 before you hit the sack tonight. Then you'll start all over again tomorrow.

Every one of those 10,000 daily thoughts represents a choice you make—a decision to think about this and not about that. Suppose someone gave you $10,000 one morning and said, "Spend it any way you like, as long as you spend it all before you go to bed tonight." You'd be careful how you spent it, wouldn't you? You'd sit down and take an inventory of what you could do with that much money.

HOW TO CHANGE YOUR MIND

All of us fight the tendency to let our minds dwell on the negative. How do you change your mind? Here are some practical suggestions for those who want to become lovers of good.

Analyze Your Input

This touches so many areas of life because we receive input from so many sources.

- What about the music you listen to?
- What about the movies you watch?
- What about the videos you rent?
- What about the radio stations you flip on in the morning?
- What about the books you read?
- What about the shows you watch on TV?
- What about the conversations you have at work?
- What about the phone calls you make?
- What about the places you go to on the weekend?
- What about the places you go to on vacation?
- What about your secret habits?
- What about your hobbies?
- What about your daydreams?
- What about the things you do when you are away from home?
- What about the magazines you look at in the airport?
- What about those porn movies they offer in the hotels?
- What about the letters you write . . . and the ones you read?
- What about the sites you visit on the Internet?

Second Corinthians 10:5 says that we should "take captive every thought to make it obedient to Christ." In order to do that, you've got to look at the sources of your input.

You may be suffering spiritually because you come to church for one hour and then spend forty hours a week cramming your mind with falsehood, evil, and impurity. Or it may be that you simply fill your mind with spiritual junk food all week. If so, don't think that an hour on Sunday is going to somehow clean you up.

Change Your Diet

This is the logical second step. First, find out what you've been putting in your mind. Then decide to change. It won't be easy if you've been filling your mind with negative input.

One suggestion: if you truly want your life to change, find a friend who will hold you accountable. In my experience, lasting change happens much faster when someone you respect is holding you accountable for your thoughts and your behavior.

Examine the Influence of Your Friends

First Corinthians 15:33 warns us that "bad company corrupts good character." Our friends often influence us in ways we never imagine. Sometimes the influence is mostly negative. If your friends love to party, you may find yourself having to party with them in order to keep their friendship. If they use coarse language, you may begin to pick up their vocabulary. If they are angry at the world, you may find their negative attitude affecting your own outlook. If they are cynical, their cynicism may rub off on you. We need to recognize what is happening and counteract it, with God's help.

These things don't have to happen, of course, and I am not suggesting that Christians should withdraw into their own ghetto. Even Jesus was called "a glutton and a drunkard" because he befriended sinners (Matthew 11:19). But sometimes Christians enter relationships (romantic and otherwise) hoping to help someone, only to find themselves dragged down spiritually.[4]

That's why it's important to examine your friendships and the impact they have on your life.[5]

Begin to Memorize Scripture

This has been one area where my own life has grown in the last several years. When Mark Bubeck spoke at our church, he challenged us all to begin memorizing Scripture. He began his message on Psalm 91 by quoting the entire Psalm from memory—slowly, with deep emotion, bringing out the meaning of every word. I felt deeply challenged by his example and determined then and there that I would begin memorizing Scripture.[6]

I started with Psalm 91. My plan was simple. I photocopied the Psalm and carried it with me on the four-mile walk I take three or four times a week. I found out that if I concentrated, I could easily memorize six to eight verses on the back side of my walk, and sometimes quite a bit more than that. It took me about a week or so to get Psalm 91 down cold. Then I went on to Psalm 90. That took another week. From there I went back to Psalm 1, which I had memorized in the *King James Version* years ago. Then I tackled Psalm 2 and Psalm 3. During a week of speaking at church camp, I memorized most of Psalm 73. Then a week or so after that I picked up Psalm 20. Soon after that I started on Psalm 34.

I'm not trying to memorize all the Psalms (although that's certainly a worthy goal), but I've found that the Psalms introduce me to God in a way I've never known Him before. Besides that, if you read enough of the Psalms, you discover the whole gamut of human emotions—anger, sorrow, fear, despair, frustration, joy, excitement, exultation, and profound worship.

More than once I have found myself waking up in the night bothered by some problem or gripped by some nameless fear. In those moments, as I begin to quote "He who dwells in the shelter of the Most High will rest in the shadow of the Almighty" (Psalm 91:1), I discover that God's Word soothes my soul, chases away my fears, and brings my problems down to their proper size.

I recommend serious Scripture memory to everyone. As you begin to hide God's Word in your heart, it will slowly but surely change your mind.

Remember: You're Not What You Think You Are—
But What You Think, You Are

This brings us back to where we started. The *King James Version* of Proverbs 23:7 reads, "As he thinketh in his heart, so is he." What you

think today, you become tomorrow. Your mind is the best predictor of
your future.

- If you think you can't, you probably won't.
- If you think angry thoughts, angry words are sure to follow.
- If you fill your mind with sexual fantasies, your body will
  find a way to fulfill those desires.
- If you dwell on your problems, they will soon
  overwhelm you.
- If you feel like a victim, soon you will become one.
- If you give way to worry, don't be surprised when you
  get ulcers.
- If you think low thoughts, low living is soon to follow.
- If you expect defeat, you'll probably lose.
- If you dwell on rejection, you will set yourself up for even
  more rejection.
- If you focus on how others misunderstand you, you will
  soon become angry and bitter.

What goes in must come out. Sooner or later your thoughts will
translate into reality. You're not what you think you are; but what you
think, you are.

The flip side is also true.

- If you focus on the truth, you will speak the truth.
- If you look on noble things, nobility will mark your life.
- If you seek out lovely things, your life will be lovely
  to others.
- If you dwell on the right, the wrong will seem less attractive
  to you.
- If you think on pure things, you will become pure.
- If you look for virtue, you will find it.
- If you search for higher things, you will elevate your
  own life.

Here is God's prescription for believers trapped in unhealthy living: "think about such things." Focus on the good, the pure, the true, the holy, the right, the lovely. Find those things that elevate the mind, and think on them.

"Find them?" you exclaim. "But where do I look?" Look all around you. Even in a fallen world, beauty is everywhere, truth is right by your side, purity is yours for the asking, and things that are admirable are at hand.

"DON'T FORGET WHERE YOU CAME FROM"

I once knew a man whose marriage had completely collapsed. The circumstances involved years of mistrust, poor communication, financial mismanagement, and some deeply-rooted personal problems. At one point I felt like their marriage was the most hopeless situation I had ever seen. I remember one session when we wrote down on a greaseboard all the bad names they had called each other. The board was literally covered with nearly seventy-five ugly expressions—some of them very inventive in their vileness.

The day came when the husband filed for divorce. It wasn't a bluff. He actually intended to go through with it. But in that desperate moment, he and his wife sat down and had a talk—a three hour, gut-level, no-holds-barred, tell-the-truth discussion of their marriage. As a result of that conversation, the husband decided to drop the divorce proceedings. Later he told me the reason: "Two things kept coming into my mind, and I couldn't think of anything else: 'Don't forget where you came from'; 'don't forget what's at stake.' I realized that I had been looking at all the negatives in our marriage. But when we talked, I remembered why I married her in the first place. She's a wonderful person, and I still love her. That hasn't changed, even though we've had our share of problems. Once I thought about it, I knew I didn't want to throw it all away."

A good memory could save many marriages. Or to put that more accurately, a good memory of the good things could save many marriages. Too many of us forget the good and remember the bad forever.

THINK ON THESE THINGS

The Bible says, "Think about such things." If you are a Christian, you have within you the power to obey this command. You can literally change your mind if you want to. How? By remembering that all that is best is embodied in a Person—the Lord Jesus Christ.

- He is the truth.
- He is the most noble Son of God.
- He is the standard of righteousness.
- He is the fountain of purity.
- He is altogether lovely.
- He is the admirable Savior.
- He is the source of all virtue.
- He is the one whom God entirely approves.

If you link yourself with Him, you are joined with the highest moral power in the universe. He is the embodiment of everything Philippians 4:8 commands us to do.

It's all in Jesus. All virtue, all beauty, all holiness, all truth—all that is good and right is found in Him.

Think on these things. This is not some abstract philosophy, but a call to a growing personal relationship. If Christ is in your thoughts, you will find it easy to love what is good.

GOING DEEPER

1. Think about the phrase "one who loves what is good." What mental images come into your mind when you hear those words? Name three or four people who fit those words. What qualities do those people share in common?

2. Read Philippians 4:8. Now take a sheet of paper and write the following words down the left-hand side of the page: true, noble, right, pure, lovely, admirable, excellent, praiseworthy. Then write at least five examples that fit into each of those categories. Put names of people, book titles, movies you've seen, places you've visited, games you've played, song titles, food you've eaten, events you've

attended, and so on. You may be surprised to see how many good and wholesome elements you can find once you begin looking for them.

3. Take the first step in changing your mind by using the questions in the "Analyze Your Input" section of this chapter. Put a star by any areas that need special attention in your life.

4. Our friends often influence us in ways we never imagine.
Is this true in your own life? Do you find that thought encouraging or discouraging?
Do you have any relationships in your life that are pulling you down spiritually? What do you intend to do about it?
How does this statement apply to the need for believers to develop meaningful relationships with non-Christians? How can we do that without compromising our own standards?

5. Consider the story of the couple whose marriage was in trouble.
Have you ever seriously monitored the negative and vile expressions that come from your mouth? For the next twenty-four hours, keep a list of every negative, cruel, unkind, or vulgar thing that you say. Or ask your wife or a close friend to call those expressions to your attention.

6. What you think today, you become tomorrow.
Why is this statement universally true?
In light of your thoughts over the last few days, what are you likely to become tomorrow? Is that the kind of person you want to become? If not, what do you plan to do about it?

TAKING ACTION

Scripture memory is a crucial discipline for any man who wants to grow spiritually. Let's begin with Philippians 4:8. Write this verse on a 3 x 5 card and carry it with you every day this week. Review the verse before every meal by reading it out loud. Ask a friend to check your progress in memorizing the words. Use it as a basis for your daily prayer time. Once you have memorized it, go on to 1 Thessalonians 5:16-18, 1 Corinthians 10:31, Psalm 119:105, and Romans 12:1-2. Set a goal of memorizing at least one verse a week for the next five weeks.

A Son's
Tribute

When I asked my friends to share their stories of the Men of Honor they had known, a close friend of mine, Chuck Thomas, wrote about his father, Charles Thomas. With his permission I share it with you here because it sums up so much of what I wanted to say when I sat down to write this book.

In my early years I knew my father as a simple dedicated pastor of a small, struggling church in Wichita. But his commitment to Jesus Christ transformed him and those he touched. I can't count the number of times he would bring home a stranger, usually a lawless, troubled youth, who would stay in our house for weeks or months. My father had a knack about such things. He'd "happen" to run into someone with serious troubles, lead them to Jesus, and then bring them to church, help them find a job, and introduce them to the importance of self-discipline and Bible study.

Later he painted his motto, "Plan big, have faith, and trust God," in 12-inch chocolate-brown letters on the cinderblock walls of his study. He lived by that motto. Everyone watched his faith with amazement. I watched him purchase commercial airliners and buses to transport U.S. Christians to the mission field to build churches, schools, and parsonages. I saw his efforts multiply as he began to link up with pastors and Christian businessmen planting churches throughout the Caribbean and Mexico and establishing hospitals and mud-thatched churches in the jungles of Central America.

His commitment to living an adventurous faith, demonstrating God's matchless love and compassion, and extending the impact of the church introduced thousands of people to the Good News. He was determined, steeled to walk in faith. He was like a small stone tossed in a pool of water. Despite his small outward significance, he was wholeheartedly committed to spreading the Gospel. God multiplied his relatively insignificant gifts and abilities beyond anything one could predict. A small preacher from the hills of Kentucky became a godly giant, with a ripple effect spreading out from the center and touching the most extreme limits of the pool. Lives are still being affected by his ministry.

A few years ago my father was diagnosed with stomach cancer. Within days of the diagnosis we began to see daily deterioration and increasing pain. Anyone that has been through such an ordeal understands the anguish my father and our family endured. But God revealed to me in a joyous, surprising way the miracle of the cross and the victory of our Lord Jesus Christ through the death of my father.

In the intense eighty-nine days that followed the diagnosis, I had the wonderful privilege to talk with my father about his life, his faith in the Lord, his love for my mother, his children and their spouses, and his intense love for his grandchildren. He searched for ways to tell his children and grandchildren and yet-to-be great-grandchildren that he loved them deeply, and yet his heavenly Father loved them even more.

In his waning days, he gathered his strength to close his final financial and legal affairs. Bearing pain so intense that at times he could not stand, he nevertheless initiated a major real estate venture and bargained like never before to guarantee financial security for his wife and an inheritance for his grandchildren.

More importantly, he always kept sight of the eternal prize. He spoke with his medical team about his faith, encouraging them and in some cases leading them to Christ. He wrote letters to his five-year-old grandson Bryson—eleven individual letters, each one designed to be given to Bryson on his succeeding birthdays through age sixteen. Each letter was full of encouragement in the faith, identifying spiritual battles yet to be fought, with words of wisdom, counsel, Scripture, and confidence.

Although each day brought deeper lines on his forehead and a grayer complexion, he was strong, bearing the pain as the cancer devoured him from the inside out. He didn't really want people to know about his illness, but somehow the word got out, and letters and telegrams arrived from around the world, filled with anecdotes, Scriptures, and words of encouragement that would make us both laugh and cry. Thousands of people, touched by his life, now reached out to him telling him how he had shaped their life and faith.

He never complained or doubted God's will. Instead he filled his last coherent weeks by hearing my mother read the hundreds of letters and listening to God's Word on taped cassettes. He was a soft, gentle man who dared to take God's promises seriously. A man of godly vision, he tried to live a life that was holy and acceptable to God. I had appreciated my father's ministry most of my life. But never before had I seen his commitment to his family more sacrificial, his faith in God's power more determined, and his future hope more evident than in those last days of his life. In his own gentle way, he was a giant. I had the privilege to call this man my father and say to him, "Dad, I'll see you again."

I cannot imagine a finer tribute a son could pay to his father! What a wonderful heritage to pass down to those who will follow you.

What are you doing with your life? And what will your children say about you after you are gone?

You don't have to be famous or rich or well-educated to be a Man of Honor for God. Any man who wants to can do what Charles Thomas did for his family. But remember this: it won't happen by accident. It never does.

THE END. . .
AND THE BEGINNING

Whative difference will this book make? That all depends.
This week I read about a man who said, "I was born a man, but
I will die a grocer." So many of us could say the same thing:

"I was born a man, but I will die a doctor."
"I was born a man, but I will die a lawyer."
"I was born a man, but I will die a coach."
"I was born a man, but I will die an accountant."
"I was born a man, but I will die a steelworker."
"I was born a man, but I will die a teacher."

Somewhere along the way we lost our humanity in the pursuit of a
career.

How much better to say, "I was born a man, and I will die a Man of
Honor for God." It can happen! If you take this book seriously, your life
can radically change.

We're finished now. In these pages we have examined the character
qualities of godly leadership found in 1 Timothy 3 and Titus 1. We started
with desire, ended with loving what is good, and briefly looked at twenty-
three other godly qualities of a Man of Honor.

IT TAKES TIME TO BECOME A MAN OF HONOR

As you think about what you've read, keep several things in mind. First,
it takes time to develop a life like this. That's the best argument for not

elevating young men and new believers to high-level spiritual leadership. That same principle applies to leadership in all walks of life.

Second, *a life like this doesn't happen by accident*. You have to work at it. If you want to be this kind of person, it will take real effort expended toward a definite goal over a long period of time. You can't read this list, pray about it, and expect to wake up tomorrow morning a totally different person. Change is possible, but for most of us real change is a slow, agonizing process. By *tomorrow* you could write down each quality on a chart and rate yourself in each area. In a *week* you could focus on one key area. In one *month* you could begin to grow in several areas. In one year you could see real change. In two *years* you could be a very different person. In five years you could substantially change your life.

DON'T BE DISCOURAGED

This daunting list is not meant to depress us, but to inspire us to be better men. A noble work demands a noble person. If after reading this book, you feel depressed, that's okay . . . as long as you don't stay depressed. Recently one of the most godly men I know—a veteran seventy-seven-year-old missionary—assessed his own life in light of this list. His evaluation was: "I'm above reproach, I'm the husband of one wife, I'm free from the love of money, I don't linger over wine . . ." Then he paused for a long moment and said, "But I could use some work in the rest of the areas." I thought to myself, "If he could say that, what about me?" As I survey this list, I see five or six areas of strength, seven or eight areas of growth, and four or five areas that need real work. And I've been a pastor for eighteen years! Does that mean I should retire? No. Because the next man won't be perfect either.

It's okay to say, "I can't meet those qualifications now."

It's better to say, "By the grace of God, that's the kind of person I want to be."

THREE FINAL QUESTIONS

We all know it's not enough simply to read a book. *You've got to do something about the truth that you hear*. Let's wrap things up with three penetrating questions. Think carefully about your own life. Please don't treat this as an academic exercise. Let the Spirit speak to your heart as you read the next few paragraphs.

QUESTION #1:
WHAT KEEPS ME FROM GROWING IN CHRIST?

Almost every week I speak with men who struggle in their walk with Jesus Christ. Sometimes the reasons are obvious—unconfessed sin, lust, greed, a refusal to read and study the Word of God, a lack of prayer, no accountability to others, lack of compassion for the lost, nonuse of their spiritual gifts. *But many times the reason touches matters involving other people.* As long as you harbor anger and bitterness, you can't grow. Bitterness is a poison that stifles the new life God has placed inside you. Pride does the same thing. So does racial prejudice or dislike of those who are different from you.

If you are guilty of any of those things, you can't and won't grow as a Christian. Until you deal with the root issues, you will remain spiritually stunted.

QUESTION # 2:
HOW MUCH OF MY TIME DO I SPEND
THINKING ABOUT MYSELF?

This is a touchy question because all of us spend a good deal of time every day thinking about ourselves. But the prevailing wisdom of the world suggests that "looking out for Number One" is the way to climb to the top of the heap. People are things to be used in your mad dash for success, we are told. Customers are ways to improve your bottom line. Students are papers to grade and empty minds to fill. Coworkers are colleagues until they get in your way; then they become enemies. Your boss is your friend when he gives you a raise; otherwise he's a pain in the neck and an inconsiderate jerk. Patients are problems. Clients are sources of income. Employees are people who work hard so you can look good and make big money. Neighbors are people who loan you things you need; other than that, you don't want to bother with them. Relatives are pests who stay three days too long, eat all your food, and criticize the way you keep house.

Sound familiar? How easy it is focus on ourselves and forget about the people around us. *The Bible tells·us to love people and use things. Unfortunately, too many of us love things and use people.* No wonder we are unhappy. No wonder our lives are filled with frustration. No wonder when we finally get to the top, there is no one left to celebrate with us.

QUESTION #3:
AM I WILLING FOR GOD TO CHANGE ME?

I am reminded of the Chinese prayer that says, "O Lord, change the world. Begin, I pray Thee, with me." How easy it is for us to pray that God would change other people. How difficult to pray sincerely that *we* might be changed.

With that thought we have now come full circle. People change slowly, if at all. We all know how true that statement is when applied to others. Stop for a moment and apply that thought to your own life. How long does it take for you to change a habit or an attitude? For all of us the answer is always the same: it takes a long time.

That's why it's much easier to pray, "Lord, change my wife" or "If only my children weren't such a problem" or "Dear God, please work on my boss—he really needs Your help." As long as we can shift the blame to other people, we don't have to look at our own failures.

Do you remember that famous Pogo cartoon that says, "We have met the enemy and he is us"? *You* may be your own worst enemy.

THE FIRST STEP

Would you like to become a Man of Honor? It's not only possible, it's well within your grasp. But you have to be willing to pay the price.

A journey of a thousand miles begins with the first step. Where will you begin? I suggest that you review the twenty-five qualities of a Man of Honor, focusing on the three or four where you need the most work. Write the names on a card, and carry it with you to work tomorrow. Share the list with a close friend, and ask him to hold you accountable for growth in those areas. Then make your list a matter of daily prayer before the Lord.

Remember, God wants you to grow in these areas even more than you do. He is fully committed to making you a godly man. All He needs is your commitment to daily obedience.

Men, you've read the book. You know the truth. The next step is up to you.

If you truly want to become a Man of Honor, with God's help you can do it.

A SPECIAL WORD
TO THE WOMEN WE LOVE

This is a book written by a man for other Christian men. But here I am, writing to the women who have picked up this book, wondering what it is all about.

First of all, let me say, thanks for caring. The very fact that you're looking at this book means that there is probably a man in your life who could benefit from reading it. He may not know that he needs it, but you know it, and that's what matters. You not only see him for what he is—you see what he could become by the grace of God.

I've often thought that most men labor under an enormous burden of guilt. We dream of being all that our wives and children want and need, of setting the kind of example that causes others to say, "There goes a real man." In our better moments, we truly want to be better men.

How can you help us? *Most of all, by praying for us.* Godly Christian men who will shoulder the burden of leadership are in short supply today. We have plenty of regular men, but not enough Men of Honor who will purpose in their hearts to love God, to serve their wives and children, to represent Jesus Christ on the job, to build close relationships with a few other men. Your prayers can make the difference.

You can also help us by encouraging us. If the truth were known, much of what we do is done because of a deep inner feeling that somehow we haven't quite measured up. One of our primary needs is to feel significant. You play a huge role in helping your man feel like he's important. As you do what you can to help meet this need, he will slowly become the man you long for him to be.

You may sometimes feel like we don't care, but we do. Deep in our hearts we want to be loving husbands, caring fathers, responsible workers; and yes, we want to be spiritual leaders at home. In our better moments, we know that God has called us Christian men to lay down our lives for our wives and our children, to set an example of godliness that others can easily follow.

Thanks for sticking with us when it would have been easier to give up.

By God's grace and with your help, we're becoming Men of Honor. We know we're not there yet, but if you'll stand by us, we'll keep going until the job is done.

NOTES

CHAPTER 1:
SEIZE THE DAY!

1. A. T. Robertson, *Word Pictures in the New Testament*, Vol. IV, *Epistles of Paul* (Nashville: Broadman, 1931), p. 572.

2. Newport J. D. White, in *The Expositor's Greek Testament*, Vol. IV, ed. W. Robertson Nicoll (Grand Rapids, Mich: Eerdmans, 1983 reprint), p. 111.

3. I first encountered many of the ideas in this section when I read Bruce Larson's book *There's a Lot More to Health Than Not Being Sick* (Waco, Tex.: Word, 1981), especially the chapter called "Are You Living by Creative Risk?," pp. 71-85.

4. A personal friend, Steve Nelson, told me this story. See also John Pollock, *Billy Graham: The Authorized Biography* (New York: McGraw-Hill, 1966), pp. 106-107, 175, and Grady Wilson, *Count It All Joy* (Nashville: Broadman, 1984), pp. 139-141.

CHAPTER 2:
COURAGE IN OVERALLS

1. H. P. Liddon, *Explanatory Analysis of St. Paul's First Epistle to Timothy* (Minneapolis: Klock & Klock, 1978 reprint), p. 28. See also Charles C. Ryrie, *Basic Theology* (Wheaton, Ill.: Victor Books, 1986), p. 416.

2. Lawrence O. Richards and Clyde Hoeldtke, *A Theology of Church Leadership* (Grand Rapids, Mich.: Zondervan), p. 118.

3. Mark L. Bailey, "A Theology of the Pastoral Epistles," in *A Biblical Theology of the New Testament* (Chicago: Moody Press, 1994), p. 362

says that this quality "enables the leader to be self-restrained in all circumstances."

4. Neil T. Anderson, *Victory Over the Darkness* (Ventura, Calif.: Regal Books, 1990), pp. 45-47 offers a helpful list of the new realities that apply to the believer by virtue of being "in Christ." See John 1:12; 15:1; Romans 8:14; 1 Corinthians 6:19-20; 2 Corinthians 5:17; Galatians 3:26; Ephesians 2:10; 4:24; Philippians 3:20; Hebrews 3:14 for some of the key teachings on this topic.

5. John Haggai, *Winning Over Fear, Pain and Worry* (New York: Inspirational Press, 1991), pp. 249-250.

CHAPTER 3:
THE FINE ART OF SELF-CONTROL

1. *The Word: The Bible from 26 Translations*, gen. ed. Curtis Vaughan (Moss Point, Miss.: Mathis Publishers), p. 2424.

2. John MacArthur, *1 Timothy* in *The MacArthur New Testament Commentary* series (Chicago: Moody Press, 1995), p. 106.

3. Samson's life divides into four parts: his godly heritage (Judges 13), his first affair with a Philistine woman (Judges 14), his victory over the Philistines (Judges 15), and his disastrous affair with Delilah (Judges 16).

4. This is a vital point because we tend to confuse outward blessing with great inner godliness, but the two don't always go together. In the words of Romans 8:13, Samson never "put to death" the deeds of the flesh, and therefore he continually made bad choices. This also explains why he "did not know that the LORD had left him" (Judges 16:20).

5. Interestingly, Hebrews 11:32 lists Samson as a man of faith. But we remember him as much for his emotional weakness as for his enormous physical strength. This paradox illustrates what happens when a man never learns the secret of self-control.

CHAPTER 4:
THE ULTIMATE HE-MAN

1. The Greek word is used only here in the New Testament. It literally means "in strength" and denotes the ability to control your inner

desires so that all your energies are bent toward righteousness. See Matthew Henry, *A Commentary on the Whole Bible*, Vol. 6 (Old Tappan, N.J.: Fleming H. Revell, reprint n.d.), p. 858.

2. I first learned this formula from Dr. Charles Ryrie, who shared it at a summer camp I attended twenty-five years ago. I believe he used the term "Habits of Holiness" instead of discipline, but the meaning is the same. For a general discussion of this principle, see *Balancing the Christian Life* (Chicago: Moody Press, 1994).

3. R. Kent Hughes, *Disciplines of a Godly Man* (Wheaton, Ill.: Crossway Books, 1991), p. 16. I highly recommend this book. He covers in great detail the material I am summarizing in this chapter.

4. Paul Peaslee shared this story with me in an E-mail message on October 9, 1995.

5. Joel Belz makes this very point in "God's Two Voices," *World*, September 16, 1995, p. 5.

6. A friend who read this manuscript asked if I was equating hard work with spirituality. The answer is no, but the word *discipline* implies concerted effort toward a goal. Hard work does not equal spirituality, but there is no spirituality without hard work. See Proverbs 10:4, 12:11, and especially 15:19 where laziness is contrasted with the "upright" man. Hard work is a virtue, while laziness is a key mark of the undisciplined life.

7. Harland Sanders tells of his conversion to Christ at the age of seventy-nine in the aptly-titled *Life As I Have Known It Has Been Finger Lickin' Good* (Carol Stream, Ill.: Creation House, 1974).

CHAPTER 5:
THE MAN I NEVER MET

1. Paul is "thinking of a man who is ever ready with his fists, a bellicose person, a spitfire or fire-eater." William Hendriksen, *Exposition of the Pastoral Epistles* in *The New Testament Commentary* series (Grand Rapids, Mich.: Baker, 1957), p. 125.

2. One friend, commenting on this point, stressed that "just because they don't hit doesn't mean they don't wound."

3. Charles Colson makes the same point in *Faith on the Line* (Wheaton, Ill.: Victor Books, 1994), pp. 57-86.

CHAPTER 6:
STOP ARGUING!

1. This word is used only here and in Titus 3:2. It literally means "abstaining from fighting" or "noncombatant." It has within it the idea of choosing not to get in a fight, and thus the idea of "uncontentious." See D. Edmond Hiebert, "1 Timothy" in *The Expositor's Bible Commentary*, Vol. 11 (Grand Rapids, Mich.: Zondervan, 1978), p. 365.

2. In writing this chapter I wish to make clear that I am not assuming the guilt of O. J. Simpson. His life story does, however, offer a compelling illustration of the need all men have to learn how to control their anger. See Susan Schindenette, "The Man with Two Faces," *People Weekly*, July 4, 1994, pp. 32-39.

3. See Romans 12:9, "Hate what is evil; cling to what is good." If we do not do the former, we will not be able to do the latter.

4. Personal communication from Brian Bill.

CHAPTER 7:
ANGRY MAN ALERT

1. Reuters news report, December 6, 1995.

2. Gene A. Getz, *The Measure of a Man* (Ventura, Calif.: Regal Books, 1995), p. 140-41.

CHAPTER 8:
SERVANTS UNLIMITED

1. Alexander Strauch, *Biblical Eldership* (Littleton, Colo.: Lewis and Roth, 1986), p. 272.

2. Homer A. Kent, Jr., "Foot Washing," *Evangelical Dictionary of Theology*, ed. Walter A. Elwell (Grand Rapids, Mich.: Baker, 1984), p. 419. Sometimes the host provided a basin of water and a towel so the visitors could wash their own feet. See Genesis 18:1-5 and Luke 7:44.

3. My thanks to Brian Bill, Bob Boerman, Bill Miller, Rose Mugford, and Terry Strandt, who all contributed to this list.

CHAPTER 9:
WANTED: GENTLE MEN

1. Alexander Strauch, *Biblical Eldership* (Littleton, Colo.: Lewis and Roth, 1986), p. 228.

2. W. Bauder, "Humility, Meekness," in *The New International Dictionary of New Testament Theology*, ed. Colin Brown, Vol. 2 (Grand Rapids, Mich.: Zondervan, 1976), pp. 256-257 notes that in classical Greek this word (and its cognates) represents the character traits of "the noble-minded, the wise man who remains meek in the face of insults, the judge who is lenient in judgment, and the king who is kind in his rule."

3. In his excellent book *Kids in Danger* (Wheaton, Ill.: Victor Books, 1995), Ross Campbell emphasizes the destructive power of anger in a child's life. In dealing with disobedient children, he urges parents to follow a three-word formula. They should be "firm but pleasant."

4. The Greek word for "restore" is used elsewhere for setting broken bones. Without gentleness, the one attempting restoration may actually do more harm than good. See Donald Campbell, "Galatians," in *The Bible Knowledge Commentary: New Testament* (Wheaton, Ill.: Victor Books, 1983), p. 606.

5. Matthew Henry, *A Commentary on the Whole Bible*, Vol. 6 (Old Tappan, N.J.: Fleming H. Revell, n.d.), p. 790.

6. R. Kent Hughes, *Disciplines of a Godly Man* (Wheaton, Ill.: Crossway Books, 1991), p. 209.

CHAPTER 10:
NOTHING HIDDEN, NOTHING TO HIDE

1. A. Duane Litfin, "1 Timothy," in *The Bible Knowledge Commentary: New Testament* (Wheaton, Ill.: Victor Books, 1983), p. 736.

2. John Calvin, *Commentaries on the Epistles to Timothy, Titus, and Philemon*, trans. William Pringle (Grand Rapids, Mich.: Baker, reprint n.d.), p. 76 offers a helpful distinction between the "ordinary vices" that are found in all men, even in those of the highest character, and those sins that give a man a "disgraceful name" and stain his reputation. To be "above reproach" does not mean sinless perfection, but rather a life of honor and integrity.

3. William Hendriksen, *Exposition of the Pastoral Epistles* in *The New Testament Commentary* series (Grand Rapids, Mich.: Baker, 1957), p. 121.

4. Warren Wiersbe, *The Integrity Crisis* (Nashville: Thomas Nelson, 1988), p. 21.

5. *Spirit of Revival* from Life Action Ministries devoted an entire issue (September 1995) to the subject of truthfulness. Included is a searching moral inventory (pp. 27-29) regarding the sins of exaggeration, flattery, lying, misleading, inaccuracy, deception, hypocrisy, inconsistency, guile, and broken promises.

6. Joseph M. Stowell, *Shepherding the Church into the 21st Century* (Wheaton, Ill.: Victor Books, 1994), p. 267.

7. William Bennett, *The Book of Virtues* (New York: Simon & Schuster, 1993).

CHAPTER 11:
A KISS ON THE LIPS

1. E. M. Blaiklock, *The Pastoral Epistles* (Grand Rapids, Mich.: Zondervan, 1972), p. 39.

2. John MacArthur notes that "the word *kosmos*, from which *kosmios* derives, is the opposite of 'chaos.' A spiritual leader must not have a chaotic, but an orderly lifestyle." *1 Timothy* in *The MacArthur New Testament Commentary* series (Chicago: Moody Press, 1995), p. 107.

3. Much of the material in this chapter comes from two sermons preached by Brian Bill at River Valley Community Church in Rockford, Illinois. The sermons are "Honesty" (January 15, 1995) and "Truth Telling" (June 4, 1995).

4. Private communication from Phil Newton, December 12, 1995.

5. Paul Gray, "Lies, Lies, Lies," *Time*, October 5, 1992, pp. 32, 34.

6. James Patterson and Peter Kim, *The Day America Told the Truth* (New York: Prentice Hall, 1991), pp. 7, 45.

CHAPTER 12:
WELCOME!

1. D. Edmond Hiebert, "1 Timothy," in *The Expositor's Bible Commentary*, Vol. 11 (Grand Rapids, Mich.: Zondervan, 1978), p. 364.

2. John Stott, *Romans* (Downers Grove, Ill.: InterVarsity Press, 1994), p. 332 notes that this passage actually tells us to "pursue" hospitality, not just to "practice" it. This touches the whole area of priority and motivation.

3. Edwin A. Blum, "I Peter," in *The Expositor's Bible Commentary*, Vol. 12 (Grand Rapids, Mich.: Zondervan, 1981), p. 246:

   In certain cultures that are strongly family-oriented, the bringing of strangers into a house may be somewhat shocking. Yet Christians overcome these conventions because God's love has made them into a single great family.

4. Letter from Mary Packard, November 1995.

5. Francis Schaeffer, "Revolutionary Christianity," *The Church at the End of the Twentieth Century* (Downers Grove, Ill.: InterVarsity Press, 1970), p. 108.

CHAPTER 13:
DO THE RIGHT THING

1. Alexander Strauch, *Biblical Eldership* (Littleton, Colo.: Lewis and Roth, 1986), p. 276.

2. This comment assumes a midwinter date for Christ's birth, which is not out of the question. See Harold Hoehner, *Chronological Aspects of the Life of Christ* (Grand Rapids, Mich.: Zondervan, 1977), pp. 25-27.

3. See Leviticus 12:6-8 and Walter L. Liefeld, "Luke," in *The Expositor's Bible Commentary*, Vol. 8 (Grand Rapids, Mich.: Zondervan, 1984), p. 848.

4. For a brief discussion of marriage customs during Bible times, see H. W. Perkin, "Marriage, Marriage Customs in Bible Times," in *Evangelical Dictionary of Theology*, ed. Walter A. Elwell (Grand Rapids, Mich.: Baker, 1984), pp. 690-693.

5. Cal Thomas, "Thank God Mary Was Pro-life," *Conservative Chronicle*, December 27, 1995, p. 27:

> Mary had a lot to fear. She lived in an era in which Jewish law allowed a woman found pregnant out of wedlock to be stoned to death. And her betrothed, Joseph, would have been justified before the law not to marry her and to cast the first stone.

6. For a delightful treatment of angelic involvement in the birth of Christ, see Billy Graham, *Angels* (Dallas: Word, 1994), pp. 123-131.

7. Bob Lustrea sent this story to me on November 16, 1995.

CHAPTER 14:
MY FATHER'S NAME

1. This verse also includes the warning against falling into the devil's snare. That happens when a man with a bad reputation is elevated to a position of spiritual leadership, causing unbelievers to mock the Lord and His church. When we ignore what others think about us, we risk bringing God's name into public reproach. The devil rejoices when this warning is ignored.

2. My oldest son is named Joshua Tyrus in honor of my father (his grand-father). Passing on an honored family name is one effective way to obey the Fifth Commandment.

3. Ken Trainor, "Just One Snapshot for a Family's Scrapbook," *Wednesday Journal*, September 6, 1995, p. 29.

4. Letter from Mary Gaskill, November 26, 1995.

CHAPTER 15:
EXPERIENCE NEEDED

1. M. R. Vincent explains that this word came to mean "newly-baptized." After their baptism, new converts wore white garments for eight days, from Easter eve until the Sunday after Easter, which was called "The Sunday in white." See *Word Pictures in the New Testament*, Vol. 2 (McDill AFB, Fla.: MacDonald Publishing Company, reprint n.d.), p. 1027.

2. Henry Alford, *Alford's Greek Testament*, Vol. 3 (Grand Rapids, Mich.: Guardian Press, 1976 reprint), p. 324.

3. *The Road Best Traveled* (Wheaton, Ill.: Crossway Books, 1995).

4. See Howard Hendricks and William Hendricks, *As Iron Sharpens Iron* (Chicago: Moody Press, 1995) for a complete description of the mentoring process, including how to find a good mentor and how to get started mentoring others.

CHAPTER 16:
JESUS PEOPLE

1. D. Edmond Hiebert notes that this word suggests personal piety, which he calls an inner attitude that causes one to conform to those things that please God. The key point here is that rather than being mystical, holiness results from a definite personal choice. See *The Expositor's Bible Commentary*, Vol. 11 (Grand Rapids, Mich.: Zondervan, 1978), p. 431.

2. When the term *holy* is applied to God, it speaks of that quality that forever sets Him apart from His creation. James Montgomery Boice, *The Sovereign God* (Downers Grove, Ill.: InterVarsity Press, 1978), pp. 164-165 identifies four elements of God's holiness: majesty, will, wrath, and righteousness. Holiness means that He "takes the matter of being God seriously, so seriously that he will not allow any thing or personality to aspire to his place" (p. 165).

3. First Peter 1:13-16 identifies practical holiness with obedience to God and rejection of evil desires.

4. Franklin Graham with Jeanette Lockerbie, *This One Thing I Do* (Waco, Tex.: Word Books, 1983), from the foreword by Richard Halverson, pp. 11-12.

5. See Psalm 39:4-6; Ecclesiastes 5:17-20; James 4:13-17. In light of the fact that no one lives forever, the only thing that makes sense is to live for God while you have the opportunity.

6. Bob Butts shared this story with me in an E-mail message, October 7, 1995.

CHAPTER 17:
MEN OF THE WORD

1. The phrase "those who oppose it" translates a Greek word that literally means "those who talk back." It anticipates that certain false teachers will aggressively attack the church by attempting to replace truth with error. Men of God must stay alert to this possibility. See A. T. Robertson, *Word Pictures in the New Testament*, Vol. IV (Nashville: Broadman Press, 1931), p. 599.

2. Mark Noll, "Confessions of Faith," *Evangelical Dictionary of Theology*, ed. Walter A. Elwell (Grand Rapids, Mich.: Baker, 1984), p. 263.

3. G. W. Bromiley, "Creed, Creeds," ibid., p. 284.

4. Doug LeBlanc, "Living in a Post-Christian Culture," *Moody* magazine, June 1994, pp. 10-17. In order to reach the "Baby Busters" (ages fifteen to thirty) we also need to show how our faith works. The younger generation is much less interested in arguments for or against; they want to know if Christianity works in the nitty-gritty. If it does, then they will pay attention to the arguments for our faith. See George Barna, *Generation Next* (Ventura, Calif.: Regal Books, 1995) and also Andres Tapia, "Reaching the First Post-Christian Generation X," *Christianity Today*, September 12, 1994, pp. 18-23.

5. See Craig Branch, "Public Education or Pagan Indoctrination," *Christian Research Journal*, Fall 1995, pp. 33-40.

6. John MacArthur offers helpful guidance in discerning truth from error in *Reckless Faith* (Wheaton, Ill.: Crossway Books, 1994). He points out that the Scriptures are the only reliable basis for making wise judgments in the spiritual arena. If we rely on our subjective feelings or personal experience, we will almost certainly be led astray.

CHAPTER 18:
THE TEACHER'S REWARD

1. Gene A. Getz develops this concept in *The Measure of a Man* (Ventura, Calif.: Regal Books, 1995), pp. 99-110. A man of God must know the Word of God, he must believe the Word of God, and he must live the Word of God.

2. John Calvin, *Commentaries on the Epistles to Timothy, Titus, and Philemon*, trans. William Pringle (Grand Rapids, Mich.: Baker, 1979 reprint), p. 80.

3. Cited by Robert Coleman, "Give Me That Book," *The Alliance Witness*, January 7, 1987, pp. 8-9.

4. For instance, see Matthew 8:19; 12:38; 22:24; 23:10; Mark 4:38; 10:20; 12:19; Luke 3:12; 10:25; 19:39; John 3:2; 8:4; 13:13-14. For a comprehensive treatment of this topic, see Clifford A. Wilson, *Jesus the Master Teacher* (Grand Rapids, Mich.: Baker, 1974).

5. K. Wegenast, "Teach, Instruct, Tradition, Education, Discipline," in *The New International Dictionary of New Testament Theology*, ed. Colin Brown, Vol. 3 (Grand Rapids, Mich.: Zondervan, 1978), p. 765 notes that teaching in the broadest sense belongs to the entire church in the sense of "handing down a fixed body of doctrine which must be mastered and then preserved intact."

6. This seems to be the clear implication of the list of gifts in 1 Corinthians 12:27-31 and Ephesians 4:11. This paragraph is not meant to make a definitive doctrinal statement regarding the reality of gifts such as speaking in tongues, interpretation, healing, working of miracles, and so on. I do not doubt that God can give any gift He chooses to give any time He chooses to give it. However, He will always act in accordance with His Word and will always do that which results in the edification of the church. See 1 Corinthians 12:7 and Ephesians 4:15-16.

7. After reading this chapter, Lisa King wrote a note raising an important issue: "Don't forget the importance of teaching children. Though teaching young ones is often seen as women's work, godly men have an important role as teachers of K-6 too." Men without children of their own could fill a great need by teaching children in their own churches.

CHAPTER 19:
A ONE-WOMAN MAN

1. For a good discussion of the various possibilities, see Robert Saucy, "The Husband of One Wife," *Bibliotheca Sacra* (July-September 1974), pp. 229-240, and Ed Glasscock, "'The Husband of One Wife' Requirement in 1 Timothy 3:2," *Bibliotheca Sacra* (July-September 1983), pp. 244-258.

2. Ed Glasscock, "The Biblical Concept of Elder," *Bibliotheca Sacra* (January-March 1987), p. 74.

3. Personal communication from Davis Duggins, October 1995.

CHAPTER 20:
WHERE MEN OF HONOR SHINE

1. John MacArthur notes that the word "well" also denotes that which is beautiful or pleasing to the eye. Since true spiritual leadership begins at home, this is where the beauty will first be seen. *1 Timothy* in *The MacArthur New Testament Commentary* series (Chicago: Moody Press, 1995), p. 116.

2. A. T. Robertson, *Word Pictures in the New Testament*, Vol. 4 (Nashville: Broadman Press, 1931), p. 573. The verb is a compound meaning "to take upon oneself." If a man cannot handle the affairs of his own family, how will he be able to take upon himself the affairs of the whole church?

3. Personal letter from Tom Phillips, October 11, 1995.

CHAPTER 21:
IS THERE A FATHER IN THE HOUSE?

1. *The Almanac of the Christian World 1991-1992* (Wheaton, Ill.: Tyndale House, 1990), p. 779. A survey of 13,000 letters from seventh and eighth graders to their U.S. Representatives revealed the following top five concerns: 1) crime/violence, 2) pregnancy issues, 3) drug/alcohol abuse, 4) gun control, 5) environment. It's obviously a very scary world for junior highers today. Source: *Executive Monthly*, October 1995, published by Christian Camping International.

2. Alexander Strauch favors the latter interpretation because even "the best Christian fathers cannot guarantee that all their children will really believe." *Biblical Eldership* (Littleton, Colo.: Lewis and Roth, 1986), p. 269.

3. Gene A. Getz persuasively argues this point in *The Measure of a Man* (Ventura, Calif.: Regal Books, 1995), pp. 211-212.

4. This, I believe, is the proper interpretation of Proverbs 22:6, "Train a child in the way he should go, and when he is old he will not turn from it." Christian parents need to take the long view when evaluating how their children are doing. Many teenagers and young adults go through a period of questioning values and testing their limits. Some will even rebel against the Christian faith. But the good seed planted in childhood will eventually bear fruit, though not necessarily as soon as we would like or as abundantly as we would like.

I believe this is also a valid implication from 1 Corinthians 7:14. Children raised in a Christian home (even with only one Christian parent) are "holy" and set apart for God. This should give us confidence in continuing to pray for our children.

5. William Hendriksen, *1 Timothy* in *The New Testament Commentary* series (Grand Rapids, Mich.: Baker, 1957), p. 127.

6. I am happy to report the children have now graduated from college. One is married, and the other is dating a fine Christian girl. They are both committed to following Jesus Christ, which is what their parents had prayed for across the years.

7. E-mail from Allan MacLeod-Smith, October 7, 1995.

CHAPTER 22:
THE BEAST IN THE BOTTLE

1. The Greek word is made up of a prefix that means "over" or "alongside" and "wine." Thus the idea of lingering over wine. The word implies a pattern of life rather than a one-time occurrence.

2. John A. MacArthur, *1 Timothy* in *The MacArthur New Testament Commentary* series (Chicago: Moody Press, 1995), p. 110.

3. In case you don't know, here are some facts. At least three million Americans are alcoholics. Alcohol-related problems are responsible for 100,000 deaths each year. Nearly half of all accidental deaths are alcohol-related. Alcohol-related traffic accidents are the number-one killer of sixteen- to twenty-four-year-olds. The aftermath of alcohol use costs the U.S. society more 100 billion dollars per year. Alcohol is a contributing factor in 80 percent of all crimes. Each month 500,000 people are victims of alcohol-related crimes. Source: 1995 Baptist Press articles retrieved via America Online.

4. One further statistic: a fatal accident involving underage drunk drivers occurs every fifty-seven minutes in America. Source: *Chicago Tribune*, March 4, 1993.

5. Jack Van Impe, *Alcohol: The Beloved Enemy* (Nashville: Thomas Nelson, 1980), pp. 156-157.

CHAPTER 23:
GIVERS AND TAKERS

1. Personal letter from Mrs. Lyle L. Leland, September 24, 1995.

2. Job 1:21 says the same thing: "Naked I came from my mother's womb, and naked I will depart." See also Ecclesiastes 5:15 and 1 Timothy 6:7.

3. Brian Bill shared these three principles with me.

4. The word "tithe" means a "tenth." It comes from the various commands in the Old Testament where the Israelites were told to give a "tenth" of their crops and flocks to the Lord. See Gene A Getz, *Real Prosperity* (Chicago: Moody Press, 1990), pp. 44-46 for a helpful discussion of the "three tithe" system. Although tithing is not commanded for New Testament believers, it serves as a helpful guideline and a basic starting point for Christian giving.

CHAPTER 24:
NO FUNNY MONEY

1. First Timothy 3:11 includes this qualification in the list of character traits a deacon must possess. Some commentators suggest that in the early church the deacons handled the financial affairs (cf. Acts 6:1-8). While this may have been true in some places, the fact that Titus 1:7 applies this standard to elders shows that all spiritual leaders must be completely above reproach in their handling of money.

2. The phrase especially applies to those hucksters who shamelessly tell people whatever they want to hear in order to get their money. We often call such people "snake oil salesmen." See Fritz Rienecker, *A Linguistic Key to the Greek New Testament*, Vol. 2: *Romans— Revelation*, trans. and revised by Cleon L Rogers, Jr. (Grand Rapids, Mich.: Zondervan, 1980), p. 306.

3. See the comments by John D. Grassmick in *The Bible Knowledge Commentary: New Testament*, eds. John F. Walvoord and Roy B. Zuck (Wheaton, Ill.: Victor Books, 1983), pp. 157-158. Many people were using the outer court as a thoroughfare, thus turning it from a place of worship into a first-century shopping mall.

CHAPTER 25:
CHOOSING THE BEST

1. Alexander Strauch, *Biblical Eldership* (Littleton, Colo.: Lewis and Roth, 1986), p. 275. He cites David's kindness toward Mephibosheth (2 Samuel 9) as an example. He also notes that the last days before the return of Christ will be marked by a notable absence of this quality (cf. 2 Timothy 3:3). "Thus, the society led by lovers of good, rather than haters of good, is truly blessed" (p. 275).

2. Amos 5:15, "Hate evil; love good." See also Psalm 97:10, Proverbs 8:13, and especially Romans 12:9.

3. Paul Lee Tan, *Encyclopedia of 7700 Illustrations* (Rockville, Md.: Assurance Publishers, n.d.), p. 1462.

4. For helpful encouragement on how Christians can impact the world today, see Bob Briner, *Roaring Lambs* (Grand Rapids, Mich.: Zondervan, 1994), and Michael S. Horton, *Where in the World Is the Church?* (Chicago: Moody Press, 1995).

5. Incidentally, I have found this negative impact happening more often through friendships with angry Christians than with actual unbelievers.

6. Mark Bubeck has written three books on spiritual warfare, all published by Moody Press (Chicago): *The Adversary* (1975), *Overcoming the Adversary* (1984), and *The Rise of Fallen Angels* (1995). All three books stress the importance of Scripture memory in effective spiritual warfare.